FAMOUS SCULPTORS
OF AMERICA

JOHN QUINCY ADAMS WARD
In his studio, in 1907; from a photograph from life

FAMOUS SCULPTORS
OF AMERICA

BY

J. WALKER McSPADDEN

Essay Index Reprint Series

 BOOKS FOR LIBRARIES PRESS
FREEPORT, NEW YORK

First Published 1924
Reprinted 1968

920
M 24f
65544
April 1969

LIBRARY OF CONGRESS CATALOG CARD NUMBER:

68-57331

MANUFACTURED
BY
HALLMARK LITHOGRAPHERS, INC.
IN THE U.S.A.

To
The Memory Of
MY MOTHER

FOREWORD

"FAMOUS SCULPTORS OF AMERICA," like the author's preceding book, "Famous Painters of America," is not primarily a work of art criticism. Instead, its purpose is to make the casual reader acquainted with some of the men themselves, who have made the noteworthy pieces of sculpture which greet us in the public square or public building, or adorn our museums.

In the past twenty-five years there have been tremendous strides not only in artistic work of this character, but also in its popular appreciation. It is within the memory of many men now living how, a comparatively few years ago, our public sculpture was limited to a stray equestrian statue which had no claim on the attention of the passer-by, beyond the fact that it commemorated some famous man. Our art galleries at the same time were limited to classic subjects in conscious imitation of some foreign school.

Then almost overnight the fuller fruitage of our art burst into blossom. With a new school of American sculptors beginning with Augustus Saint Gaudens, and a newer impetus in public architecture and civic pride, we turned our backs upon the past with

[vii]

its slavish adherence to foreign models, and set out to achieve something distinctively our own. How well this movement has succeeded and is succeeding is matter of common knowledge. The carving of a battle monument in Georgia is a matter of national interest. The setting-up of a statue to Civic Virtue in a New York park arouses a spirited, and healthful, controversy.

It is high time, therefore, that we of America—not merely art students but every class of citizen—should become better acquainted with the group of men who are aiding largely to make this new movement possible. If we can get a glimpse of them as they model the clay or wield the chisel, we may perhaps derive a better understanding of this, one of the most imperishable aspects of our national life and art.

The list here included is not intended to be either definitive or exclusive. The limits of the present volume do not permit us to consider all who have done yeomen service in the interest of American Sculpture. But those here discussed are undoubtedly in the foreground. Ward, the dean of the modern school, Saint Gaudens, French, MacMonnies, Barnard, Bartlett, Borglum, and other able artists, both men and women, most of whom are still working among us, have almost in a single generation brought our art up to a high level comparable to the best contemporary work of

FOREWORD

other countries. It is a marvelous achievement, of which every American can be proud; for its visible results are our common heritage.

In the preparation of this work the writer has been assisted by general books on art subjects already in print; still more by articles in current periodicals; and most of all by the artists themselves. I have found—as doubtless other searchers have discovered—that general works on the subject of American sculpture are sadly out of date; it has gone forward so rapidly in the last two decades that they have been left far in the rear, in both data and opinions. This has been remedied somewhat by miscellaneous essays in both technical and popular magazines, but naturally these are too widely scattered and inaccessible to be of use to the general reader. I have cited many such sources in the Bibliography as well as in footnotes, and wish to make further grateful acknowledgment to them for their aid.

To the sculptors themselves, whose friendship and coöperation I have keenly enjoyed, my heartiest thanks are due. They have granted interviews without stint, giving freely of their time, talking without reserve, and in many other ways giving cordial assistance. The memory of the hours spent in their studios will always be pleasant to me.

Finally I wish to thank officials in the New York

FOREWORD

Public Library, the Metropolitan Museum of Art, the Montclair Public Library (in my "home town"), and other officials and friends for courtesies and suggestions. To one such friend, Lindsay Morris Sterling, herself a sculptor of high promise, a special word of thanks is due.

J. W. M.

NATIONAL ARTS CLUB

June 1, 1924.

CONTENTS

[xi]

ILLUSTRATIONS

[xiii]

ILLUSTRATIONS

ILLUSTRATIONS

[xv]

I

JOHN QUINCY ADAMS WARD

THE DEAN OF OUR MODERN SCULPTORS

I

JOHN QUINCY ADAMS WARD

THE DEAN OF OUR MODERN SCULPTORS

"THERE, thank Heaven, that's done!" said a young man as he climbed down weariedly from the scaffolding encircling a large bronze horse. It was a part of an equestrian statue in Union Square, New York, and one of the first and most ambitious attempts of the sort yet made in America; for the time was before the Civil War.

"Yes, that's done," assented an older man with a sigh of relief, as he watched his assistant carve upon the pedestal the final touch: "H. K. Brown, Sculptor."

"Now," said the older man, "put your own name on it as assistant sculptor." And as the other demurred through modesty, the master seized mallet and chisel and added with his own hands the signature, "J. Q. A. Ward, Asst., 1854." where it may be seen to this day.

This simple incident marked the entry into American art of a man who for the next half century was

[3]

to take an active part in it, and exert a lasting influence upon its development. When he first entered the scene our sculpture was almost negligible, being limited to a few examples by such pioneers as Greenough, Powers, and Brown. When he laid aside his mallet for the last time, he saw a thriving school of younger men who were rapidly bringing our country into step with the world of sculptured art. As Charles H. Caffin says: "His career connects the past with the present, spanning the long interval like a bridge: one pier embedded in the old condition of things when American sculptors first began to make America the scene and inspiration of their art, its arch meeting above the indifference to, and ignorance of, things artistic which prevailed before the influence of European art began to be felt here, and its other pier firmly incorporated into the new order."

John Quincy Adams Ward came by his American tendencies honestly, as his patronymic would indicate. Only twenty-five years after the first settlement of Jamestown, Virginia, a certain John Ward came over from Norfolk, England, and started a plantation. His grandson, Colonel James Ward, was killed while fighting Indians on the Virginia border, in 1774. The latter's son, William, moved across the mountains into Kentucky, and became owner of some large tracts of land in what is now Ohio. In 1805 he laid out and named Urbana; and this was the birthplace of his grandson, John Quincy Adams, on June 29, 1830.

The boy grew up as any other farmer lad in the rugged Middle West. His schooling was without any frills; and it is one of the many unsolved mysteries which surround native talent, how he first felt the impulse or necessity to model and draw. The story goes that he and some of his playmates discovered some good pottery clay one day on his father's farm, and taking a good-sized lump of it he proceeded to fashion a negro's head, giving it the features of an old slave who lived in the vicinity. "Wonderful!" exclaimed the others, and thus encouraged the boy began dabbling in clay in all his spare moments. He was especially fond of fashioning small animals. A local potter became his friend and gave him the freedom of his workshop.

At sixteen he was taken from school to assist on the farm, and he stayed there for three years, but didn't like it. Then his parents suggested that he take up the study of medicine, but again it was something foreign and distasteful to him. His own aspirations, to be an artist, were secret. He did not dare voice them, lest he become the laughing stock. At that time, art, particularly sculpture, was a thing almost unheard-of, outside our larger cities. When Hiram Powers exhibited his "Greek Slave," it created a

[5]

furore and no little scandal. This beautiful nude female figure was something to be discussed guardedly in certain circles other than art, and to go to see it was a mild form of dissipation! When it was exhibited in Cincinnati, a committee of clergymen went to view it, to ascertain whether or not they could give it a clean bill of health. Young Ward made a visit to the city especially to see it; and then and there decided that he must become a sculptor, cost what it might.

"I would have gone through any imaginable privation," he said years later, "had I been able to speak to the sculptor that day."

Fortune was to favor him in another way. His health began to fail, and his father gave up the project, for the time being, of making him a doctor, and sent him on a visit to his sister in Brooklyn, to recuperate. Henry Kirke Brown had a studio not far away from this sister's home, and Ward soon discovered it and began to haunt it. Finally he confessed to his sister this longing to become a sculptor, and after his return home she talked to Brown about the boy. He was not very encouraging, for she wrote to her brother: "If you have genius of the *highest order*, you may come on and study."

Young Ward was anything but certain of the quality of his genius, but he prevailed upon his family to let him try for at least a year. With many misgivings upon their part and his own, he began with Brown at the age of nineteen, entering as a paying pupil. The one year became seven in all. Brown was impressed by his tremendous earnestness and soon made him his assistant. He learned modeling, drawing, carving in stone, and casting in bronze. The latter was especially difficult for both master and pupil, as there were few facilities for it in this country at the time. Nearly all of the casting was done in Paris. For some of his larger pieces Brown imported French workmen.

About this time Brown received his most important commission, and the one by which he is best known to-day,—the equestrian statue of General Washington, for New York. They encountered innumerable difficulties in the completion of this great bronze piece. Castings made at a local foundry sagged, and it looked as though the work could never be assembled. To add to their difficulties, the workmen struck.

"What in creation are we to do now?" said the harassed sculptor turning to his assistant.

"I think I can finish the job," replied Ward; and he did.

"I spent more days inside that horse, than Jonah did inside the whale," he said afterward. "But the rivets held."

How the grateful Brown insisted upon giving him a graven credit for his share in the task, we have already seen. As for the statue, it remains to-day one of the best of its type and one of the worst placed, in America. Union Square, New York, for some reason has always had a down-at-the-heels look; and every time it has one of its periodic upheavals, poor Washington and his neighbor, Lafayette, stretch out entreating hands to each other from amidst piles of débris. Perhaps some day when this historic old square comes into its own, the gallant charger and its rider will have a point of vantage which they have so long been denied.

Not long after the completion of this statue, Ward decided to strike out for himself. He was now a man of twenty-six eager to try his own powers. His first accepted piece was "The Indian Hunter," which depicts a young brave holding his dog in leash. Simple as is the composition, Ward was not content to draw from models at hand, but took a trip into the Northwest, visiting Indian tribes and making many sketches and models. The result was an exceedingly faithful likeness, which was as fortunate in its final placing, as Brown's "Washington" was unfortunate. It was

[8]

accepted by the Park Commission of New York, and set up in Central Park.

"It is one of our few public statues which are suitably placed," said Taft, some twenty years ago.[1] "The same group in a museum would be quite another thing. There one might wonder whether this is a real Indian, and of what tribe, and if Indians wore their clothes in that way; might compare his tense muscles with the suaver works of men of Parisian schooling. Such refinements of curiosity do not occur to one when he looks upon the original in its fortunate setting of trees and shrubs. There he is—a sudden apparition, low-bent amid the foliage. His copper glow, his preoccupation, his silence, make the illusion complete. It is a glimpse of a forgotten past evoked by the skill of a master."

And Clark adds:[2] "Both the dog—which fairly quivers with excitement, and which is barely stayed by the cautionary hand of his master from rushing on his prey—and the Indian who advances with stealthy step, his eye intently fixed upon the object against which he is advancing, and his whole being absorbed in the eagerness of his pursuit, are instinct with an intense vitality."

This is high praise for the first formal work of a

[1] "History of American Sculpture."
[2] "Great American Sculptures."

young and untried sculptor. It showed clearly that his days of probation were over; that he had come into his own. "The Indian Hunter" was exhibited in a Broadway art shop, prior to its placing in the Park. A gentleman who walked with a slight limp saw it there, and hunted up the artist.

"My father-in-law is Commodore Matthew C. Perry," he began. "Could you do a portrait of him?" The speaker was August Belmont. Commodore Perry had achieved fame, in 1854, by opening up the ports of Japan to civilization. Ward gladly consented to undertake the commission, and the completed work was afterwards set up at Newport, Rhode Island. It was his first private commission, and he was never idle thereafter.

A visit to Washington in 1859 broadened his acquaintance with men and affairs. These were the troublous days just before the Civil War, and the Capital was a seething caldron. Ward was fortunate in being given several portraits of distinguished men, among them, Senator Hale, of New Hampshire, Joshua R. Giddings, of Ohio, and Alexander H. Stephens, of Georgia, who afterwards became Vice-President of the Confederacy. Ward went with Stephens to Georgia to complete this portrait, and thus had opportunity to study Southern types. One product of this visit, done a few years later, was "The

Freedman." This was a statuette which, however, attracted as much attention as some of his larger works. For one thing, it possessed a peculiarly timely interest. It was a thoroughly live subject. Said one contemporary critic: "A naked slave has burst his shackles, and with uplifted face thanks God for freedom. It symbolizes the African race of America, the birth of a new people within the ranks of Christian civilization. We have seen nothing in our sculpture more soul-lifting or more comprehensively eloquent."

We of a later time are not aroused to such emotions by the sight of a little study such as this. Ward himself felt that it was truckling merely to a passing phase. "But they wanted to glorify heroes," he said one day in explanation of this and other contemporary War work; "and they were right. It was good-bye to ideal subjects." He sighed as he looked at a copy of his "Indian Hunter"—*that* was the sort of thing he most liked to do. "From that time to this," he added, "I have never been without an order for a portrait statue—almost always of contemporaries."

After a visit to his old home in Ohio, he opened up a studio in New York, on Forty-ninth street—then out in the suburbs—in 1861. He was elected a member of the National Academy of Design, in 1863; his "Indian Hunter" was set up in Central Park in 1864; and three years later he exhibited both the "Hunter" and the "Freedman" at the Paris Exposition. These events marked his formal entry into the world of art.

It will be seen from the foregoing that Ward was preëminently an *American* artist. He drew his inspiration from this soil, and all his life long he eschewed foreign models. He paid one visit to Rome, that Mecca of painters and sculptors, but he resolutely kept aloof from its siren song. He found it delightful but dangerous.

"There is a cursed atmosphere about the place," he asserted. "The magnetism of the antique statues is so strong that it draws a sculptor's manhood out of him. A modern man has modern themes to deal with; and if art is a living thing, a serious, earnest thing, fresh from a man's soul, he must live in that of which he treats."

While he advised every young artist to go abroad, he cautioned them against remaining there.

"In sculpture no man can ignore the grandeur and the beauty of the antique," he said. "Adhere to nature by all means, and correct your taste by the study of the best Greek works. If one is faithful and conscientious he will find that every good Greek work is verified in nature. After years of observation I have found things in nature that I once doubted, and the joy of discovery was intense."

Reiterating his plea to our artists to come back

home to work, he contended: "We shall never have good art at home until our best artists reside here. God knows how much we sculptors suffer from not living in an art atmosphere—from the absence of proper assistance of fine examples, of sculptors to talk with and commune with, and of the thousand other elements that produce such an atmosphere. But an American sculptor will serve himself and his age best by working at home."

This was said, be it remembered, when the sculptors of this country could be counted on the fingers of one hand. It was the heroic message of a pioneer who lived to see his dream realized, of a self-respecting and self-sustaining American art—thanks to sturdy men such as he.

Then came the Centennial Exposition of 1876, with its first assembled display of American sculpture. Sparse indeed would it seem if compared with such a display of half a century later; but it was significant as marking the birth of this phase of our art. Ward was at this time the president of the National Academy of Design, to which office he had been elected in 1874. It was due no little to his personal efforts that the exhibit was noteworthy.

His own work at this period and in the next decade comprised a large group entitled "The Good Samaritan," in honor of the discovery of anæsthetics in sur-

[13]

gery, and placed in the Boston Public Gardens, in 1866; "Shakespeare," in Central Park, New York; "Lafayette," in Burlington, Vermont, in 1883; "The Pilgrim," in Central Park, in 1885; the equestrian statue of "General Thomas," in Washington, in 1878; the standing figure of "Washington," in front of the Sub-Treasury building in New York, in 1883; and the "Garfield," erected in Washington in 1887. This is but a partial list, but enough to show the tremendous energy and invention of the man.

Ward's method of work was first of all to draw a sketch on paper—sometimes several—for composition, pose, expression, and placing. He next made several small models in clay; meanwhile referring constantly to nature. On an equestrian statue especially he felt thoroughly at home. Note, for example, the spirited lines of General Thomas's horse, even though it suffers to the spectator from being placed on too high a pedestal. A small detail like the loose rein gives tremendous freedom to the whole piece. There spoke the skilled horseman; for Ward himself was fond of horses and of riding.

He was also fond of other outdoor sports, and kept himself in fine physical trim through his long and active life by exercise in the open. He liked to whip a trout stream in the Catskills, or go on a wild turkey hunt in the South. He was fond of rambles in the

WASHINGTON

By J. Q. A. Ward; in front of Sub-Treasury Building,
New York

woods, and his companion on more than one occasion was the poet, William Cullen Bryant who, in his "Thanatopsis" and "Waterfowl," has left us a permanent voice for Nature.

Bryant was among those who signally honored Ward on the occasion of the unveiling of the "Shakespeare" statue in Central Park. This was made a gala day by the committee in charge. It was a beautiful afternoon in May, 1872. Thousands of spectators were grouped about on the smooth lawn, in a huge semicircle facing the veiled statue. Thomas's Orchestra, then one of the most famous in the country, discoursed sweet music. Edwin Booth recited a poem written for the occasion by Richard Henry Stoddard. Bryant was the orator of the day. And when the drapery was drawn away revealing the pensive figure and lofty brow of the Bard of Avon, a great shout went up, and the artist was called forward to acknowledge the applause. It was one of those rare days when an artist receives his perfect reward. And not content with this public expression, a souvenir volume was printed, and a thousand numbered copies were struck off to commemorate it. A copy of this handsome volume is still on file in the New York Library.

Aside from this tribute to the sculptor, it is gratifying to note such early response to the work of an American. It showed unmistakably that Ward was right when he contended that our artists must stay at home if they would express themselves and represent their country.

His "Shakespeare," by the way, was practically the only foreign subject which Ward undertook; and this was done on commission. His subjects, like the man himself, were American. Especially noteworthy among his later works are his "Beecher," which stands in front of the Court House in Brooklyn, and his "Horace Greeley," in New York, because of the fact that in each instance he turned his back upon the classic, and made his portraits realistic at the risk of being dubbed homely. Since then, others have done likewise—as, for example, the Saint Gaudens' "Lincoln" in Chicago —but Ward it was who blazed the trail.

"I am not afraid of the modern frock coat and the trousers," he said, referring especially to the "Beecher." It was a far cry from the neoclassic style of Greenough, who pictures Washington as a semi-nude seated figure, a sort of Virginian Jove, down in front of the Capitol at Washington!

Ward was essentially a man's man, not only in his friendships but also in his work. This does not mean that he was a woman-hater. He was happily married, and was always chivalrous toward women and children. In welcoming some women members to the Sculpture Society, of which he was then president, he said: "We shall be glad to meet you at the council-table of this Society. Enter the race asking no odds. Sex will not handicap you, if you are true to your own instincts and feelings. Do that which your woman's mind tells you to do, regardless of what any man has done. There may be subtle phases of art for you, too fine for the coarser range of the masculine sense."

Ward himself was exclusively masculine in his work. It is practically devoid of female or allegorical figures. He dealt with men of the time, and preferably warriors. He was a purveyor of history in everlasting stone. Take as an illustration his "Garfield," which stands in the Capitol grounds at Washington. The high pedestal gave him an opportunity to place subordinate figures around the base; and these are three in number, typifying the "Warrior," the "Statesman," and the "Student." Says Mr. Taft:[1]

"It can hardly be claimed that Mr. Ward was inspired in his treatment of the 'Garfield.' The figure is said to be an excellent likeness, and the pose to be characteristic; but the interest of the monument is in the three figures which recline on the radiating bases below. The graceful 'Student' is a general favorite; but there is much to admire in the massive, Agrippa-faced 'Statesman' and yet more in the play of light and shade which gives surface charm to the powerful frame

[1] "History of American Sculpture."

[17]

of the 'Warrior,' a remarkably statuesque conception."

"I think," said Daniel Chester French, "that Ward's masculinity always impressed me more than anything else about the physical man. His powerful build, his strong, deep voice, his forceful choice of words, his motions and gestures,—all contributed to this impression. And this quality pervaded whatever he did. Incisive and straightforward he was—intolerant of sham, impatient of sentimentality—all this showed in his work as in his character—naturally."

"After talking with Ward for half an hour," said another sculptor, "one felt that all the rest of the world was half asleep."

Adeline Adams, a woman critic adds:[1] "Male in the highest sense are his most characteristic works— the 'Washington,' the 'Beecher,' the 'Garfield,' the 'Shakespeare,' the 'Thomas.' And if no one has surpassed Saint Gaudens in his presentation of the Angel, a being beyond sex, yet with a strangely compelling charm—a lofty, contemplative being from another world—then few have equalled Ward in setting forth the Man, the virile, real, active presence in the world that lies about us."

Ward himself was his own greatest "slave-driver." "There is no rest for the individual artist until his faculties are dead," he said.

[1] "J. Q. A. Ward, an Appreciation."

"How long are you generally at work upon a life-size statue?" he was once asked.

"I usually have more than one work under way," he replied; "but there are stages in every work when you cannot be flying back and forth but must concentrate your energies. The time necessary for composition is of course a variable quantity, but nearly every figure I model spoils a year."

"When is the moment of your greatest enjoyment?"

"When I first begin to realize my idea—when I first feel that I am succeeding in reproducing what I intended to reproduce. One has generally a sense of dissatisfaction when his work is complete and ready to leave his hands. The cause of this dissatisfaction lies, I suppose, in the growth and development of his perception, as he proceeds with the undertaking. The longer he labors, the more he sees to be done. He has visions of twenty different ways of doing the same thing. Sometimes it is positively painful to contemplate a finished work."

At another time he remarked: "I am always glad to get help from anybody. A conceited fellow, you know, shuts out the light and cannot make progress in his art, because nobody dares say anything to him."

To a young sculptor he once said: "I curse your stuff—I curse it roundly—but, I beg of you, keep on with it, keep on in your own way. For it may lead to something yet."

He was more charitable to the faults of others, than to his own. "I want to see every statue that was ever made," he averred. "I like to observe how an artist has treated a subject, and above all how he has wrestled with his difficulties."

"What do you consider your own best work?" he was asked.

The sculptor smiled and shook his head. "My best work? Oh—the one I am going to do next. As for the things I have already done—I am always afraid to ride near one of my own statues in the Park. I don't believe I have stopped in front of one of them since it was put up; though perhaps if I saw anybody throwing stones at it I might defend it." [1]

"What is the secret of successful work—nature, or the classic models?"

"No man can ignore the antique in art," Ward replied positively; "and yet it is not wise to pore over casts too long. Sometimes a young sculptor finds that nature puts him out; he cannot model from life at all. There is no hard and fast rule; it is largely a matter of temperament."

At another time he remarked: "I have never yet seen a really good art work go begging. We artists

[1] *Harper's Magazine*, June, 1878.

sometimes whine about the lack of appreciation, but in nine cases out of ten the cause of our sorrow lies in ourselves. A true work of art will meet the wants and, therefore, stir the feelings of the ordinary human heart. It is sure to win recognition."

Speaking of criticism, he said one day to Lopez: "Contemporary criticism is always of doubtful value. If an artist has an individuality, it cannot be compared with the individuality of another. Each takes his own point of view of a subject, and gives us something different—so different and yet so interesting that it would be perilously near foolishness to say, this one is the greatest painter, and that one is the greatest sculptor of the day."

He was at all times helpful to the younger artists both by advice and encouragement. Perchance he remembered his own early days in the studio of H. K. Brown. Jealousy or petty rivalry was not in him. When the Farragut statue was being planned for Madison Square, New York, some of the committee favored Ward, and some the younger man, Saint Gaudens. As soon as the difficulty of the committee came to his ears, Ward advised, "Give the young man a chance"—which they did.

Beyond the strong impress of his art, Ward left the impress of his sturdy personality. He was the right man at the right time to stand at the helm of our dawning sculpture. He was not only the president of the National Academy of Design, and the National Sculpture Society, but was also chosen, in 1874, president of the American Academy of Arts and Sciences—the only sculptor to be thus honored. One of his fellow Academicians, William M. Sloane, pays him this tribute:

"He was a fine figure of an American, vigorous, supple in his frame, in later years a trifle bowed, but always erect in spirit and self-reliant in bearing. His brow was massive, his eyes keen and observant, his nostrils full and broad, and there was a play around his mouth and chin which argued the nervous readiness of a man able to uphold the beliefs which he held. Perhaps of all his limbs, his arms and particularly his hands were the most characteristic; the hands that obey the behests of the mind but give limit and proportion to its ideals."

Examples of Ward's work are found in many scattered places, chiefly along the Atlantic seaboard. In Burlington there is the "Lafayette"—again a conventional rather than a heroic treatment; in Boston the "Good Samaritan"; in Newport the "Commodore Perry"; in Hartford the "General Putnam"; in Gettysburg the "General Reynolds"; in Washington the "Garfield," "General Thomas," and others; in

Spartanburg the "General Morgan" of Revolutionary Fame; in Charleston the "Simms." But it is in New York, where he lived and worked for so long, that he has left the most. All these reveal him as one of our finest interpreters of national life.

So busy was he all his life long on commissions, that he never had time to turn aside to the purely artistic conceptions such as are in every true artist's dreams. His very prosperity hampered him. And one of the few pieces other than portraits or memorials which he did has unfortunately not been preserved to posterity. This was the fine allegorical group which surmounted the Dewey Victory Arch for its brief day, on Fifth Avenue at Madison Square, New York.

Admiral George Dewey was on his way home from the Philippine conquest, at the end of the Spanish-American War, and the reception committee in New York was in a buzz of excitement. The great arch of welcome had been decided upon, and must be erected in a few short weeks. True it was to be done in plaster, but the work of designing was no less exacting upon the artists. To Ward and his confreres in the National Sculpture Society the committee turned confidently; nor were they to be disappointed. Ward himself was by this time beginning to feel the weight of years, but his spirit was as active as ever. He personally directed the younger men, in the huge improvised studio beneath Madison Square Garden. For two months they worked almost night and day, but at the appointed time the graceful arch flanked and surmounted with its figures stood ready to greet the conqueror. To Ward himself was assigned the central group on the summit—"Victory" in her sea chariot drawn by plunging horses just emerging from the foam. It was a beautiful and inspiring conception, but aroused in the beholder two emotions—one the wish that at least this group might have been spared from the speedy destruction of the splendid monument; and the other the regret that an artist capable of such fine emotions should be limited all his life to portraiture, no matter how excellent.

That there was no diminution in the quality of his work, even in old age, is shown in the statue of "General Hancock," which was not unveiled until after his death. Of this work Herbert Adams says:

"I believe that the very latest work of Ward's lifetime, the equestrian statue of 'General Hancock,' will stand as one of the very finest examples of his achievement. Its large, monumental impressiveness has seldom been surpassed; and in these swift moving times of ours, what an example to his fellow artists to live up to their highest ideals is seen in his struggles throughout this enterprise! In spite of advanced years and failing health he worked with all his old time strength of conviction, all his passionate love for his art. His lifelong habit of doing his best was upon him.

"After the one-fourth size model had been completed, and the figure of the General finished in the full size, declining health made it necessary for him to entrust the work of finishing the enlargement of the horse to a younger man. Mr. Ward had become too ill to supervise these final stages, but even then his solicitude was of the keenest. He had expressed a wish that I should see the work. Two days before his farewell to us, I went to tell him that the heroic model was complete, and that to my mind this last equestrian statue of his was a masterpiece. The valley of the shadow was very near. His eyes were glazed with suffering and with desire for the long sleep, yet his work was still in his thoughts. I shall not soon forget his look when, on hearing my words, he turned to his wife and murmured, 'Now I can go in peace.'"

The Dean of our modern sculptors passed away after the new century had been well ushered in (May 1, 1910). He was busy until the last; and he had lived to see his own wish and prophecy of a purely American art come true. Who could desire a finer success than this?

Near the end of his life in one of their public gatherings, Ward said to his younger associates: "I will say adieu, and when the waste mold that encloses my personality shall have been broken, I ask no greater honor than to have my brother sculptors meet here and say a kind word in my memory." For, after all,

[25]

the memorials in bronze and stone which one sets up are valueless unless behind them there is not the spirit of brotherhood and service—and this was the message of John Quincy Adams Ward.

II

AUGUSTUS SAINT GAUDENS

THE SCULPTOR WHO TYPIFIED AMERICAN CHARACTER

II

AUGUSTUS SAINT GAUDENS

THE SCULPTOR WHO TYPIFIED AMERICAN CHARACTER

AMONG the immigrants who landed upon the old Boston wharf in the fall of 1848 were "a short, stocky, bullet-headed, enthusiastic young man of about thirty, with dark hair of reddish tendencies and a light red mustache," and a woman with a babe at her breast. The woman was about as tall as her husband, "with the typical long, generous, loving Irish face, with wavy black hair, a few years his junior, and 'the most beautiful girl in the world,' as he used to say."

This newly-landed couple who had come to try their fortunes in the great America were the parents of Augustus Saint Gaudens, and he, in fact, was the babe in arms already noticed. This was how near he came to being a native-born American. The description of his father and mother are in his own words written, of course, some years after, for upon the autumn day when we first make his acquaintance he knew almost as little about their appearance as of this great

new country into which his childish fortunes were
launched.

Saint Gaudens the elder, an adventurous Gascon
whose patronymic was Bernard Paul Ernest, had
grown up in a little village at the base of the Pyrenees,
where he had plied the family trade of shoemaker.
When a boy he had been apprenticed for a time to a
plasterer—a suggestion here of the son's later calling
—but soon went back to the cobbler's last of his
fathers. The Saint Gaudens family, indeed, were
noted throughout that province for their skill in making shoes, and they must have continued at that trade
for more than a century, for many years later when
the sculptor visited southern France he found the
identical little shoe store in which his father had
passed his childhood, and on it still the sign "Saint
Gaudens."

After completing his apprenticeship Bernard Saint
Gaudens traveled northward from his native village as a journeyman shoemaker and a member of
the *"Compagnons du Tour de France,"* a popular
trade union of the time which aided workmen to travel
from town to town, the members being pledged to help
one another to secure employment. The young man
spent three years in London, going from there to Dublin, where he lived seven years. Like the patriarch of
old, in these seven years of labor he secured a wife—

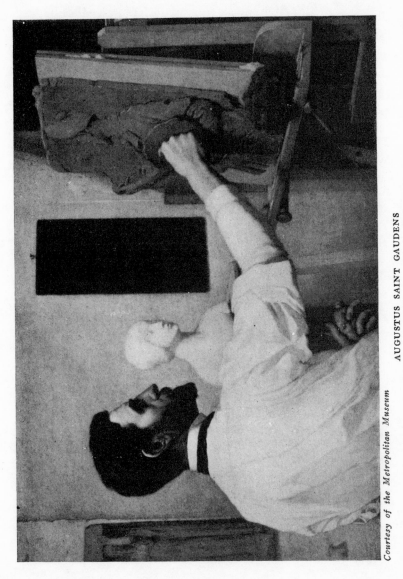

AUGUSTUS SAINT GAUDENS

From a painting from life, by Kenyon Cox

a rosy-cheeked Irish lass, Mary McGuiness by name, who worked in the same shop—he making shoes, she binding slippers. The young couple had two sons in Ireland who died in infancy. When the third, Augustus, was six months old the famine compelled his parents to emigrate. The date of his birth by the parish register was March 1, 1848.

Mother and child were left in Boston temporarily while the Gascon went on to New York to find work. This was soon obtained, and in a few weeks the little family was reunited in lodgings in Duane Street. But the child's first impressions came two or three years later in a home on Forsyth Street.

"Ecstatic, dream-like playing and picking of flowers in the twilight among the graves of an old burying-ground, just over the fence from the first house I have any vision of, blended with similar ecstatic enjoyment of the red wheels of the locomotive in some journey out of New York, are my first impressions, vaguely discerned in the gray, filmy cobweb of the past. But soon we went to the Bowery, whence delightful reminiscences of the smell of cake in the bakery at the corner of the street, and of the stewed peaches of the German family in the same house, have followed me through life." [1]

The boy, a little later, recalls vivid memories of his

[1] "Reminiscences of Saint Gaudens."

[31]

home life and the ups and downs of his father's business. The Gascon had two crotchets which interfered with his success. The first was his overweening fondness for fraternal societies, of which he was usually the "Grand Panjandrum." "In the daytime, notwithstanding mother's gentle pleadings, instead of preparing work, he was constantly writing letters about these societies, all naturally to the serious detriment of his affairs. This condition he complicated to a still greater extent by his remarkable theories as to how shoes should be made, which he propounded and carried out with the greatest insistence, in the face of the protests and tortures of his customers. . . . The only time when the shoes were properly completed in his establishment was during a six weeks' absence abroad when mother had charge of the store."

Nevertheless the personal foibles of the shoemaker were counterbalanced by other things, not the least of which was the fact that this was a real French shoe store, and so the little shop prospered to an extent and numbered many of the great and fashionable among its clientele,—such as Governor Morgan, General Dix, General Sickles, the Astors and the Belmonts. Horace Greeley was a steady customer, and he alone agreed with the Gascon's peculiar ideas about the proper form of lasts.

As Augustus and his two brothers, who were born

in America, grew up into sturdy boyhood the scope of
their adventures increased. The future sculptor was
a "combative and morose" lad who delighted to follow the volunteer fire companies and participate in the
free-for-all fights which often ensued between the
juvenile adherents of the rival companies. Life at
school also lent its zest to this period.

"There were about fifteen of us bad ones who were
collected every afternoon and lined against the wall
of what was called the private class-room for our daily
punishment. 'Pop' Belden, whom I recollect mainly
through the mass of dandruff on his shoulders, would
begin at one end of the line and administer the rod
to the extended hands of the boys, who would receive
the blows without other sound than perhaps a low
whine, but with much squeezing of fingers under arm-
pits, so that by the time he had finished there were
fifteen or twenty squirming boys. Occasionally a
youngster would withdraw his palm before the blow
came down, and then he would receive a double dose."

In the midst of these school days good and bad the
first artistic impulse came. First it took the form of
war-like sketches scrawled upon the school slate when
the master's back was turned—for this was the
troubled time just before the outbreak of the Civil
War. Next the boy began to draw pictures with
charcoal upon every available fence and wall, one of

his most ambitious efforts, as he recalls it, being a ragged pickaninny whose bare knee peeping through a rent in his trousers furnished an excellent target for his crossbow and arrow! His father, who in many ways recognized in the son a kindred spirit, happened to see this anatomical target.

"Isn't that bulls-eye crooked?" he asked. "Wait a bit and I'll draw you another."

And he worked patiently over the sketch while the boy looked on in wonder. It was his first art lesson.

After and between school hours the boy ran errands and delivered shoes for his father. But when thirteen the father said to him, "My boy, you must go to work for yourself. What would you like to do?" It was the first year of the Great War and perhaps the shoe trade had fallen off.

"I don't care," replied the boy, "but I should like it if I could do something which would help me to be an artist."

The father had his misgivings in the matter, but there was a strain in his Gascon blood which responded and so he cast about for some work of the artistic sort which should still be remunerative. He finally apprenticed the boy to a cameo-cutter named Avet, a moody Savoyard whom the elder Saint Gaudens may have known abroad in the old days, and one of the earliest, if not the earliest, stone cameo-cutter in

America. Avet was first employed by a firm on the corner of Spring Street and Broadway, and later did some work for Tiffany. The young Augustus was his first apprentice, and found him anything but an agreeable master. Avet was either scolding, swearing, or singing at the top of his voice, his temper being as variable as an April barometer.

But Augustus was very much in earnest at this time and thenceforward on the subject of being an artist. As soon as he was apprenticed to Avet he applied for admission to the drawing school of the Cooper Institute, and every evening after his return home from work he would snatch a hasty meal and then go to this class. Years after, in grateful remembrance of the aid which he had received at this school he modeled the benign figure of Peter Cooper which is seated in the little square just in front of the old Institute building. Even at this early age his destiny was being worked out, for it is probable that his apprenticeship in cameo-cutting turned his steps definitely toward sculpture. Certain it is that this work gave him the finest possible training in technique and draftsmanship. These were long, busy days for the ambitious lad toiling early and late, and they were made none the easier by the fault-finding Savoyard. "I can only describe my years with him as being ones of miserable slavery," said the sculptor in later years; but he also wrote in a letter to his own son (1898), "I believe the terrible discipline of my apprenticeship from thirteen to twenty is what has made me accomplish anything."

Into the reminiscences of apprentice life at this time come side glimpses of the great War as seen in the streets of New York. First came the intense political meetings, the processions before the election with carts bearing rail fences in honor of "Honest Abe, the Rail-Splitter," then the assembling of bodies of troops in the various city squares, the marching, the recruiting, the proclamations, the drilling, and general excitement. Avet's shop at this time was just north of Eleventh Street, on Broadway, not far from Union Square, one of the chief centers of interest. "From my window I saw virtually the entire contingent of New England volunteers on their way to the Civil War, and profoundly impressive it was, even to my youthful imagination."

Then followed the years of the War, the reading of the bulletins, the temporary hospitals, and the vision of some great man as he passed through. He remembered especially "a tall and very dark man, seeming entirely out of proportion in his height with the carriage in which he was driven, bowing to the crowds on each side." It was Lincoln on his way to Washington. He saw the face of Lincoln on another never-to-be-forgotten occasion; after the assassination, when his body lay in state in the City Hall. Augustus was one of the "interminable line that formed somewhere down Chatham Street and led up by his bier at the head of the staircase. I went back to the end of the line to look at him again. This completed my vision of the big man." This incident is worthy of emphasis when we recall the famous statue of "the big man" which links for all time the names of Lincoln and Saint Gaudens, in Chicago.

At last came the day when his apprenticeship with Avet was ended. The master in a fine fit of rage discharged him, and the boy went home feeling as though the sky had fallen in upon him. But although Avet sent for him again the same day offering an increase in wages, he refused to return. He felt that three and a half years of his life had been wasted, and that this was the end of his artistic career, but his proud spirit rebelled at the thought of any more indignities. He told Avet so in an heroic speech, while the elder Saint Gaudens stood by hiding a smile behind his mustache. But the incident opened the second by-road in the career of the sculptor-to-be.

Augustus soon obtained employment with a shell cameo-cutter named Le Brethon, who also allowed him to continue his work in stone. The three years or so of apprenticeship with him were as day to night compared with his previous employment. Then the young man took another step forward by entering a class in the National Academy of Design, at this time on Twenty-third Street. Here came his earliest appreciation of the antique and attempts to draw figures from life; but it was still the formative, or dream period, with ideas unresolved.

The next definite impulse came with the opening of the Paris Exposition, in 1867. Augustus was just turning twenty, and when his father asked him if he would like a trip abroad we may well believe that he assented eagerly. The kind-hearted Le Brethon also aided him at this time by presenting him with a purse containing one hundred francs in gold, "To pay for a trip to father's village in France." Truly the *bonhomerie* days of the *"Compagnons du Tour"* were not yet over! The traveler's last few days at home were spent in making a bust of his father and a drawing of his mother, possessions which he later treasured more than anything else in the world.

With the arrival of young Saint Gaudens in Paris the second chapter of his life began. He had burned his bridges behind him and was now an art student. The Exposition had attracted him at the outset, but he was now in the great art center on more serious business. He meant to stay and make his own way. Employment was easily found at his trade of cameo-cutting, but admission to the School of Fine Arts came more slowly; in fact, did not come for nearly a year. Meanwhile he studied anatomical drawing in a smaller school near the School of Medicine and called by that name. This school was conducted in a noisy, stuffy room holding about fifty pupils, and much given over to rough jokes and merrymaking. But some serious work was done there withal, and Saint Gaudens had the satisfaction of winning first prize during the term. However, as he gave his mornings and evenings to the school, and cut cameos only in the afternoons, he became miserably poor, earning barely enough to keep body and soul together. He contrived to live a happy-go-lucky life, nevertheless, with other boon companions of the Latin Quarter, just as ambitious art students have done before and since. Finally his joy was complete when on top of the École prize he received official notification that he had been admitted to the Beaux Arts.

He wisely chose the atelier of Jouffroy, who was just then at the height of his reputation, and under this appreciative master his progress was rapid. At first he was the only American in the class, but Olin Warner followed him a few months later. Jouffroy was attracted to his first American pupil not only by the brilliant quality of his work but also by his infinite capacity for taking pains, a valuable trait, by the way, which never left him.

Thus passed two more years in Paris—years of constant progress, of widening horizon, and of valuable inspirations and friendships. He fraternized with Alfred Garnier and Paul Bion, brilliant students like himself. He came to know Mercié and Bastien-Lepage, artists of acknowledged genius. It was an atmosphere alive with endeavor and inspiration. Mercié had received the "Prize of Rome" before the American entered school, and Saint Gaudens decided to follow in his footsteps to Italy, the fountain source of classic modeling. But first he went with friends on long delightful walking tours through France and Switzerland, and he likewise nearly became involved in the Franco-Prussian War which broke out at this time (1870). A pathetic letter from his mother received at the critical moment prevented him from enlisting in the army, and he wisely returned to the south of France. But he was in Paris long enough to witness the entrance of the troops from Brittany, "while crowded with them in utter confusion and dust were droves of sheep and cattle being led to the Jardin des Plantes, in preparation for the coming siege. That was a vision of war that I can never forget."

Life in Rome, whither he now directed his steps, furnished an agreeable contrast to the bleak, war-swept Northern city. Indeed, it seemed to him like paradise, and he entered into his modeling with greater zeal than ever. Here he was also fortunate in finding several staunch friends and a better market for his cameos, so his more pressing wants were relieved. But his day-dream was to do the big work which should at once lift him from poverty and free him from the necessity of cutting cameos at once and forever. The subject of this first masterpiece was at last hit upon as Hiawatha, the Indian, musing in the forest. It seemed poetic and appealing to the young sculptor and he worked zealously at this, his first Indian piece—and his last. But when the figure approached completion the vexing problem was, how to get it cast, for this was an expensive item. The worry and fatigue over this composition, coupled with the previous hardships he had endured, made the young sculptor ill. It was a critical moment in his fortunes, but here fortunately the old adage proved true that it is always darkest before dawn.

A wealthy American, Mr. Montgomery Gibbs, was then stopping in Rome with his wife and two daughters. The circumstances of his meeting with Saint Gaudens are told in a letter by one of the daughters. She writes: "Mr. Gibbs asked a few ladies about having a cameo cut of Mary Stuart. They told him of a young American who had designed some for them and who greatly needed work, and they gave his address to Mr. Gibbs. It was the address of Augustus Saint Gaudens's studio. Upon going there, Mr. Gibbs found only a little boy, who told him that his master was very ill, but that he had taken care of 'the model' and had kept it wet. He then undid the wrapping from the clay figure of Hiawatha, which so impressed Mr. Gibbs that he hastened to discover the sculptor. He found him dangerously ill in a low attic, and immediately had him removed to better quarters and nursed. On his recovery, Mr. Gibbs undertook to support him while he finished the Hiawatha, and to obtain an order for a bust from his friend, Senator William M. Evarts. . . . Mr. Saint Gaudens cut the cameo before anything else, as he said that the search for a cameo-cutter had brought him his friend."

This commission was the beginning of better things, the actual beginning of the career of the sculptor, Saint Gaudens. The statue of Hiawatha was completed and cast. It was finally purchased by Governor E. E. Morgan, of New York, and now stands in Hilton Park, Saratoga.

The young sculptor's next commission was for a portrait bust of Senator Evarts, who was then in Europe. The delight in this and other "real work" was marred only by the intermittent attacks of Roman

fever, from which he suffered much, and from the
dunning of a fat restaurant keeper to whom he was in
debt. His friend, Mr. Gibbs, again came to his relief
by advancing him sufficient money to enable him to go
home on a visit. This was in the autumn of 1872.
"So I reached home," he writes, "to the surprised delight of my family; for, as I was a very bad correspon-
dent and wrote to my parents only on rare occasions, I
had given them no idea of my project, and marched
into father's store without warning." He had been
gone five years, and perhaps one reason for his scant
letter-writing was his proud reserve as to the matter
of his immediate needs. He felt that he should earn
his own way, and although his parents had helped him
from time to time, as they were able, it was always
with a sense of reproach that he accepted it.

This return visit to America, though limited to a
few months, was productive of result. He was enabled to complete the bust of Senator Evarts in the
Senator's own home, and this piece of work was so
satisfactory that other commissions rapidly followed.
Mr. Evarts proved a valuable ally, giving him letters
to several prominent men, and when Saint Gaudens
finally set sail again for Europe, it was with a pocket
full of commissions which made him feel richer than
Crœsus. Among other orders he had two from Mr.
Elihu Root, for copies of classics, and one from Mr.

L. H. Willard to model an original figure of "Silence," to be placed at the head of the staircase in the Masonic Temple, New York. This figure, while interesting as an example of his early period, falls far below his maturer conception of a somewhat similar theme,— the figure sometimes called "Silence," or "Grief," in Rock Creek Cemetery, Washington.

On his return to Europe he spent several months in Paris, living again the old life of the art student and gaining new impressions for his work in hand. But Italy was calling him, and again he found himself in Rome. These were busy, delightful days. His health and strength were renewed, the financial wolf was driven to bay at last, and his studio was being sought out by notables as that of a rising American sculptor. It was at this time that Governor Morgan called upon him and arranged to have the Hiawatha, then in plaster, cut into marble. "I have forgotten what the price was," he writes, "I think in the neighborhood of eight hundred dollars. I suppose I danced with glee when I reached my studio after that visit, for here again was one of the happiest days of my life."

There were many "happiest" days thereafter, as if to compensate for the leaden-colored days which had gone before.

The sculptor's busy life in Rome was pleasantly interrupted by a walking trip from Rome to Naples—

his old-time diversion in France and Switzerland. He was accompanied by two friends, Dubois, the landscape painter, and Mayor, a Swiss architect. Mayor was about as short as Dubois was tall, and the trio must have made an odd-looking picture as they plodded along laden with knapsacks and blankets, and with pistols ostentatiously thrust into belts to scare off possible brigands who just then infested the mountain passes.

There is an old picture of the group still preserved, showing the young sculptor as he looked, on the threshold of his life work. His head would have attracted attention anywhere, with its shock of red hair, massive brows, long, thin face—he did not yet cultivate the familiar red beard of later years—deep-set eyes and long, sharply-pointed nose. It was the face of a dreamer, and at the same time a man of action. He was a good comrade, but one who reserved his friendships only for a few. Fond of jests and with a strong vein of humor, there was yet a vein of melancholy underlying it, which was not always easily shaken off. Another trait to which he often alludes in his "Reminiscences" was his romantic love of the gentler sex. From the time of his school-days there was always some one absorbing passion, or perhaps more, which was only conquered by the arrival of a new divinity in his sky. Naturally diffident, however, he usually buried these love affairs deep within his own breast, so they never could have been very exciting. It was during this second sojourn in Rome, however, that he met Miss Augusta F. Homer, who was to prove the one girl of later years.

Saint Gaudens remained in Rome for two years, at this time, working industriously on the marbles ordered from America, but also finding time to make many agreeable acquaintances both among the American visitors and influential Italian families. When he returned to America, bringing his sheaves with him, it was to enter a larger and what might be called the national phase of his career.

The year 1875 found him hard at work in his first studio in America, a room at the top of the German Savings Bank Building, on the corner of Fourteenth Street and Fourth Avenue. He was the first tenant and for a long time the only one, and he tells of many dreary hours spent in study and waiting for the patrons who are often slow in coming, under such circumstances. Meanwhile, he tried to "break in" to the salon of the National Academy of Design, which must have been somewhat of a charmed circle in those days, and when his work was rejected he became a leading spirit in the famous opposition movement on the part of younger artists and sculptors who felt that the doors of the Academy were closed to them.

AUGUSTUS SAINT GAUDENS

Mr. Richard Watson Gilder writes an interesting letter in regard to the establishment of this Society and the part our sculptor had in it. "I have often said that the Society of American Artists was founded on the wrath of Saint Gaudens. . . . Just then the old Academicians were carrying things with a pretty high hand, so I spoke to a few of the younger men of our American renaissance about starting a new organization. When I mentioned it to Saint Gaudens he said that the time had not yet come. But one day —June first, 1877—he called, as mad as hops. He declared that they had just thrown out a piece of sculpture of his from the Academy exhibit, and that he was ready to go into the new movement. I told him to come around that very evening. We sent, in addition, for Walter Shirlaw and Wyatt Eaton, and the Society was that night founded." [1]   All art-lovers know of the immediate success of this Society and how for a quarter of a century it gave a fresh impulse and impetus to art in this country until the battle-ax was finally buried and the Society was merged into the Academy.

Two kindred spirits whom Saint Gaudens met at this time were John La Farge and Stanford White, the friendship proving of the greatest value to all three. The name of White, the architect, is especially

[1] "Reminiscences."

[47]

associated with his in several important public monuments, as we shall see further on. While through La Farge he obtained the commission to execute the relief work in the beautiful church of Saint Thomas, which La Farge was also rendering notable with his mural paintings. Saint Gaudens's carvings, in high relief, were known as "The Angels Adoring the Cross." This fine church was destroyed by fire a few years later.

The year 1877 was a notable one in the sculptor's life, for it was then that he obtained his first public commission, the Farragut statue, and then that he was married to the lady of Roman days, Miss Augusta Homer. Following the Farragut commission, Governor Dix asked him to model a statue of Robert R. Randall, for Sailors' Snug Harbor, Staten Island, "so that, before I knew it I had the making of two public monuments." It was a light-hearted bridal couple who set sail at once for Liverpool and the closing days of the French salon of that year.

Once more in Paris the sculptor was further honored by being appointed one of a jury of three for the American Art Exhibit in the International Exposition, which was about to take place in that city. The next two or three years were especially busy ones here. Saint Gaudens hired a large studio which would accommodate casts of the heroic size demanded. He finished his work for La Farge and for the two public monuments in astonishingly quick time—for him—as he was proverbially slow and conscientious in all his work, measuring, experimenting, and constantly changing.

"People think that a sculptor has an easy life in a studio," he once remarked to a friend with a rueful smile, as the friend was admitted into the workshop, a maze of clay models, plaster casts, scaffolding and ladders, in which two or three assistants were busily employed. "You can see for yourself—it's hard labor, in a factory."

The unique pedestal for the Farragut statue was designed by Stanford White. The statue is known to everyone familiar with Madison Square, New York, as it stands sturdily facing Broadway. It was cast in Paris and unveiled in New York in May, 1881. Mr. Joseph H. Choate delivered the address on this gala occasion, but few realized, as the guns saluted and the flags dropped from the figure, that the event marked the artistic birth of our greatest national sculptor. With the unveiling of the "Admiral Farragut" Saint Gaudens became a public character. He took his place at once at the head of the new school of sculpture, a position which he was thereafter to retain.

"It is well to remember the date of the Farragut monument," says Royal Cortissoz. "At that time we were still more or less held in thrall by the facile

[49]

makers of 'soldiers' monuments,' those dreary, lifeless products which cheered our patriotism and ought to have shocked our taste. Saint Gaudens pointed the way to a better order of things."

The stern old Admiral challenges the attention of any passer-by who may pause to contemplate him. He stands quiet and dignified. His hands are not raised in gesture, and his legs and feet are planted squarely and firmly as though accommodating himself to the roll of the man-of-war underneath him. But his pose in its very immobility suggests action and power. The sculptor has caught the spirit of the leader, just as he has caught the salt of the sea and the sweep of the buffeting winds. The figures in extremely low relief, which are the sole ornamentation of the broad phalanges of the pedestal, might not be noticed at all at the first glance, but a careful study of them will reveal distinctive and appealing beauties of their own. It is unfortunate that this statue was placed directly upon the sidewalk and set low, instead of being given the proper elevation and approach which its treatment and merits deserve. The force of the whole work, especially this fine pedestal, was considerably weakened. Public commissions have learned much in such matters, since those days.

For the next fifteen years Saint Gaudens remained in New York, having studios in Fifty-seventh Street and Thirty-sixth Street. He finished the work on the Randall statue, and accepted his first commissions for portrait medallions—those of Mr. S. G. Ward, the sons of Mr. P. H. Butler, and Miss Sarah Lee. These medallions, especially those of the Butler children remain some of his most pleasing work in this field. Shortly afterward, through Mr. H. H. Richardson the architect, he received the order for the Boston monument to Colonel Robert Gould Shaw. About fifteen thousand dollars had been raised to erect a memorial to this leader of colored troops in the Civil War, but the project had been suffered to languish for some years, as the usual type of street-corner statue was not felt to be fitting for the peculiar subject in hand. With the advent of Saint Gaudens the promoters took heart again. They felt that perhaps here was a man who could strike the original note they required. They had no reason to regret their choice, barring the matter of time, for it gave Saint Gaudens the opportunity to create a masterpiece, to strike a new and a definite note for all time, in American sculpture. But the fruition of it was not to be for many years thereafter—when the committee had almost despaired of seeing the work in their own lifetime!

"Fourteen years the Shaw relief remained in the Saint Gaudens studio," says his son, "while other commissions came and went, and during these fourteen years he clung to his work winter and summer, with unflagging persistence. Even the hottest of August days would find him, from half-past seven in the morning till the fall of dusk, high up on a ladder under the baking skylight wearing only a bit of silk for a loin-cloth, pausing scarcely to munch an apple for luncheon as he altered, developed, and eliminated the details of his task." To the appeals of friends for a needed vacation he would only reply, "Nothing would please me better, but I'm in the midst of my work, in the best of spirits, and in the mood; too much vacation would demoralize me." And even after the unveiling of this statue the sculptor desired to make certain changes which his fancy had suggested to him—a petition which was refused.

"You could alter it, but you could not improve upon it," said a friend in regard to another work upon which the sculptor had toiled in similar fashion, and this remark is probably quite as true here.

From this point it would be difficult to give an exact chronology of the sculptor's work—even if such were necessary in the present study—as such commissions naturally overlapped. He usually had several commissions in hand at once, and they were apt to extend forward into years. We have already noted that his slowness and laborious care were proverbial. Of the Shaw memorial he said at another time, "I had this many years in my studio, my interest making me do a thing beyond the sum contracted for justified me in doing."

He also tells an amusing story about his work on the negro troops which form the field work of this monument: "The models I used for the undertaking, a horse and countless negroes, all furnished me with the greatest amusement. In the beginning, when I met a colored man whom I thought well of, I would approach him politely, and, after hemming and hawing, I would explain that I was a picture-maker who wanted to take his picture, and that if he would come along with me I would do it for nothing. Anyone who knows the negro of that class can readily understand what followed. They would look at me suspiciously. Some would accompany me part of the way and suddenly go off. Others would refuse altogether. A few would follow as far as the door and then leave. One I remember saying as we reached my threshold, 'You don't kotch me in dat place!' While those that I did succeed in trapping trembled and perspired in utter terror as I stood them up with a gun over shoulder and a cap on head. However, at last an intelligent chap told me that no doubt they feared I was a physician trying to lure them to their death and to cut them up for anatomical purposes, and that their terror was augmented by seeing plaster heads,

[53]

painted a brown color, lying about. So, following his advice, after that, when I desired a man, I succeeded somewhat better by simply saying, 'Do you want a job?' And upon his affirmative reply, adding, 'Well, come along with me. I will give you one.' But I had little real success until I found a colored man to whom I promised twenty-five cents for every negro he would bring me that I could use. The following day the place was packed with them, and I had not only a great choice, but endless trouble in getting rid of them and stopping their besieging the studio."

The next important piece of work—done long before the Shaw was finished—was the Lincoln monument for Lincoln Park, Chicago. Stanford White again assisted him with the pedestal, and the monument was unveiled in 1887. This statue is recognized as one of the noblest conceptions of the character of the Great Emancipator. It is of bronze and is eleven and a half feet high. The severely simple pedestal which supports it stands in the center of a platform some sixty by thirty feet, on a slight elevation. The simple but impressive figure inspires dignity despite the homely everyday attire. With his firmly planted feet, his erect body, squared shoulders and resolute bearing, Lincoln is here depicted as a tribune of the people, as a man accustomed to face a mob, if need be, and bend them to his will. In con-

ABRAHAM LINCOLN
By Augustus Saint-Gaudens; in Chicago

trast to this is his slightly drooped head, sad features, and quiet but expressive hands, betokening Lincoln the thinker, who pondered his utterances well before giving expression to them.

In swift contrast to this work stands the Deacon Chapin statue—more popularly called "The Puritan," which was the next piece engaged upon. This monument, set up in Springfield, Massachusetts, and later duplicated, very nearly, for the city of Philadelphia, has been called the finest embodiment of Puritanism in our art. Surely those stern old seekers after a "liberty of conscience" which was not, after all, broad enough to include the liberty to differ from their own beliefs, —surely, if they should come to life, they could hardly fail to recognize a kindred spirit in this on-striding, resolute old chap, staff clasped in hand as though it were the sword of Gideon, and Bible held tightly as Moses must have held the tables of stone. He is not merely a Puritan of the Puritans, he is also a man of primitive courage, a rough-hewn son of Adam who would travel to the ends of the earth in order to carry out his idea of creation; and as we study this whole chapter of American life set in a single stalwart figure, we feel that thus, and thus only, the old Puritan forefathers must have looked.

Says Mr. C. Lewis Hind:[1] "The years between

[1] *The Studio,* 1908.

1880 and 1900, which saw the completion in 1887 of the 'Lincoln' and 'The Puritan,' and the 'Shaw' ten years later, were strenuous. As if with prevision that he would die all too young, he would bewail, one of his intimates tells me, the brief time there was to do all that he meant to do. He was a reticent man, talking little in company, not averse to Bohemian gatherings, but filling the part of onlooker rather than participator. I have heard him described as *nevrose* but with his nerves well under control; often indifferent to opposition, but capable of sudden outbursts, as when he ground a plaster medallion beneath his feet when the criticism of the subject had irritated him to exasperation. Work calmed him. An assistant tells me that sometimes he would arrive at the studio in a state of suppressed nervous excitement, but that the moment his hands touched the clay and began to shape and press the material, he would gradually become quite calm and intent.

"One of the intimate friendships of his life was with Robert Louis Stevenson, who sat for him when delayed in that city by illness on his way to the Adirondacks in 1887. The Puritanic, mystical part of Stevenson, combined with his charm, ease of expression and the range of his frolic imagination, fascinated Saint Gaudens. He was forever quoting him, the prayers as well as the poems. Readers of the

'Letters' know what Stevenson thought of 'My dear, godlike sculptor.' Stevenson's philosophy of happiness in the shadow of death must have affected Saint Gaudens, who disliked speaking of death, although suggestions of our common end by symbol or by implication are not infrequent in his works."

Those of us who are familiar with the exquisite portrait medallion made of Stevenson at this time will remember that the invalid, propped up in his couch, is engaged in writing. The sculptor tells an interesting story of the circumstances. He says that he had taken his son, Homer, then a child of eight, to see the great author.

"I then asked Stevenson to pose, but that was not successful, all the gestures being forced and affected. Therefore I suggested to him that if he would try to write, some natural attitude might result. He assented, and, taking up a sheet of paper—of which he always had a lot lying around on the bed—pulled his knees up and began. Immediately his attitude was such that I was enabled to create something of use and to continue drawing as he wrote with an occasional smile. Presently I finished and told him there was no necessity for his writing any more. He did not reply, but proceeded for quite a while. Then he folded the paper with deliberation, placed it in an

[57]

envelope, addressed it, and handed it to me. It was
to 'Master Homer Saint Gaudens.'

"I asked him, 'Do you wish me to give this to the
boy?'

" 'Yes.'

" 'When? Now?'

" 'Oh, no; in five or ten years, or when I am dead.'.

"I put it in a safe, and that delightful letter can be
found in the second volume of Stevenson's 'Letters to
his Family and Friends.' "

Closely in touch with the Stevensonian attitude toward death may be regarded the Adams statue, executed about this time. The popular story as to the
origin of this noble study, by many considered the
finest conception of this artist hand and brain, is well-
known: How that a bereaved husband asked the
sculptor to chisel a figure which should not be a portrait or symbol, but should only give utterance to an
all-consuming grief. Saint Gaudens accepted the
commission without hesitation. It was precisely of
the sort which appealed to his poetic side. Who shall
say that his intimacy with Stevenson had not further
ripened him for just this work? And thus arose the
nameless figure seated in front of the mass of granite
marking the Adams tomb in Rock Creek Cemetery,
Washington,—a figure which has caused endless discussion and speculation, and about whose silent head

some of the mystery of the Sphinx has already gathered. The sculptor did all that the patron had desired, and more. He expressed the universality of grief that has in it all the sorrow of the world, and yet has found the strength to endure it with calmness. In the stern, hopeless quiet of that face there is no thought of revolt, but rather of a steadfast courage, a prescience of something which looks beyond transient earthly loss and awaits patiently the time when all things shall be made clear.

The figure is variously known as "Grief," "Silence," "Death," "The Mystery of the Hereafter," and "The Peace of God," the last being the happiest. There is a suggestion of Buddha in the pose, and La Farge always contended that this idea of Nirvana was in the sculptor's mind. It has also been noticed that the figure suggests neither sex. It is universal, just as grief is universal.

"Just what he has meant," says Lorado Taft,[1] "the great artist has carefully abstained from telling us, but that he has charged the figure with significance, at least with the appearance of meaning, cannot be gainsaid. It is as perplexing as the look of Leonardo's 'Mona Lisa.' Some one has written of it despairingly: 'It appears to know all that there is to know, and is a positive and negative to every sentiment one

[1] "American Sculpture."

[59]

can suggest concerning the unknown.' Baffled, but ever fascinated, one lingers there, indifferent to the flight of time, dimly conscious of the song of birds overhead and of the shadows of leaves trembling upon the Silent One opposite. Strangers who stroll in speak to one another in subdued tones and move away softly. The bronzed figure with closed eyes compels it; one is awed into reverence. You may recognize beautifully proportioned moldings on the granite background, or may perceive that the shrouded form is seated upon a boulder of different material; that the modeling of the drapery is very broad and coarse in texture; but these things seem to mean very little in this presence. One feels no concern in trifles when confronting eternity. And that is where one finds himself when under the spell of this amazing work."

Thomas Nelson Page recently said regarding this single masterpiece of Saint Gaudens: "Should future generations demand of us what we have done in art—there sits our answer. We have done that—and *me judice*, no other people in modern times have equaled it. . . . Whatever the judgment of the ages may be as to this work or that, Augustus Saint Gaudens has with his chisel carved his name with those who are immortal."

"The Adams monument," says Cortissoz, "is for a kind of restrained grandeur not only the finest thing

THE ADAMS MEMORIAL

By Augustus Saint Gaudens; in Rock Creek Cemetery, Washington, D. C.

of its kind ever produced by an American sculptor, but an achievement which modern Europe has not surpassed."

Saint Gaudens's New York studio was given up when he went abroad for the third time, in 1897, after the unveiling of the long-delayed Shaw monument, and the Logan, of Chicago, to work upon his statue of Sherman. The latter commission was given him in 1892, and the statue itself did not see the light of day in its final form until Memorial Day, May 30, 1903. But committees had long since found that they could not hurry the sculptor, and that he was one for whom it was worth while to wait. Meanwhile the New York studio with its constant interruptions and grind of smaller work was not conducive to these big things, and hence the trip abroad. He never again made his home in New York. In 1885 he had purchased a summer home at Cornish, New Hampshire, being the first-comer of what became later an artistic colony, and when he returned to this country in 1900, bearing fresh honors but broken in health, he settled at Cornish permanently. He called his place Aspet, after his father's birthplace, which he had lately visited, and he added two studios, in which he finished the Sherman statue, the seated figure of Lincoln, for Chicago, the Parnell statue, for Dublin, the Philips Brooks monument, for Boston, the Peter Cooper statue for New York, and other work. All this was prosecuted with almost feverish energy, despite his failing health. It was upon his return in 1900 that he underwent an operation at Boston, and during his enforced idleness while convalescing he wrote the "Reminiscences" which give so many revealing glimpses of the man himself. So the illness, unfortunate in other respects, was not without its good results.

The famous Sherman statue which stands at the entrance of Central Park, upon Fifth Avenue, New York, has been regarded by many critics as not only the crowning achievement of Saint Gaudens's genius, but as also the finest example of American equestrian sculpture, up to that time. General Sherman had given him a series of sittings for his bust in 1888, and the sculptor was therefore already at home in his subject, when the commission was given him four years later. His first sketch which was completed in a few months had been immediately accepted. He then made the horse and rider in smaller studies and modeled the on-marching Victory from the nude. When he went to Paris he modeled the full-sized group, and in 1899 a portion of it was exhibited in plaster at the salon of the Champs de Mars, where it was given a place of honor. At the Paris Exposition, in 1900, the whole group in plaster was seen for the first time, where it was given the Grand Prize.

But in spite of these honors the sculptor, always his own severest critic, was not satisfied with it, and when he returned to America he continued to make changes. The group showing these changes, still in plaster, was sent to the Pan-American Exposition, at Buffalo, where it was the cause of an unusual honor being paid to the sculptor. Upon the recommendation of the Jury of Fine Arts, composed of painters, sculptors, and architects, he was awarded a special diploma and medal of honor, "apart from and above all other awards," a distinction which marked him as the foremost of American artists, as previous honors had marked him as one of the greatest sculptors of his time. But this success, like former ones, seems only to have been a signal for him to recommence his struggles toward that ideal which distinguished his whole life. The bronze was brought to his New Hampshire home and set up in the open air, in order to get the outdoor effect, and experiments in gilding and toning were begun, while the base was remodeled and twice cut in granite. Finally in 1903, the sculptor was persuaded to desist, to give his last loving touch to the whole, and the completed work was sent to New York and set up.

"The group is about twice the size of life in each dimension, so that the figure of the General, if standing, would be about twelve feet high. Tall and erect

he sits his horse, his military cloak bellying out behind him, his trousers strapped down over his shoes,
his hat in his right hand, dropping at arm's length
behind the knee, and his bare head, like that of an
old eagle, looking straight forward. The horse is as
long and thin as his rider, with a tremendous stride;
and his big head, closely reined in, twitches viciously
at the bridle. Before the horse and rider, half walks,
half flies, a splendid winged figure—one arm out-
stretched, the other brandishing the palm—Victory
leading them on. She has a certain fierce wildness of
aspect, but her rapt gaze and half-opened mouth indicate the seer of visions: peace is ahead and an end
of war. On the bosom of her gown is broidered the
eagle of the United States, for she is an American
Victory, as this is an American man on an American
horse; and the broken pine bough beneath the horse's
feet localizes the victorious march through Georgia to
the sea. One of the most remarkable things about
the group is the extraordinary sense of movement and
of irresistible force conveyed by it. The gait of the
horse is only a quick walk, but horse and rider and
striding Victory move onward with a rush, and one
feels that nothing can arrest their progress." [1]

Another incident which emphasizes Saint Gaudens's
keen sense of detail occurred a few years earlier, at

[1] Kenyon Cox, "Old Masters and New."

the completion of the Madison Square Garden tower in New York. His friend, White, the architect, asked him to model the light figure of the huntress Diana, which poises airily on one foot at the top,— strangely enough the only example of the nude which he has left us. After the figure was in place, Saint Gaudens was not satisfied. He felt that it was out of proportion. So he and White had it lowered again, at their own expense, and a figure five feet smaller was hoisted in its place.

The bulk of Saint Gaudens's work was, as has been pointed out, not allegorical or imaginative, but types of American portraiture and character. Besides his personal portraits, such as the Phillips Brooks of Boston, the Stevenson of Edinburgh, and others of his later period, he was fortunate in being given the opportunity of depicting so many different types of historic Americans. In the Deacon Chapin he embodied for all time the early Puritan. In the Farragut we have the typical seaman. In the Lincoln the homely type of American manhood which yet illustrates the noblest qualities of statesmanship. The Logan, with all its theatrical pose, illustrates the dashing soldier, just as the Shaw, the practical leader. While the Sherman combines in one all the higher traits which mark both the warrior and the conqueror.

In 1904 Saint Gaudens's Cornish home was visited

[65]

by fire, and one of his studios was destroyed, a loss which the sculptor never ceased to deplore, as some of his most cherished art treasures and mementos were burned. The next year was marked by a pleasant event. The artistic and literary colony which had gradually grown up about his home celebrated the twentieth anniversary of his coming to Cornish by a fête and open-air masque held in the beautiful groves of Aspet. The grace and poetry of this pageant are still among the fine memories of this place.

A pen picture of the man himself at this time, by one of his most discerning friends and critics, is of value: "Some part of the vivid and lovable personality of Augustus Saint Gaudens must have been visible, almost at a glance, to anyone who ever came in contact with him—to anyone, even, who ever saw his portrait. In his spare but strong-knit figure, his firm but supple hands, his manner of carrying himself, his every gesture, one felt the abounding vitality, the almost furious energy of the man. That extraordinary head with its heavy brow beetling above the small but piercing eyes, its red beard and crisp, wiry hair, its projecting jaw and great, strongly-modeled nose, was alive with power—with power of intellect no less than of will. His lack of early education gave him a certain diffidence and a distrust of his own gifts of expression. He was apt to overrate the mere verbal facility of others, and to underestimate himself in the comparison—indeed, a certain humility was strongly marked in him, even as regards his art, though he was self-confident also. When he was unconstrained his great powers of observation, his shrewdness of judgment, his bubbling humor, and a picturesque vivacity of phrase not uncommon among artists, made him one of the most entrancing of talkers." [1]

Another tells this incident of him: "He was of a nervous temperament, and a man who loved the retirement of his own studio, but he would freely give of his energies whenever they seemed to be needed in a good work. His generosity came out, too, in all the private relations of an artist. No one could have been more helpful than he was to young men of talent. I remember the delight and pride a sculptor of my acquaintance had in a visit Saint Gaudens once paid him. My friend had put a fine piece of work to his credit. Saint Gaudens did not know him, but when he saw it he demanded the stranger's address, jumped into a cab, and though he was not by any means in good health made the rather long journey to the young man's door. 'I am Saint Gaudens,' he said when it was opened, 'and I've come to tell you

[1] Kenyon Cox, in *Atlantic Monthly*, March, 1908.

what I think of the beautiful work you have done.'
He stayed long enough to give his grateful and be-
wildered listener such happy stimulus as he had never
known before." [1]

Still another writer says: "It was my privilege to
spend a few days at his Cornish home. I roamed
through his haunts, lingered in his studios, and
sleighed over the beautiful upland country which he
loved. It was good to hear of the enjoyment he derived from open-air relaxations—skating, skiing,
tobogganing, and sleighing. More than once he
turned out the whole studio of his assistants, crying:
'Sculpture isn't in it with tobogganing.' " [2]

Saint Gaudens himself writes: "I would never
have believed it, nor do I suppose you will believe me
now, but I am enjoying the rigorous young winter
up here keenly. Snow over all, sun brilliant and su-
preme, sleighs, sleigh-bells galore, and a cheerfulness
that brings back visions of the halcyon winter days
of my boyhood. We skate, and I play games upon
the ice as I played them thirty-seven years ago. I
am a little more stiff, but that makes no difference,
since I still feel young. . . . It is very far from the
terrible, black, sad days of the winters of London and
Paris, and even New York."

[1] Royal Cortissoz, "A. Saint Gaudens."
[2] C. L. Hind, *Studio.*

AUGUSTUS SAINT GAUDENS

It is not the purpose of this sketch to give a complete list of the sculptor's works, nor to state the circumstances or dates of these achievements. They were many and varied, from the great public monuments, most of which we have noticed, to his portrait medallions, the designs for the two gold coins which he executed for the United States mint, at the suggestion of President Roosevelt, the Caryatides for the Vanderbilt home, the Whistler Memorial at West Point, and many another charming piece in bronze or marble. The wide range of his labors was not more remarkable than its uniform excellence. While the minute fidelity of detail was at once a tribute to the master's painstaking skill, and to the long apprenticeship he had served in the cutting of cameos.

Even with the shadow of death threatening him for the last six or eight years of his life, he was serene, cheerful, enthusiastic. He kept his two studios filled with eager workers, such as MacMonnies, Fraser, Martiny, and Louis Saint Gaudens; and he developed the happy faculty of communicating his ideas to others and of producing through their hands work essentially his own. He was the impulse behind an entire school of younger artists. But it was at a great physical cost. As his strength failed him, and when too weak to stand, he would sit by his assistants sketching his ideas upon a pad; when too weak to sit,

[69]

he was carried in an improvised sedan chair from one studio to another, where he reclined on couches directing and suggesting.

Thus Death finally found him, busy to the last. The summer of 1907 was a conflict against great odds, and the end finally came on the evening of August 3, 1907. He died as he had lived, a member of no church, but a man distinguished by his nobility of character. "He left the world a little better than he found it." With these words, Mayor McClellan closed the memorial oration, held in New York a few months later,—the city which is associated most intimately with his life work. And of no man could this more truly be said, nor could there be greater fame than this. If the trend of a man's life is ever upward toward the stars—if out of toil and privation he yet achieves nobility of thought and deed—and if he leaves behind him monuments in enduring bronze and stone whose mere presence is a constant inspiration to every passer-by—then the world is indeed better for his having lived in it.

And such a man was preëminently Augustus Saint Gaudens, the sculptor who typified American character.

III
FREDERICK MACMONNIES
THE PAINTER-SCULPTOR

III

FREDERICK MACMONNIES

THE PAINTER-SCULPTOR

BACK in the year of our Lord 1893 when the Columbian Exposition was in its glory, a Southern youth with big eyes was among the throng who were busily engaged in trying to drink it all in. One of his most vivid memories which persisted in after years was the Court of Honor with its majestic figure of the "Republic" standing on guard (that was French's work) and the lagoon with its ornate fountain in the center. He asked the name of this stately ship rowed by nymphs and attended by sea-horses and dolphins, and was told that it was "the MacMonnies Fountain." That, indeed, was the name which was popularly bestowed upon it—instead of "the Columbian Fountain," and the sculptor thereof became famed in one short year from Maine to California, as the visitors to the "Fair" narrated its beauties to the folks back home. Frederick MacMonnies could not have chosen a more auspicious time or method of making his artistic début.

[73]

At that time the artist was just turning thirty. He had been born on September 28, 1863, in Brooklyn, and his formative years—like those of other successful artists—were marked by struggle, hardship, and perseverance; his first brilliant success, therefore, was honestly earned.

William MacMonnies, his father, was Scotch, of Clan Menzies. He had come to America as a young fellow bringing his "burr" with him, plus an innate Scotch thrift and acumen. He established a successful grain business in New York and was on the highroad to comfort if not opulence, when the Civil War swept his business away. It was in these parlous times that Frederick was born. He is said to have revealed a fondness, if not a talent, for modeling things when a very little fellow of five. He used to beg bits of dough from his mother for this purpose, until he discovered a better medium. At that time white chewing gum or "wax" was in style among the younger generation. Frederick saved up his pennies until he could obtain a sufficient supply of the wax to make his horses, dogs, and persons. His *chef d'œuvre*, the product of a vast amount of mastication, was a mounted Washington, which was treasured among the family heirlooms.

Another vivid early incident was the coming to Brooklyn of Barnum's Circus, the "greatest on

FREDERICK MACMONNIES

At work in his studio on a detail of the Marne statue

earth," with its marvelous street pageant including its string of elephants. The small boy watched these huge beasts entranced, and then rushed madly home to model one of them from memory. His medium this time was clay, as he did not have enough wax saved up for such a bulky animal. Wax, after all, was unsatisfactory, so as a next venture he tackled "real sculpture"—the actual carving out of a pet bull-frog in a slab of paving-stone, his chisel being an ice-pick!

There is only one family explanation of this art instinct, if we must trace such impulses to heredity. His mother, Juliana West, was a grandniece of the famous Benjamin West, a pioneer among American painters. Certain it is that young MacMonnies liked to draw as well as model, and at ten is said to have painted a very creditable likeness of his father.

The state of his father's finances at this time, how-ever, did not permit the boy to follow his inclinations. He was sent to the public schools for a few years, but was obliged to leave early in his teens and go to work. His father found him a position as a clerk in a jewelry store; but the boy through it all never lost sight of his original ambition. He had long since decided that he wanted to be a sculptor. How to realize that ambition, and at the same time earn a living, was his big problem.

In a fortunate moment he heard that Mr. Saint Gaudens needed a helper in his studio, and he lost no time in applying for the job. He got the place, but it was some time before the busy man discovered the talent of his apprentice. The story of these early days is told with much verve by René de Quélin, a French sculptor who for a time assisted Saint Gaudens:[1] "In the studio I was much attracted toward a lad of seventeen—pale, thin, gaunt and anæmic-looking—seeming better fitted to be a patient in some good sanitarium in a more congenial climate. It was Frederick MacMonnies. His duties combined keeping accounts with the regular studio chores—mixing clay and serving it as requested, keeping the models wet and covering them with cloths at night, attending to fires in winter, answering the door, and running errands.

"It was easy to see, however, that his heart and purpose were quite above and beyond the tasks assigned him. He wanted to model, and that was the reason he was there. It was not difficult, therefore, to imagine what was going on in the breast of one with that constant longing to handle clay from the expressive standpoint, and not just to water it, mix it with a spade, or knead it into a more intimate mass. No doubt the strain of circumstances at the time,

[1] *Arts and Decoration,* April, 1922.

[76]

coupled with the vagaries and idiosyncrasies of genius, diverted Saint Gaudens's mind from all but most pressing matters; for he gave no heed to MacMonnies's persistent plea to model, thus delaying discovery of the unusual talent that awaited his training. Deprived of the opportunity he sought, under pressure from his parents to cease such menial work, and his own ambition suffering through continued postponement of the chance to enter upon the work he had really come for, MacMonnies was almost brought to the point of giving it up. He persevered, however, and clung to the determination to achieve his ambition. I admired his character, and we became good friends. He was always rather quiet and most courteous."

Mr. De Quélin goes on to give a graphic account of the Saint Gaudens studio at this time (1881) and of the master himself. He says that in those early days of struggle for recognition in the world of sculptural art, Saint Gaudens was constantly confronted by the obstacle of finding funds to carry out his artistic projects, and to pay his studio helpers. The strain of financing his ventures as well as the labor of designing kept his highly-strung nerves on edge.

"In Augustus Saint Gaudens, as in most geniuses, was equal capacity for extremes of feeling—for sudden bursts of sunshine and as sudden storms with all their exciting accompaniments. He was a thorough good fellow and possessed a generous, noble, and poetic spirit, inspiring all who worked with him; but unfavorable circumstances at times drove him into excessive irritability, and he became irregular and erratic. He would work furiously for a few days, then remain long away from the studio, possibly returning in a morose and churlish mood. The pressure for money was always unbearable to him."

Finally one day the overwrought nerves gave way, and Saint Gaudens vented his wrath by hurling lumps of clay at everything in sight, in his studio. His brother came in just in time to calm his outburst of fury, and persuaded him to go home and rest. There was no doubt that he was a sick man. De Quélin continues:

"Saint Gaudens stayed away nearly three weeks. In the interim his brother Louis and I were in charge, and MacMonnies found his chance; for when he asked what he should do, we told him to do what he liked. He immediately mustered two grocery boxes such as hold canned goods. Seated upon one and using the other for a stand, he quickly modeled several full-length little comic figures. He made four or five. We were watching him with keen interest. The miniature figures were really well done—full of character and very humorous. MacMonnies had talent;

that was obvious. We had a talk and decided he should do something serious; so we set him to work copying one of Donatello's bas-reliefs. He did it beautifully, with an excellent touch. This was kept to surprise Saint Gaudens upon his return. At last he came, and on his tour around the studio he took the wet cloth off the panel to see what it was, asking excitedly: 'Who did this?'

" 'MacMonnies,' we told him.

" 'No, impossible; you're joking,' he said. 'Don't fool; who did it?'

"We assured him we were quite in earnest, that the panel was really MacMonnies's own work.

" 'Well,' said the master in amazement, 'we must set him to work at once. De Quélin, you take him and give him something to do; he may assist you.' "

Saint Gaudens, with his accustomed generosity to budding talent, made up thereafter for his first neglect of this Scotch lad. He took a personal interest in his progress, criticized his work, and gradually gave him more and more important work to do in the studio. And his pupil never disappointed him in his first promise. He was quiet and hard-working. He would do a subject over a dozen times, if so be he could please the eye of the master. Further, the master included him in the studio talk, when fellow-artists, painters, architects, and sculptors, would drop in, as they frequently did to exchange views. Stanford White, the architect, was a colaborer with Saint Gaudens. Then there were John La-Farge, Edwin Abbey, Blashfield, Maynard, Cox, and many another. The lot of the young student had at last fallen among pleasant places for him; for nowhere else in America could he have obtained both the atmosphere and the training that were his in these years with Saint Gaudens.

At the master's suggestion, MacMonnies entered a class in the National Academy of Design, to learn the technique of drawing. In order to "make" this class he was required to present an original drawing, and this he did at the studio, under the direction of Louis Saint Gaudens and De Quélin. It was accepted, and he proudly entered upon his new work with the same zest he had shown in the modeling. He attended the life classes at the Academy at night and worked in the studio in the daytime. Of course, it was not all smooth sailing. The pinch of poverty while not actually present, was often just around the corner; and many a lunch was a bowl of soup or a sandwich eaten in some cheap restaurant. But he was not alone in these privations; they were then as now the fate of many happy-go-lucky art students, and regarded as part of the game.

By this time MacMonnies's family had awakened

to his talent, and were almost as anxious as he to see him succeed. His father was able to obtain for him a few small commissions and an older brother advanced funds which enabled him to go to Paris for further study. His master, Saint Gaudens, also helped by obtaining lodging for him with a relative, at very low rates. He had hardly begun his work in Paris, however, when his brother met with an untimely end by drowning. It looked as though the young student would have to return home, but again the generosity of Saint Gaudens paved the way for his remaining abroad.

A further interruption occurred in this fateful year. The dreaded scourge of cholera broke out in the French capital, and on the urgent advice of his home folks, Frederick forsook the city and went to Munich, where he devoted most of his time to the study of painting—for, as we have seen, his artistic bent lay almost as much in the direction of color as of modeling.

Then followed a "hike" (as we would call it today) through the Alps, with many leisurely stops to visit interesting nooks, or to study types of people. His purse was not too well supplied with cash, but he had enough for the ensuing week, so why worry? Thus he made his way back by easy stages to Paris, ready to resume work in the life classes—only to receive a message from Saint Gaudens: "I need your help on some big pieces of work; come home as soon as possible." He obeyed the summons, but was enabled to return to France the next year, with still broader experience, and enough funds to see him through the winter.

Although only twenty when he first began work in Paris, he at once impressed his teachers as something more than a novice. His practical experience in Saint Gaudens's studio and other study in America had given him a maturity far in advance of the average student of twenty. He entered the École des Beaux Arts, in the atelier of M. Falguiere, one of the foremost sculptors of the day; but it was not long until his master took him from the class and made him his assistant, to criticize the work of other pupils.

At twenty-four he won the Prix d'Atelier, and he won it again two years later,—this being the highest prize open to foreign students. There is a legend that one day on presenting himself to Falguiere, the latter said with mock impatience: "Here, get out! I can teach you nothing more!"

About this time he opened up his own little studio on the Impasse du Maine, in the Latin Quarter, and began work, among other things, on his first "big" piece—a "Diana." Long and faithfully he worked upon it in the clay, and then one day in his absence from the studio, Falguiere wandered in. The master looked upon the figure at first critically, and then approvingly. As he began to study it, he forgot for the moment that it was not his own, and began to set to work to improve it. He twisted and pulled and dug and punched poor Diana, to alter her pose to his liking. Then at last he stopped for breath and stepped back satisfied.

"Voila, mon ami! J'aime mieux ca. (There, my friend, I like her better so)" he cried, and took his departure.

He had really intended to do his pupil a great favor, and it was a sincere compliment; but poor Mac-Monnies was crestfallen, upon his return. His master had unwittingly given his "Diana" the exact pose of one of his own compositions! So the younger man went painfully to work to punch the long-suffering goddess back into her former likeness. That she emerged from this second ordeal is a matter of record. She won for her modeler an honorable mention at the Salon of 1889.

This same year marked a definite turning point in his career; he entered the American field as a full-fledged sculptor and "on his own." Of course, the powerful influence of Saint Gaudens meant much to him—so much, that in later years at a public gathering which both attended, he turned toward his old master and said: "Gentlemen, this is the man to whom I owe everything I have accomplished." However, no influence could have pushed him forward, if he had not more than measured up to his opportunities.

Three important works belong to this opening period. The first was a trio of life-size angels in bronze for Saint Paul's Church down on lower Broadway, in New York. This is generally regarded as his first commission. It was followed by his "Nathan Hale" for the City Hall Park; and a portrait statue of "James Stranahan," for Prospect Park, Brooklyn. Both of the latter works were executed abroad, and when shown at the Salon of 1891 they won a "second medal"—"the first and only time that an American sculptor had been so honored at the Salon."

The "Nathan Hale" still remains one of his best-known compositions, partly because of its prominent position, where millions of persons pass by in the course of a year. It is not intended as a life portrait of the patriot-spy, but an idealized conception. MacMonnies had no photograph or other likeness to work from, but did not much care for one. He himself says: "A statue in stone or bronze should never be a photographic likeness, but should be so conceived as an ideal that the figure should symbolize the life-work of the subject." This artistic creed he could put

[84]

into full execution on the "Nathan Hale," without fear of reprisals from the critics; and so.he has given us an ideal of a patriot with fettered hands and feet, yet with chin held high and gaze fixed proudly aloft— the face and figure of a man who could well say: "I only regret that I have but one life to lose for my country!" The sculptor tried earnestly to convey this message to the man in the street—to give him an enduring lesson in patriotism—and not merely to carve a pleasing statue. He sums up his own state of mind in these words: "I wanted to make something that would set the bootblacks and little clerks around there thinking—something that would make them want to be somebody and find life worth living."

The "Stranahan" statue was hardly less successful, and although more closely a portrait—having been done from life, with all the accessories of contemporary apparel—it aroused the cordial appreciation of the critics. Here was the wielder of a new chisel which could never be commonplace, they said; and it is true to-day as yesterday. No matter what commission the sculptor has undertaken, he has had the happy faculty of investing it with a certain distinction.

However, up to the year 1893 Frederick MacMonnies was still unknown to the general public. His work was much better known in France than at home, but even there was limited largely to a small circle of artistic friends. This, we say, was in 1893. By the year 1894, he had become known all over the land. What had worked the magic transformation? It was his ornate fountain, already referred to, at the Columbian Exposition.

The "World's Fair," as we all persisted in calling it, took form at Chicago at a happy time. It marked both an industrial and an artistic awakening. It awakened us to the sharp realization that we had within our own borders artists and artisans who could create works of beauty of the highest type. We were further favored by the then recent invention of the incandescent electric light from the Edison workshop; and the thousands of tiny, gleaming bulbs now employed for the first time to set off the majestic white buildings at night added no little to the fairy-like splendor of the scene. Nowadays, our "Great White Ways" and gaudy illuminations have made electricity an old story; it requires an unusually elaborate display to make us turn our heads. But who does not still recall with a continuing thrill the Court of Honor in Jackson Park, ablaze with these new jewels of the night? They were shattered into a million facets by the dancing waters of the lagoon in the center, and lighted up a fairy ship rowed by nymphs. It was the lordly Ship of State, steered by Father

Time and heralded by Victory blowing a trumpet; while on a dais sat the stately figure of Columbia. Such was the Columbian Fountain which, by spontaneous tribute to its designer, was popularly called the "MacMonnies Fountain"—and has so been called to this day.

Here again the good genius of Saint Gaudens had been in evidence. He was a member of the Advisory Board of the Exposition, and had urged that they employ sculpture as freely as possible, in order not merely to decorate the grounds and relieve the long straight lines of the huge buildings, but also to demonstrate the ability of America in this field. His recommendations carried, as we know. Many scattered commissions were given out for smaller groups, but there were two big commissions. To French was entrusted the heroic figure of the "Republic" for the Court. Who should do the Fountain, the *pièce de résistance* of the whole setting? With fine faith, Saint Gaudens advocated his former pupil, and largely on his recommendation the highly-important commission was entrusted to MacMonnies. He was still a young, comparatively untried man, of less than thirty; yet the Board voted him the sum of fifty thousand dollars for this project, and gave him a free hand in its design.

Of his special problems we have not space here to

[87]

treat. The Fountain, no matter how big in conception, was likely to be dwarfed by the huge structures surrounding it; consequently the sculptor could gain no idea of relative values until the composition was set up in place—and then it would be too late to rectify mistakes! At the same time, it must be big enough to "carry," no matter from what part of the lagoon it might be viewed. The artist solved his problem by treating it as an ornate and highly embellished composition—a picture in its frame, as it were,—and with a grace and seeming ease which belied the tremendous labor which had entered into it. The Ship seemed to float upon the water, a dream vessel indeed, and whether seen by day or night was the pivotal point of vision in the great Court.

Incidentally, before MacMonnies completed his task he had expended the last dollar of his appropriated fifty thousand, but he gave no thought to that. He held and used this money only in trust; and he obtained his larger reward in the tremendous prestige which the completed work gave him. Thereafter, he did not have to seek work; it flowed naturally to him.

"I did not regret my work on this Fountain," said Mr. MacMonnies to the writer recently, "nor the fact that I made no money out of it—for I ended just where I had begun financially. To me it represented something vastly more than either labor or cost. Why, it cost me ten thousand dollars to get the completed work transported over to America. It had all been done in my Paris studio, because there I had every facility and could work more quietly, besides having my own skilled assistants; but getting it across the seas and set up in its final position presented some interesting problems. You see, it was done in plaster—exceedingly fragile stuff—which meant that every piece and every figure had to be doubly wrapped. Fortunately nothing broke in transit, but the railroads were so congested at the time, with exhibits from everywhere coming in, that we couldn't get our stuff delivered. I remember yet what a time of it we had. The last week rolled around, and some of the nymphs got lost in the freight yards. I went into the yards personally and searched frantically—it seemed to me that I checked up thousands of cars—and luckily found the strays just in time. We got them opened and the Fountain set up on the evening just before the 'gong sounded.'

"I have never worked so fast in my life, before or since, as I did on that Fountain. They gave us only fourteen months from first to last. Nowadays I take longer to work out things. And, by the way, that was the first and last work of the sort that I have done for expositions. Why? Partly because of the temporary character of the work; it is only for the time being, and then it vanishes. To me, sculpture means more than work for the day—it means work for eternity. And my other reason is that I think such work should be left for the younger men, just as I was a young man. It is good apprenticeship work, but leads nowhere. I have had numerous opportunities since—as, for example, at the Paris Exposition of 1900—but have always declined them."

Certainly, he himself could not complain of lack of recognition, once his reputation was achieved in this meteoric fashion. It was not long before orders and inquiries began to come to him from all parts of the country. The American decorative sense was being awakened at last, as other sculptors also were discovering. A little later on, he found himself so busy that he made it a rule not to enter into any competition with other sculptors for a prospective order.

"In this connection," says French Strother,[1] "a story is told of an American city that asked him to enter a design for army and navy groups for a soldiers' and sailors' monument. He declined to compete. Then the commission was tendered him outright. He submitted sketches of his idea for the groups. The committee in charge of the monument wrote him, asking, 'How many tons of granite do you intend to use in the base?' His reply was, 'If you are in the

[1] *World's Work*, December, 1905.

business of buying granite, you may use as much as you want, one ton or one hundred thousand tons. I am an artist, and I have never yet heard of art being bought by the pound.' The question was dropped until the contract for the commission was drawn. When Mr. MacMonnies received it he discovered in it a clause providing that in case the bronzes were ever thrown down from their base, by any cause whatever, and any person or property should be injured, he and his heirs and their heirs forever should be liable for the damage sustained. He returned the contract without comment, unsigned. When the committee wrote him asking the reason, his brief reply was, 'Your lawyers are too sharp.' "

Harking back again, however, to the days immediately following the Columbian Exposition—there was a second bit of work in entirely different *métier* which brought the artist almost as much into the public eye, as his Fountain had done. It was his "Bacchante." Had the artist deliberately planned it as an advertising "stunt"—which most assuredly he did not—the results could not have been more satisfactory from a publicity point of view.

The "Bacchante" was born of his work in Paris; it betrays the French influence; but it is also frankly pagan in conception. Here is a live, alert nymph, dancing with the riotous joy of life, her graceful body and limbs absolutely unfettered. She is poised airily upon the toes of one foot—a creature apparently wild, free, and irresponsible. But at the same time a human note is struck: in the crook of her left arm she holds an eager child who fixes hungry eyes upon a bunch of grapes that she holds high in air and temptingly beyond his reach. Her smiling face is one of teasing mirth. It is a cunning compound of idealism and realism.

This bronze group, done life-size, was intended for the corridor of the Boston Public Library, that shrine of letters which contains the mural decorations of Sargent and Abbey. But when the frivolous "Bacchante" tried to enter these walls a stern note of protest went up. They would have none of her. It is hard to understand why they disapproved. The Volstead Act which to-day the nymph might be accused of putting to scorn—was not then in force. As to her lack of attire, she was by no means the first nude figure to greet Boston eyes; and there is no suggestiveness whatever in her dancing pose. In the thirty years which have elapsed since then, many another public revealment in painted or modeled guise of the human form divine has been set up. Howbeit, poor "Bacchante" knocked at Boston's door a few years too soon—and promptly got her walking papers! But succor was at hand. The Metropolitan

BACCHANTE

By Frederick MacMonnies

Museum of Art, in New York, heard of the maiden's plight, and at once offered her a home; and here she has remained ever since. Naturally, her wanderings caused a deal of comment at the time—comment which overflowed the purely art periodicals and got into the daily newspapers—and as a net result, the name and fame of the young sculptor became still further bruited abroad. To-day "Bacchante" remains one of his best-known compositions; and the critics regard it as one of the half-dozen best studies of the nude in the United States. The copy at the Metropolitan Museum is of bronze, now turned quite dark and (when last seen) placed in a particularly dark portion of the hall. Another copy is in Paris, also done in bronze; while a third, in marble, is in the Brooklyn Museum of Fine Arts.

Meanwhile, the artist was divided in his allegiance between the respective merits of America and France, as the location for his studio. His patriotic instincts led him to return to America more than once, but each time the roar and upheaval of New York drove him away again. At Paris he had found a congenial colony of friends and pupils, and he had a pleasant country home in Giverny. In 1888, while yet unknown, he had married another art student, Mary Louise Fairchild, of St. Louis, who also won considerable fame as a miniature painter. Their home, while abroad, was a favorite rendezvous of the American colony.

More and more, however, the pull came from America. We had need of this facile sculptor, and were not backward about telling him so. Some of his finest public work, about this period, was done for Prospect Park, Brooklyn. This city was his native heath, and as a boy the park had been a chosen playground. He designed a clever group for a small fountain, at one such spot—his "Boy with the Duck"—splashing merrily in the spray from jets of water spouting from the mouths of small turtles. But at the entrances to the Park some much larger works were set up. Facing the principal entrance a beautiful Memorial Arch has been erected. It is not as large as the Arc de Triomphe, in Paris, but so commanding is its site that the effect of grandeur is no less apparent. Mr. MacMonnies was given the entire commission for embellishing this Arch; and his work consists of two closely-wrought groups, the "Army" and the "Navy," decorating the piers on each side, while the top is surmounted by a quadriga of symbolical figures. The two lower groups are executed in the same general manner that he employed some years later for the Battle Monument at Princeton—a mass of blended figures in action against a common enemy. Mr. Mac-Monnies says that he conceived the group as an "ex-

[94]

plosion"—a mass hurled against a stone wall, which scattered as it burst and then became petrified into its final form. In the "Army" group, the soldier in the lead, brandishing his sword, is said to be a fair likeness of MacMonnies himself at the time; while in the "Navy" group, the likenesses of some of his friends have been discerned. The surmounting group, "America" in the center, flanked by winged Victories and prancing horses, forms a silhouette vibrant with life and action.

However, at another entrance to Prospect Park are steeds of still finer breed and mettle. These are two groups called originally "The Triumph of Mind Over Brute Force," but since called variously, "The Wild Horses" and "The Horse Tamers." Each of the two groups consists of a pair of powerful leaping brutes, which a slim youth is holding in check. To obtain these spirited poses, MacMonnies purchased two wild Andalusian horses and brought them to his Paris studio. Here by means of stout ropes and tackles the horses were made to assume their difficult postures scores of times, until he had caught this play of restrained, leaping muscles for all time. The magnificent bronze stallions formed part of a collected exhibit at the Paris Exposition of 1900, which won for the sculptor the Grand Prize of Honor, the highest award in the gift of the Jury.

That Mr. MacMonnies, after the lapse of a quarter of a century, still regards "The Horse Tamers" as among his best work, came out in the course of a conversation with him recently.

"Mr. MacMonnies," I ventured to remark, "among all your works which I have seen, there is nothing quite so satisfying to me as those wild horses."

"I am glad you think so," he replied, with an emphatic nod of his head; "for I consider them as good as anything I have ever done. And there is another early work of mine over in Brooklyn, of entirely different character, which I still rank among my best. I refer to the portrait statue of Mr. Stranahan."

As further illustration of the sculptor's versatility —to this first period belong also the heroic bronze "Victory" for the Battle Monument at West Point, the pediment having been designed by Stanford White; a portrait statue of "Sir Henry Vane," a courtly cavalier for the Boston Library; and a portrait statue of Shakespeare for the Congressional Library; not to mention sundry fountain pieces and smaller conceits of purely decorative nature. As we compare any of these with other products of the same time—the two nudes, "Diana," and "Bacchante;" the leaping horses; the fairy "Ship of State;" the Army and Navy groups; the "Hale" and "Stranahan"—we can but marvel at the many-sidedness of the man.

And yet, wide apart as they are in conception, the same technique, the "MacMonnies touch," is readily discernible in all.

Not content with this achievement, in 1900 the artist announced to his friends that he intended to lay aside his chisel and devote himself to painting! True to his word, and despite many remonstrances, he pushed back the clay platform, set up an easel in its stead, and went to work. We have already noticed how his allegiance was divided between these two forms of art in his student days, and now the urge had come again so strongly that he felt he could not ignore it. He showed his first canvases in the Salon of 1901 but, lest the Jury should be prejudiced either for or against them, he witheld his name. The anonymous paintings, nevertheless, received honorable mention. Later he received medals for other exhibits in oil. Several noteworthy portraits from his brush were done at this time; and at intervals later we find him turning to the same medium. A writer in *The Studio*, discussing "Frederick MacMonnies, Portrait Painter," tells of his change of mediums as follows:

"Two or three years ago, anyone visiting Mr. MacMonnies's studio would have found himself in a huge, dusty, barn-like workshop, filled with all the unsightly paraphernalia of a sculptor. . . . The work of the moment, the clay models, the visitor would have

[97]

found concealed under dank, shapeless masses of wet, gray rags. But to-day what a change! Spacious Renaissance tapestries cover the walls; soft Oriental carpets cover the polished floor; furniture of rare design abounds; and in the midst of the rich color and fastidious forms are Mr. MacMonnies's new triumphs in the struggle of art—great, striking paintings, whose variety and range of color complete the contrast."

After discussing some of these canvases in detail, the writer continues: "But though by his change of medium Mr. MacMonnies has not denied his older gods, he has now, of course, found new expression for his faithful love of realities. He has reproduced color, painted it truthfully and directly, not rearranging and composing backgrounds, not looking out for a possible monotone, but reproducing existent colors, however bafflingly brilliant. . . . One of the reasons why he has been able to reproduce color so accurately and brilliantly, is a triumph on the more practical side of painting. He began his career as a painter by a systematic study of processes of painting, of the properties of pigments and media, and of different kinds of canvases. 'In any art,' he says, 'your materials must be of the best, when the pursuit is so infinitely difficult.' His portraits are painted on canvases prepared by himself, and in colors ground and mixed in his own studio."

FREDERICK MACMONNIES

The same writer states that MacMonnies followed sculpture rather than painting, from force of circumstances. So promising had been his drawings and sketches, while as a young man with Saint Gaudens, that the latter advised him to study both arts if possible. He had sent letters of introduction not only to Falguiere, the sculptor, but also to Paul Baudry, the painter of the mural decorations of the Paris Opera House, and to John S. Sargent, the portrait painter. But Sargent had left Paris, and Baudry was ill, so these two letters were useless. However MacMonnies later criticized classes in painting as well as sculpture. "Indeed his influence as a painter has already perceptibly counted. For his manner of criticizing, his power of teaching, is unusual, is simple and forcible in no ordinary way. His liking for fact, for reality, prevents him from ever taking refuge in theorizing."

And a writer in *Century* adds: "The rendering of character is startling in its reality. Selecting the sitters who appealed to him, Mr. MacMonnies has presented the dramatic quality of interesting personalities, unusual, attractive, compelling curiosity and attention. Without any psychological or literary aids, we are made to realize the general characteristics, the thoughts, the aims of these people, what they stand for in life. Too often in modern painting the

[99]

sitter is but a model; here are men and women."

One of his canvases of this period is "Mrs. Frederick MacMonnies and Children in the Garden of Giverny," which shows a delightful vista of trees and shrubbery, while in the foreground and center are four figures—Mrs. MacMonnies in a reclining chair, their two children, Marjorie and Betty, and a French maid in a white cap, who, seated on the ground, leans against a tree, knitting.

The home at Giverny must have been truly delightful. The place had been a convent once upon a time, and was a retired spot situated near a quiet roadway and amid the rambling radiance of a picturesque old garden. Vines, shrubs, and trees ran riot, and shaded walks led off here and there to sequestered nooks. In different parts of this garden the sculptor had established two studios—the one a huge barn-like affair which, in fact, had formerly been the barn, for work on equestrian statues and other large pieces. Here he would have his horses conducted and put through their paces, day after day, until he got the exact pose he required. The other studio was smaller and was used for painting. It is interesting to note that, at one time, he worked coincidentally upon the heroic equestrian statue of "General Slocum," and upon his portraits in oil.

Mr. MacMonnies himself does not regard this love

of painting as especially remarkable. "I turn from modeling to painting, in order to rest my faculties," he told the writer not long ago; "not that painting is easier, but because it is different. After a long siege at modeling, it is a great relief to sit down before a plane surface and work in colors. All arts are coequal—no one is more important than another. Music, sculpture, painting, writing,—all are a part of the eternal scheme of things. An artist may express himself in many ways. However, I personally regard sculpture as the most difficult of arts; it is more difficult than painting, because every side needs separate attention, and the onlooker can and does pass entirely around it; whereas, the painter can compel the beholder to view his work from some one chosen position."

One result of his taking up painting was necessarily the slowing down of his modeling. The ensuing ten years were not nearly so productive in this field as the first decade had been. From 1888 to the end of the century he had worked with almost feverish haste. As we have seen, it was remarkable for its diversity and no less remarkable for its volume. The painting gave him the chance to catch his second wind, so to speak. During the next few years he was to produce such works in stone or bronze as two handsome bronze doors for the Congressional Library; an equestrian

[101]

statue of "General Slocum," for Brooklyn; an equestrian statuette of "Roosevelt"; an equestrian statue
of "General McClellan," for Washington; two fountains for the Knickerbocker Hotel, New York; and
numerous smaller studies. However, this output in
no way compared with that of the earlier period, and
one cannot help regretting that he did not stick to one
medium. Since the time of Michelangelo, for that
matter, every great sculptor has probably felt the
urge to try his skill with the brush and palette.

"Yes, it is a temptation," said another artist,
George Grey Barnard, to me not long ago. "We all
feel the impulse to try our hand out with the paints.
I have done a few canvases from time to time, and
always lay them aside regretfully. I want to go on
with them."

Since this book is a treatise on sculpture, we must
hurry past the array of glowing canvases which invite
inspection, and consider MacMonnies's later work
with mallet and chisel. Down in the university town
of Princeton, at the intersection of the Lincoln Highway and another important thoroughfare, in a V-
shaped square, stands a great monument commemorating the defeat of the British by Washington's men,
at the Battle of Princeton. It may be styled a "high
relief," the bronze figures of the General on horseback
surrounded by soldiers charging forward to victory

forming an unforgettable picture against the classic background of the stone entablature. The principle of a congested mass is the same as that employed in the Army and Navy groups for the Brooklyn Memorial Arch. The modeling is so involved that it eludes the passing glance, which fact is unfortunate for the thousands of motorists who dart swiftly by. But it repays and satisfies the prolonged scrutiny; while the contour of the whole resolves itself into a definite architectural line.

Over a hundred years ago, Congress resolved upon such a Battle Monument, and it is quite interesting to read their specifications for it: "It shall be of bronze, the General to be represented in Roman dress, holding a truncheon in his right hand, and his head encircled with a laurel wreath"—another old Roman evidently, such as now ornaments the Capitol grounds! Furthermore, it was to be done by "the best artist in Europe."

When I quoted these original specifications to Mr. MacMonnies, he smiled at the conception of Washington in Roman garb. "But that is the classic notion of sculpture," he remarked, after a pause. "It was the accepted thing a hundred years ago, and it still is in some circles. Some of our critics still assail the sculptors on the ground that we are too realistic.

"Now in this Princeton Monument I did not want

to depict Washington as an aloof figure, a demigod. I tried to show, in the whole group, the struggle and uncertainty of the battle—how at first there was defeat, then indecision, then a rallying to final victory. I wanted to show Washington as a 'patriot with the toothache,' if you please! Again, there are no heroics in the composition; there is no laudation of war—only its misery. You will note this in the general air of dejection, the drooping lines, the 'rain' lines, as I call them. That is my conception of warfare, and the same note that I strike in my Marne Monument."

The latter work, which will be considered presently, is one of the four large commissions that have occupied his time for the past ten years. The Princeton Monument, unveiled about two years ago, was the second; the two fountains for the New York Public Library, a third; and a certain much-discussed fountain group in the City Hall Park, New York, a fourth; not to mention in detail some smaller works such as a particularly charming group done for Mr. George Gould of his small daughter and her pet goat. This was finished in both marble and bronze.

The above does not seem like a large volume of work for ten years, and the artist admits the fact without argument. "I do not work as fast as when I was younger," he says; "but for one thing, the subjects themselves are more difficult. I think nothing now of working for five years, if necessary, on a single subject. It took me that long to work out my 'Civic Virtue'; and it is taking me that long on my Marne Monument."

His casual mention of "Civic Virtue," which made him the storm center of public discussion when first set up, recalls the "Bacchante" furore of earlier days. If at that time New York made merry over "prudish" Boston, the latter has had abundant opportunity to laugh in her own turn. It all arose over the heroic statue for the center of the new Fountain in City Hall Park, New York, entitled "Civic Virtue." This is a nude male figure of sturdy limbs and stern aspect, with a sword resting upon one shoulder. At his feet lie sirens whom he spurns unheeding. The preliminary design for this group was approved in 1915, but it was not until the spring of 1922 that it was completed. Then the voice of protest arose—chiefly from some women's organizations which maintained that it was "a degradation to womanhood," and that "his man was trampling woman underfoot."

We have not space here, nor inclination, to take sides in this controversy, or to describe the hue and cry of voices striving to be heard. It was a typical tempest in a teapot. But in justice to the artist, we quote a letter from Mr. MacMonnies which clearly states his position: [1]

"The youth has one foot behind one of the sirens who is impeding his progress by entwining herself and her fish's tails about it, and the other foot is planted on a rack in front of the other siren, who is attempting to snare him with her net. He is not 'trampling,' 'kicking,' nor 'stepping' upon, but escaping from the sirens.

"I am blamed for choosing a male figure to suggest strength, female to suggest grace and beauty, forms of sea monsters to suggest treachery and guile. I did not invent this. I have to take things as they are. An artist is not responsible for verities. He only records them. He is observer—spectator of life. He will not lie to please anybody. To flatter the ambitions of women he cannot pretend that their graceful fragile forms give an impression of strength.

"The Creator has willed otherwise. He cannot express his idea at all unless he bases it on the verities. He cannot get it across. The attainment of suffrage by women has not yet changed the fundamental verities, nor altered the laws of creation. When it does, some artist will be there to record the change.

"The gem-like City Hall recalling another age, lying at the bottom of the well formed by the canon-like wall of surrounding skyscrapers of the present city, required a design that would harmonize the old and new. To make the fountain emblematic of our treasured antique jewel and a living part of modern New York; to 'throw back' and indulge in the

[1] *Architecture,* April, 1922.

[106]

CIVIC VIRTUE

By Frederick MacMonnies; in City Hall Park, New York

ease of archæology and build a graceful miniature fountain
and figures such as might have been done when the City Hall
was built (when horses trotted about drawing dainty ladies
and elegant casual gentlemen in fragile carriages, and the sky
line of New York was uncluttered as far as the Palisades),
would have been to make the neighborhood as dead as the
Roman Forum or St. Paul's Churchyard.

"I believe my titanic Youth will bring down some of the
strength of the towering structures about, and by his robust
scale only add by opposition (if such a thing is possible) to
the grace and dignity of the City Hall and light up the park
with life and modernity."

Mr. MacMonnies returned to this country in 1916,
as war conditions in Paris made artistic work difficult.
He thought at the time that he would probably go
back in a few months, but he has remained here ever
since.

"I like New York, in spite of the noise and hurry,"
he told me, on a recent visit to his studio on West
Tenth Street. This studio is a big, plain structure,
and may have been a stable once upon a time—who
knows? Now, however, it is transformed into an excellent workshop. At the back, where the light can
strike in from above as well as at the front, there is
uninterrupted air space of perhaps twenty-five feet in
height. Here, on this particular afternoon, stood the
one and only piece of work that the large studio
contained.

"I work on only one thing at a time," he remarked, noting my glance around the room; "and this has occupied my sleeping and waking moments now for many months past, and will doubtless do so for some months to come. It is my Marne Monument of 'Victory.' "

When completed, this will be a war memorial, an American gift to France made possible by the small contributions of thousands of school children. The sum of $250,000 has already been subscribed, and the artist is practically donating his services. It is a labor of love, and in a sense a return gift to France for the Bartholdi Statue of Liberty, in New York Harbor.

"I wanted to place this in Paris, and went over there especially to find a site," Mr. MacMonnies said. "But the city has become so built up that it is impossible to find an open space sufficient to give this group the space it requires. So we have determined to place it near the village of Meaux, overlooking the River Marne, at the point where the first German advance was halted, in 1914."

The general contour of the group is a narrow pyramid—"like a mountain peak," he said, "the base gradually growing broader giving the impression of stability, of lasting endurance." "Victory," the central figure, is represented as a splendid nude female figure, brooding over her fallen soldiers and still protecting them with her shattered sword, while her face is uplifted to the sky in a gesture of mingled entreaty and defiance. "They shall not pass!" she seems to cry.

"She is like Niobe, weeping for her sons," said the sculptor. "But while she weeps, there is no note of weakness; she will fight to the end. You see here only the horror and tragedy of War—not its glorification. Modern sculpture does not seek to glorify conflict; it glorifies suffering."

The interviewer could and did confirm this changed attitude toward War. He has heard not merely one, but several of our foremost artists speak of memorials which should emphasize the sacrifice of conflict, and not its tawdry glory.

The composition, which to the casual eye is approaching completion, stands nearly ten feet high, in the clay model. The final work, which will be done abroad, will be about fifty feet high and of granite. It is so planned that it will carry its message, no matter from what side it may be viewed. As the sculptor talked to me that day, he continued at work putting on minor touches, in order to satisfy his own exacting requirements. His medium was a fine French clay about the color and consistency of fresh putty.

"You see," he explained, "how the addition of certain figures to the pediment on this side requires a supporting line on the opposite side. That is one of the features which makes sculpture the most difficult of all the fine arts. There are a thousand little depressions or protuberances, each of which must be exactly treated for light and shade, as well as balance of line. That is why a work of this character is so long in the finishing. That is why it required so long to complete the 'Civic Virtue.' Every day as I come into the studio I ask myself, 'What can I demolish to-day?' I once knew of a French sculptor whose life ambition was to carve a 'Jeanne d'Arc.' As he worked on it, he became imbued with the entire spirit of the 15th century, and began collecting everything he could pertaining to it. He had a remarkable collection, but when he died, at seventy-five, his statue of the Maid was not yet completed!"

As I listened to Mr. MacMonnies talk, and watched his busy fingers with the clay, I gained a still further insight into the genius which fires men's souls. Like the Frenchman of whom he told, he did not value time except as an opportunity for further labor. Day after day, now for over three years, he has concentrated upon this one subject—toiling for long, lonely hours upon endless details. And when I asked him if it was nearly done—for it looked so to me—he shook his head. "I'm afraid it will hold me pretty closely to the city this summer," he said.

As the artist talks, his face lights up and banishes for the moment the look of weariness, born of these long days of toil. He has the renewed enthusiasm of the young man of the early nineties. However, MacMonnies was never of robust type. He is slender but of good height and carries himself well except for a slight stoop. His face has few lines, and his hair which curls riotously over his head is still more brown than gray. He is quiet in demeanor but has a kindly courtesy that puts his visitor at once on a friendly footing. His manner is absolutely free from pose. To him, it is not the artist that is important, but his message.

"The man is nothing; the work is everything," he says. "Art is the expression of one's self. It is character wrought into enduring stone or bronze. When I pause to think that these things upon which I labor may endure for centuries, a feeling of awe comes over me. One might well spend one's life on a single work that is to be irrevocable, immutable, unchanged throughout all the centuries. It is not so much the quantity, but how well the thing is done. I have read that certain of the priests of India spend a life-time carving upon a single Buddha; that is a fine conception. When the ruins of Pompeii were unearthed, in the first century, they uncovered a beautiful figure that we now call 'Narcissus.' No one now knows the sculptor, but the work of his chisel persists, and has survived the ruin of that splendid city. There it is for all time.

"I think that is the secret of sculpture—its fascination. We are working upon something as near eternal as man is given to do, on this planet. It is a piece of eternity itself. Into my hands is given a huge, shapeless block of stone, and in it I am permitted to express myself, my thoughts, my feelings, my emotions. The finished work is my impress, however feeble, upon future ages and civilization itself!"

IV
DANIEL CHESTER FRENCH
THE SCULPTOR OF MEMORIALS

DANIEL CHESTER FRENCH

"**Y**ES, half a century is a long time to be at work," mused Daniel Chester French, one afternoon not long ago, as he sat in his New York studio talking with the writer.

Outside, a belated March snowstorm was falling, its big flakes swirling in gusts and eddies before a capricious wind. But in the roomy studio under the big skylight all was bright and cheerful, and even quiet, despite the trucks and trolleys which rushed by in the busy street. The studio was in the rear of the building and fortunately escaped most of the street sounds.

"It was just fifty years ago that I began work upon my first public statue, the 'Minute Man,'" he continued, "and as I look back over all the work since then and view it *en masse*, it seems a century. But when I take it up year by year, it seems only a short time, and the total product quite disappointing."

Thus spoke, with a modesty which was not assumed, a sculptor who has probably contributed more than any other one man to the public memorials, historic and personal, of this country; whose output has been uniformly high in quality; and whose fertility of invention and grace of flowing line have invested each and every subject with potent charm. That a man could have wrought as long and as steadily as Mr. French, without growing stale, is in itself an achievement—and he has kept young. He told the writer the secret.

"I have always enjoyed my work. When I get interested in a subject I lose all track of time, and thoroughly enjoy myself. I am not like my old friend, Saint Gaudens, who took things more seriously. He actually fought his work, studying it from every angle, worrying with it, puzzling over it. Now I never worked that way, and I used to feel guilty— as though I were having too good a time. But I suppose there is more than one way of doing things."

There are so many tales of struggling genius, of poor boys who fought their way upward through poverty to success, that it is pleasant to note exceptions to this economic scheme. Fortune is not always hardhearted, and genius not always under a cloud.

As in the case of Bartlett, whose artistic way was smoothed for him by his parents, so also was that of Daniel Chester French made plain. But, unlike his

DANIEL CHESTER FRENCH
From a photograph from life

DANIEL CHESTER FRENCH

New England contemporary, French stumbled upon his talent by accident. He was nearly grown when, one day, the mood seized him to carve a turnip into the grotesque likeness of a frog dressed in clothes. He carried it into the house, more in jest than earnest, and his stepmother said: "Daniel, there is your career!"—and so it was.

Mr. French comes of a long line of New England ancestry. His forbears held positions of prominence in both local and national affairs. His paternal grandfather, Daniel French, was Attorney General of New Hampshire. His maternal grandfather, William M. Richardson, was Chief Justice of the same state. His grandmother, Sarah French, was related to Daniel Webster; while his great-grandmother, Dorothy Whittier, was a kinswoman of John G. Whittier. His father, Henry Flagg French, was a Judge and also Assistant Secretary of the United States Treasury. At the time of Daniel's birth, April 20, 1850, his parents were living at Exeter, New Hampshire, where their home surroundings are spoken of as charming and delightful. His mother died when he was six years old, leaving three other children, two sisters and a brother. The latter, by the way, was also artistically inclined and later became the Director of the Chicago Art Institute. The children spoke of their mother as "a gentle and judicious woman," and of their father as "the wittiest person they ever knew"; that "he was a man of great activity, energy, and dignity," and one who "beautified every place in which he lived."

When Daniel was ten, the family moved from Exeter to Cambridge, Massachusetts, where their father married again. The children became much attached to their second mother, and always spoke of her also in terms of deep affection. It was she who discerned the young man's budding talent for sculpture, and both she and his father encouraged him to cultivate it.

An earlier bent which Daniel as a boy displayed was the collecting and mounting of birds. At Cambridge he found a congenial friend in a William Brewster, and together they made a practical study of ornithology—following the same bent of George Grey Barnard, as a boy, on the Mississippi River. In young French's efforts at taxidermy and study of contour and plumage, he was unconsciously laying the foundation for his later calling. However, it is interesting to note that the sculptor of maturity did not choose either bird or animal subjects.

Daniel's boyhood was divided between attendance at the Cambridge public schools and work upon his father's farm; with one year spent at the Institute of Technology at Boston. His father did not urge him to take up any particular profession, but waited to see what line the boy would choose for himself. When the little incident of the turnip occurred, both parents encouraged him to go in for art.

Mrs. Helen B. Emerson, who gives a pleasing sketch of this period,[1] says: "Young French's vocation, then chosen, was entered upon with a quiet but steady enthusiasm. May Alcott, the 'Amy' of 'Little Women' and the artist of her family, was then teaching drawing in Boston, and as she and Daniel's father traveled to and fro upon the cars, they conversed upon the future of the young artist. She saw his work, was much interested in it, and offered to lend him her modeling tools. The French family lived on a farm near Concord; and the evening is still a memorable one in their annals, when Daniel was bidden by his father to harness the horse and go and bring from the village Miss Alcott's material. Upon his return the family gathered around the dining-table, and all had an evening of modeling, Daniel making a dog's head. It is a curious fact that although he began his artistic career with the modeling of dogs, birds, and other animals, he turned aside from them later on, and even employed other artists to add such figures to his groups. And yet he had an aptitude for animals. Of a wounded deer made by him in his

[1] *New England Magazine,* May, 1897.

youth, Mr. Cobb, himself a sculptor, said that 'it was better than anybody in Boston could do.' "

There was then no art school in Boston—this was just after the Civil War, and before the awakening of our art which came with the Centennial—so Daniel was largely self-taught at first. He attended a class in anatomy conducted by Dr. Rimmer in Boston, but had little opportunity to study works in sculpture, beyond a few antique casts. He became interested in portraiture and made several busts of members of his family and of neighbors. Then for about a month he had the great privilege of working in the studio of Mr. Ward, in Brooklyn; but circumstances did not permit him to continue there. It is remarkable, in view of French's later achievement, how little expert guidance he had in these formative years. He actually accepted his first paid commissions and carried them through, almost without instruction.

At the age of twenty he visited his brother in Chicago, and there exhibited a bas-relief of his sister, Sarah. This won favorable notice and brought him an order for a similar portrait of a Chicago lady.

And now comes one of the most interesting anecdotes in the entire history of American sculpture, with Daniel French as the chief actor. His home town of Concord was, as we know, the scene of an opening engagement of the Revolutionary War. Here the embattled farmers had withstood the British regulars and "fired the shot heard round the world." Now nearly a century after that lively little disturbance a local movement was set on foot to erect a monument to commemorate it. The village selectmen met to discuss ways and means, and young French, encouraged and aided by his father, presented himself at the meeting with a sketch showing his notion of what such a monument should be. He said with natural diffidence that he would undertake to make the statue heroic size and deliver the plaster cast to the town, if they would defray expenses to the extent of four hundred dollars. This, he stated, would just about cover such expenses, and if they wanted to allow him anything additional, well and good; otherwise he would rest content. They accepted his design, told him to go ahead, and eventually paid him one thousand dollars.

The result of this conference was the well-known "Minute Man" which stands "by the rude bridge" to-day—one of the most familiar bits of historical statuary in all America—and the work of an untried, untutored sculptor! Mr. French confessed some time afterwards that he had no models to guide him, but that he took the general pose from the classic statue of Apollo Belvidere, dropping the arms slightly and clothing the figure to represent the young farmer who hastily forsook his plow and seized his gun, to defend his homeland. The stride of the legs and attitude of the body do indeed recall the Apollo.

The monument was unveiled in 1875, on the centennial of the Concord Fight. A distinguished audience was gathered together for the occasion. Ralph Waldo Emerson, who was a neighbor and friend of the young sculptor, made a brief speech; James Russell Lowell read a poem; and George William Curtis was the orator of the day. When the concealing flag fluttered away from this maiden work of a local artist, the audience burst into rounds of hearty applause. The sturdy farmer standing there told the story; and while this work may lack the ease of line and assured touch of the mature artist, it remains still a worthy child of his imagination. The amazing thing is that the amateur could have done so well.

And the little town of Concord might reckon itself indeed fortunate. It had furnished the men for the battle, the poet for its celebration, and the sculptor for its outward commemoration,—all without going outside its own borders!

Fifty years after the completion of this work, Mr. French confessed that he was not ashamed of it. "It has some good points to it," he told the writer. "I myself am amazed that I came out so well!"

Daniel French himself was not present at this unveiling. It was not through trepidation that he stayed away, but he had a longed-for opportunity to go abroad and study, and at this particular moment he was on the high seas. A friend, Preston Powers, had invited him to visit him in Florence. He remained there a year, studying in the studio of Thomas Ball, one of the best of our earlier school of artists. We can believe that the student made the most of these few short months, in that city beloved of all artists. He absorbed the atmosphere like a sponge. He must have realized, what afterwards proved to be the case, that this one year of foreign schooling, in addition to the desultory training which he had already received, was practically all the instruction that he was to receive. But French was later to prove the truth of that old adage, "True artists are born, not made."

The only visible product of this year abroad was his "Sleeping Endymion" which he brought back with him, and which for a long time adorned his studio at Concord, built in the orchard of his father's farm. The statue, which is recumbent, is chiefly interesting as being done in conventionally classic style—a style which the artist fortunately forsook when he got back to the shores of America. He may not have known it at the time, but classicism and the adherence to foreign models was the incubus which had prevented our native work from flowering sooner.

One of the first clients whom he was privileged to model upon his return was his old neighbor, Emerson. The Seer of Concord was a congenial subject but withal a difficult one. Mr. French himself says: "I think it is very seldom that a face combines such vigor and strength in the general form with such exceeding delicacy and sensitiveness in the details. James speaks somewhere of 'the over-modeled American face.' No face was ever more modeled than Mr. Emerson's; there was nothing slurred, nothing accidental, but it was like the perfection of detail in great sculpture—it did not interfere with the grand scheme. Neither did it interfere with an almost childlike mobility that admitted of an infinite variety of expression and made possible that wonderful lighting-up of the face so often spoken of by those who knew him. It was the attempt to catch that glorifying expression that made me despair of my bust. When the work was approaching completion, Mr. Emerson looked at it after one of the sittings and said, 'The trouble is, the more it resembles me, the worse it looks!' When it was at last complete, however, he looked at it long and contemplatively, and said, 'That is the face I shave.'"

Another portrait of a distinguished neighbor, and hardly less difficult of execution, was that of A. Bronson Alcott, the father of May Alcott his first mentor, and of Louisa M. Alcott, the author. The Alcotts he had come to know quite well. These two portrait busts are still among the artist's finest examples. They prove at first glance that he had arrived and was henceforth a force to be reckoned with, in American sculpture. Some years later, French used the Emerson bust as the model for a full-length seated figure, for the Concord library.

Mr. French was fortunate at this time in having two members of his immediate family who were in position to advance his work. His brother's connection with the Chicago Art Institute was soon to give him an entry to the West. And his father at this time was Assistant Secretary of the Treasury, and was able through the Supervising Architect's Office to obtain commissions for the decoration of public buildings. Such family influence, it is hardly necessary to add, would have availed him nothing, if he had not been eminently fitted for the task. During the next ten years we find him engaged upon huge ideal figures for the embellishment of Custom Houses in St. Louis, Philadelphia, and Boston, fine training for later work in outdoor sculpture, but by no means all of his activities at this period.

His work by this time was becoming well-known, and orders for portraits and small pieces came in from many sides. One of the first and most representative of these was the statue of "John Harvard," which was unveiled at Cambridge, in 1884. Here he strikes the same vigorous note which made his "Minute Man" immediately popular; but it is also tempered by a fine dignity and simplicity which was to be a dominant note of his succeeding groups. This seated figure has also been called "The Puritan Scholar," a title which faithfully describes it.

The following year, he exhibited at the Architectural League, New York, a frieze entitled "Greeks Carrying Offerings," both the subject and the method being a departure from his accustomed manner. About this same time he executed with great fidelity several small figures and groups, which were put in parian and plaster. Among the best of these were: "The Owl in Love," "Dolly Varden and Joe Willett," "Dick Swiveller and the Marchioness," (these two groups being from Dickens) and some studies of dogs which were practically the last of his animal work. In marble he wrought out "Daybreak," "The May Queen," "Elsie Venner," and "The Awakening of Endymion." But the great work in marble of this time was a colossal group for the St. Louis Custom House, entitled "Peace and War."

In reviewing Mr. French's life-work we find that it logically divides itself into three periods. The first may be called his "Apprenticeship," and extends from boyhood to his visit to Florence. The second period, from 1876 to 1886, may be styled "Formative," and ended with a second visit abroad. The third period is that of the "Master Workman."

On his second trip to Europe, he went to Paris, that magnet of American artists and students. He studied for a time in the studio of Leon Glaize, but drew most of his inspiration from the public galleries. The immediate work he had then in hand was a marble likeness of General Cass, which the State of Michigan wished to place in the Statuary Group in the Capitol at Washington—a doubtful compliment when we consider that amazing collection!

The statue of Cass did not altogether please his French critics. He had purposely depicted the doughty General as standing solidly upon both feet; this the critics felt was a mistake. No statue modeled along classic lines rested its weight equally on the two legs, they insisted. Mr. French said afterwards with a smile that evidently they thought he "did not know any better," but he had given the soldier his pose to depict an outstanding trait of his character, his sturdiness. It was the same note which Saint Gaudens struck so successfully in his statue of "Admiral Farragut," which adorns Madison Square, New York.

Again the sculptor limited himself to a twelve-

[127]

month abroad, not entirely from choice, as he had many commissions awaiting him. And there was a still more intimate reason. On his return, in 1888, he married Miss Mary French of Washington, and went to New York to live. A magazine writer thus describes his home life of that time:[1] "His studio and home are combined, for he took a house in a quiet street, and completely remodeled it to suit his requirements and artistic ideas. The studio, a lofty room, occupies the whole of what was the yard in the rear, and is a grand apartment, severely plain, and without the properties scattered in every direction which are so dear to his brothers of the brush. If you reach this studio from the dwelling part of the house, you emerge upon a balcony and can look down upon the work in progress. For the house Mr. French designed many charming things, among them a fireplace with bas-reliefs, and upon whose hearth a fire is kept alive in a tripod of classic design. At his summer home in Glendale, Massachusetts, he has given even freer rein to his fancies, and frequently tests his statues on the lawn among such surroundings as those in which they will ultimately be placed. No name as yet has been given to this country home, but some of Mr. French's friends have dubbed it 'Chesterfield,' a name which so far Mr. French repudiates.

[1] *The Chautauquan,* September, 1903.

DEATH AND THE SCULPTOR
By Daniel Chester French

DANIEL CHESTER FRENCH

A recent addition to this house is a large arched loggia, a sort of out-of-door dining room, with wide open arches facing south and east. Into the plaster walls are set a madonna and two Italian escutcheons, one a lion rampant, the other a lily. These are colored, and to continue the decorations all around the apartment his artist friends have painted festoons of brightly colored fruits bound together and suspended by blue ribbons, which flutter off in endless convolutions. It makes an ideal room, looking off over the formal garden and lawns. Here is much genial hospitality dispensed, and art work passed in review."

In the beginning of this third period of Mr. French's work we note two striking groups, yet widely dissimilar. The first was "Gallaudet and His Deaf-Mute Pupil"—a seated figure with a child by his side. The story is fully given by its title, and radiates a homely kindliness. The group done a little larger than life, in marble, is now in the possession of the Columbian Institution for the Deaf and Dumb, in Washington. The other subject is one of the most famous, if not the most famous, of all his works: "Death Staying the Hand of the Sculptor." Countless prints of this beautiful group have been sold, and it is still one of the most popular subjects of the art shop. The design was for a memorial to a young sculptor, a friend of French's, Martin Milmore. He was a Boston artist of much promise, who had done, among other things, the Soldiers' Monument, in Boston Common; also a Sphinx for the Mount Auburn Cemetery. In the French design, the youth is cutting out with mallet and chisel a sphinx's head, when Death in the guise of a fair and benign young woman reaches forth and stays his hand. The youth betrays no fear, and the angel no threat; for in the other hand she carries flowers. There is a tender simplicity, a universal appeal to the human heart about this group, which is the underlying cause of its widespread popularity. The work, however, rests on far firmer grounds than this, for its permanence. In ease and grace of line, in action and pose, in the deft handling of both the nude form of the youth and the draped form of the angel, there is a mastery of touch which is invincible.

With the advent of the World's Fair in Chicago, in 1892, Mr. French became nationally known as a sculptor of heroic subjects. He modeled the gigantic figure of the "Republic," among other things,—that stately goddess standing guard in the Court of Honor, her flowing robes, uplifted arms, and "stern, sweet face," making an unforgettable picture. There was a fine blending of the classic East with the democratic West, which made of this figure at once a symbol and a type. It was endlessly photographed and made into innumerable small replicas, until it became in many homes the only symbol of America. Certainly it would be hard to find a more gracious or impressive prototype. The original plaster statue which stood in the Fair Grounds was sixty feet high. After it disappeared, a permanent bronze figure twenty-five feet high was set up. So the beautiful "Republic" was perpetuated.

Mr. Royal Cortissoz, the art critic, says of it: "I used to think, as I studied this gigantic statue, and remembered vaguely certain rather decorative busts by Mr. French in long past exhibitions, that the requirements imposed by his architectural surroundings at the Fair had called out a new impulse in him. I thought that he had had the severity of his Columbian work forced upon him, more or less. I find now that he has always cultivated the peculiar tone of simplicity there disclosed so impressively. Looking back over the work which he has put forth since the 'Minute Man' at Concord, of 1875, his first statue, one is aware that his *métier* was settled then. I like to think of it as being settled on such a figure in American history. It has been said over and over again that the earliest effort of an American sculptor is bound to be an effigy of an American Indian; but Mr. French appears to have escaped that, and to have plunged at once into an analysis of the American genius as we

[131]

know it best, the American idea as it was founded on New England character and courage."

Again he says: "I have never seen anything of his that was trivial in subject. I have never known him to fall below his theme; and his subject has always been worth while."

This remark made some years ago has proved increasingly true as the scope of the artist widened and his works multiplied. The year 1900 found him in the height of his powers, and the quarter of a century since then has been crowded with achievement.

He has done much work upon individual portrait statues: the "Rufus Choate" at the Boston Court House; the "Roger Walcott" and "General Bartlett" at the State House, Boston; the "Thomas Starr King," in Golden Gate Park, San Francisco; the "Governor Pilsbury," in Minneapolis; the "Commodore Perkins," in Concord, New Hampshire; the "Governor Oglethorpe," in Savannah, Georgia—and many another. The record is impressive. From Maine to California his works are found, and always with the great fundamental theme of glorifying and perpetuating American traditions.

He, like Bartlett, was paid the high compliment of being invited to contribute a monument to beautify a setting in Paris. Bartlett's theme was "Lafayette"; French's was "Washington." Both were equestrian statues. French had gotten away from his early work with animals, and did not attempt to create the horse for his statue; it was the rider that interested him. However, he was fortunate at this time in being thrown in contact with Edward C. Potter, another sculptor of talent, who was fond of equine subjects. The two artists exchanged views freely and were able to collaborate to great advantage. Mr. French completed the man, and Mr. Potter the horse for this as well as later groups. The "Washington" is a spirited pose. The General leans well back in his saddle, with sword raised on high, while his steed with arched neck and high-stepping foot, seems conscious of his own importance. This statue stands in the Place d'Iena, in Paris. A replica of it was later erected in Washington Park, Chicago.

Mr. French has done many martial figures, all of which are stamped with quiet dignity. The "Washington" is marked by a lofty expression of countenance, as he lifts his face to heaven as if in silent appeal for the success of the American cause. The "General Grant" in Fairmount Park, Philadelphia, shows the calm determination which was an essential trait of this commander. Then there are those of "General Hooker," in the State House grounds, Boston; and the "General Devens," at Worcester, Massachusetts, which further illustrate the artist's ability to catch the love of country which fired these men in life, and to transform it into bronze and marble.

"Why did you forsake animal subjects, Mr. French?" I asked one day, in commenting on the fact that Potter collaborated with him on equestrian statues.

He seemed amused that I had made a note of this point. "Why, I didn't do it deliberately," he confessed. "When I first started out, it was with animals, and I thoroughly enjoyed doing them. Then I tasted human flesh—and I have not been able to resist it ever since. On the 'Washington' I did not confine myself to the human figure; neither did Potter stick to the horse; we swapped work and ideas constantly, and I think the group benefited by it. But there are two equestrian studies that I did, horse and all. One is the statue of 'General Draper,' now in Oakdale, Massachusetts; the other is the 'Lafayette' over in Prospect Park, Brooklyn."

The latter is a pleasing bas-relief, or semi bas-relief, done entirely in bronze, in which the figure of the French General is standing alongside his horse— somewhat in the same fashion that Massey Rhind has treated his 'Washington,' in the Newark square. I commented on this fact, stating that it was a pleasing variation from the accepted form of equestrian statue.

"Yes," laughed Mr. French; "I told Rhind that I

hadn't intended to steal his thunder. As a matter of fact, we both hit upon the same idea about the same time.

"The 'Lafayette,'" he continued, "is to my mind a good example of the union of the architect's work with that of the sculptor. I was aided in it, as in many other things, by Henry Bacon. I shall miss him terribly. You know, he passed away only a short time ago. He stood back of me constantly in all of my outdoor pieces. He told me recently that we had done together no less than forty things. I was amazed at the total, but it extends over a considerable period of years. It only goes to show that these two branches of art—architecture and sculpture —are coincidental. The one cannot exist without the other. Take this model, for example—do you not see how the figure would be almost valueless, without the supporting back and foreground?"

He paused, in his studio, before a small sketch for a memorial fountain, which is soon to take form in the Boston Public Gardens. It is to the memory of George R. White, a philanthropist who left several millions of dollars to the city of Boston. Mr. Bacon had provided the setting for the fountain, a circular background of shrubbery framing a pool, and approached by a formal court. At the back of this pool stood a gracious figure, an angel with outspread wings, who scattered seeds from a bowl. The ensemble was most satisfying; it abundantly proved the artist's contention of the union of the two arts. The angel is so placed that the onlooker will never get too close to it, or at the wrong angle, to destroy the perspective; and furthermore it is only an integral part of the whole decorative scheme.

I mentioned that this setting reminded me of the very successful treatment of the Spencer Trask Memorial Fountain, at Saratoga Springs. "Yes," quickly assented Mr. French; "I regard that as one of the most successful things that I have ever done; and there again I owe no little to Henry Bacon."

As illustrating further the aid which the architect can give to the sculptor, Mr. French continued: "I never know how a figure will look until it is actually in place—either as to pose or proper dimensions. On the larger subjects I work, of course, from small models here in my studio. But when they are hoisted into place, they may be all wrong. That is why I like to set things up out-of-doors, if possible, up at my studio in the country. I can study them against a natural background. It is astonishing how different some things will look when you get them outside, or lifted up at some other elevation."

I recalled the anecdote about Saint Gaudens and Stanford White, who pulled the "Diana" down from

MEMORY

By Daniel Chester French

the Madison Square Tower, because it was too large, and put up a smaller figure, at their own expense. "Yes," said Mr. French, "the larger figure would have made the Tower itself look too slender."

"What do you regard as your most distinctive work?" I asked, risking a bromidic question for the sake of his reaction.

"Oh, I hardly know. There are some things that I have taken especial delight in doing, that the public might not regard as so remarkable. The 'Death and the Sculptor' is perhaps my most popular group. Of the larger things, I like the four 'Continent' groups for the New York Custom House as well as any. Then, of course, there is the large seated 'Lincoln' down in the Memorial Building at Washington. Of the smaller subjects, there is the 'Memory,' up at the Metropolitan Museum; but—shall I confess it?—I very nearly gave that work up unfinished, and was only persuaded to continue it by a fellow artist. I had worked on it too long, and had gotten too close to it, so to speak."

"How long had you worked on it?"

"Some ten or a dozen years—not constantly, of course. I had picked it up for my own delectation, and at first was enthusiastic about it; but the longer I worked, the more dissatisfied I got; but I finally finished it."

As we talked, he pointed out a replica of this beautiful nude figure, in his studio, and one wondered how he could have become dissatisfied to the point of quitting such a work! In satisfying beauty it stands almost alone, among modern studies. It is already a classic.

Many writers have added their praise to this subject. Royal Cortissoz says: "This is his finest work in the treatment of the nude, and his most imaginative contribution to American sculpture; an achievement in true creative art." And Maria Dewing, in the *American Magazine of Art*, compares it with the Venus of Milo, in these words: "It is less removed, more human and lovable, but not less perfect, not less noble."

However, when these and other critics passed judgment on the "Memory" they had not seen a work which at a single bound takes its place as one of the finest nude studies produced thus far in America. It was exhibited for the first time in the spring of 1924, in the Grand Central galleries, at the time of the Sargent exhibit of paintings. A replica of this group was in French's studio when I last visited it. There are two figures—a winged male bending down as from a great height to seize and carry off a maiden who has no wings. She does not struggle, but lifts her face to his, and both figures seem to be floating upward, so ethereal and graceful are they.

"What is the title of that?" I asked.

"I gave it no title, but a friend has suggested the Biblical quotation, 'The Sons of God looked on the Daughters of Men, and behold they were fair.' That seems to fit it as well as anything."

"What then was your own inspiration for it?"

Mr. French smiled, and by way of answer produced a photograph of a geyser in action in Yellowstone Park. The ascending column of water and steam had assumed a fantastic shape and was actually almost identically the contour of these two ascending figures! The quick eye of the sculptor had caught it, and had wrought the fantasy into imperishable marble. It is one of his finest creations, worthy of being listed with his "Memory." It betrays the spirit and freshness of eternal youth—and this recent *tour de force*, be it remembered, is from the chisel of a man who has toiled steadily for fifty years!

In his studio at this time were examples of his work extending over a period of nearly half a century, and it would have been hard indeed to differentiate between the old and the new. Here was an "Emerson," a replica of that in the Concord Library; a seated "Lincoln" in plaster, from the Washington statue; a standing "Lincoln" in bronze, with bent head and brooding brow, from the one at Lincoln, Nebraska; the "Memory" and the "Sons of God" already referred to; and a dozen other things, culminating, in the outer atelier, in a stately angel in white plaster, ten feet high, which still lacked its wings, and upon which Mr. French was then at work. It was the model for the centerpiece of the White Fountain, at Boston. As his assistant slowly turned the platform, and the light from overhead struck directly upon the angel, it seemed transfused with life and almost on the point of striding out into the room, so vigorous were its lines.

The four groups for the Custom House, New York, which Mr. French "likes as well as any of his work," are indeed excellent examples of the new order of things in American sculpture, where the decoration on the exterior of our public buildings really means something. These impressive seated figures will repay careful study; they are the dominant notes of a wealth of sculpture which adorns a remarkably fine structure, designed by Cass Gilbert, the architect. The four seated figures, done in heroic size, of Tennessee marble, represent the continents of "America," "Europe," "Asia," and "Africa"; while grouped at the bases or sides are supplementary figures. Standing out in bold relief from the building itself, they must of necessity be viewed from any angle and all sides. They were therefore worked out in such detail that, no matter how viewed, each forms a harmonious whole and a pleasing contour. The present writer has seen studies of these groups, taken from the front, both sides, and the rear,—and always the picture was complete and satisfying.

Of this work, Charles DeKay writes: [1] "Only an artist can realize what it means in mental strain and hard labor to compose and carry through their various stages four groups on this scale, having a common motif, but varied so that each emerges distinctive, each representing a series of ideas different from the other. Can a layman understand what studies must precede even a single group of this sort? And is he likely to appreciate how few sculptors there are who can master such a task? Surely congratulations are due to the genius and profound skill which have combined to produce such results. These groups differ radically from any previous work by Daniel French, and mark a stride forward in his career. They are cast in a larger, more masculine mold than any hitherto, and show a richer vein of imagination, as indeed befits the task of expressing through large group sculpture large elemental ideas by the channel of human and other forms. . . . In the groups the sculptor has held a middle path between realism and extreme symbolism. . . . It is more than likely that the four groups by French will be the most admired

[1] *Century Magazine,* January, 1906.

of all the statuary of this building, not because of their size and prominent place, but for their intrinsic dignity and beauty. Certainly they are worthy of prolonged study. They are the strongest work of one of our greatest sculptors."

However, in point of size and impressiveness, this work must yield to another done at a still later period of his busy life. I refer to the "Lincoln" which he made for the Lincoln Memorial, at Washington, and which was finally unveiled in 1921. The building itself was designed by French's friend and associate, Henry Bacon, and is justly regarded as one of the noblest structures in that city of fine structures. The Lincoln statue is so placed in this shrine as to be almost overpowering in its simple dignity.

The actual manual labor of preparing such a colossal work was tremendous. In order to gain any adequate idea of what the construction of this great mass of carved stone means, let us consider its dimensions. The height of the seated figure exclusive of the pedestal is twenty-two feet, the total height from the floor over thirty feet, and its weight two hundred and seventy tons! Of course, it would be impossible to carve such a mass from a single block of marble, even if such a block were available. It was necessary to quarry out and transport to the great studio which was devoted especially to this work, twenty-eight blocks of

Georgia marble, perfect and without fissures or seams. These were of varying sizes, and weighed from five to forty tons. The total mass measured over four thousand cubic feet!

The sculptor called to his assistance a family of Italian sculptors, a remarkable group of six brothers, each skilled in individual work as well as expert in carrying out the designs of others. They were the sons of Giuseppe Piccirilli, himself a marble-cutter and artist of ability. To have such a band of men behind him at this time was a godsend to Daniel French.

His first work was to prepare a small working model of his design, which was about three feet high. This model still stands in his studio, not far away from another model of about life size.

"I executed the head the full size of the completed work, later," said Mr. French. "This was about four feet in height, and was done in plaster over a supporting framework. With the head in exact size, and the measurements from the models, my assistants were enabled to go right ahead carving out the sections and afterwards assembling the whole work. It only remained for me then to go over their work, pointing up the features and other details."

This all sounded very simple as he explained it; but if one could have peeped into that busy workshop of

the Piccirilli brothers, and have seen the men themselves darting here and there amid great fantastic
shapes of disjointed clay or marble; watched them
taking minute measurements and correcting infinites-
imal errors amid the flying clouds of marble dust from
the drills and chips from the chisels; and finally have
observed the great mass of the completed "Lincoln"
take shape in the stately building in Washington,
piece by piece so perfectly that it seemed a monolith,
—he would have ended with a new and profound
respect for the word "sculpture" which no amount of
book-writing could convey!

However, with French and his helpers it is all in a
day's work. Each new piece may, and often does,
present some special difficulty. They expect them
and are there to solve them.

"Some things work out easily," Mr. French said to
the writer. "They almost seem to do themselves.
Oftentimes the big things work out far more readily
than the little ones—I mean, in size. I have told you
how much trouble I had with 'Memory.' I usually
have several subjects going forward at once; it rests
me to turn from one to another; keeps me from going
stale."

Mr. French spends six months of the year on his
country place at Glendale, near Stockbridge, Massachusetts, where he has a large studio. He has

resided there for the last twenty-five years. He is fond of the outdoors and of great open spaces. "For six months in the year I live in heaven," he said smilingly. "The other six months I spend in—New York!"

Space has not permitted me to enumerate even his most important works in any detail. He is a sculptor of memorials, and in thus perpetuating others, he has left an imperishable record of himself. From one seaboard to the other his works in bronze and marble may be found to-day. When the "Oglethorpe" was unveiled in Savannah, Georgia, the State declared a public holiday, and the event was celebrated by the marching of troops, by public games, and finally by a souvenir volume of the occasion. When the "Lafayette" was set up at the College of that name in Pennsylvania, the grateful collegians made him a Doctor of Laws. Columbia University regards as her most distinctive emblem the gracious figure of "Alma Mater" in gilded bronze, which guards the portal of the Memorial Library. Almost the only memento which now remains of the great Columbian Exposition at Chicago is the great bronze statue of the "Republic," which replaced the gigantic plaster one of other days. And thus the record goes year by year for half a century!

Daniel Chester French has won many honors, but

[145]

withal he is one of the most unassuming of men. He talks of his work with a certain diffidence, as though it were by another. He is quite unspoiled by success, and lives simply and quietly. In appearance, he is slender and of medium height—not at all the robust type that his heroic designs would lead one to suppose. His hair, which has become sparse, is streaked with gray, but his face shows few lines. He is vivacious, cordial, and frank, without mannerisms or affectations. As he talks his features light up with a smile, much as he himself describes the face of Emerson whom he modeled in his youth.

"As I look back over the years," he says, "I am proud and glad of one thing: that my work has been coincident with the rise of our modern American art. In my boyhood we had practically nothing worthy of the name; we had to fall back upon European and classic models. I have lived to see the full flowering of our national genius. It is no longer necessary to adhere to foreign models; we have demonstrated a native American art which is comparable with the best of any other nation to-day. It is my proudest boast that I have had a part in this movement—that I and the group of men I knew have worked in this formative period. With the group of men now working, the future of American art and particularly sculpture is assured."

[146]

V

PAUL WAYLAND BARTLETT

THE CRAFTSMAN-SCULPTOR

V

PAUL WAYLAND BARTLETT

THE CRAFTSMAN-SCULPTOR

IN a little village on the outskirts of Paris, not
so many years ago, a small boy and a small goat
were the chief actors in an animated scene. The
boy crouched in front of an improvised table, on
which were clay and a few modeling tools. The kid
evidently felt that it had an important engagement
elsewhere, for it struggled desperately to wriggle out
of the arms of a lady who was laughingly trying to
hold it. Finally the animal grew more tractable; and
the boy fell eagerly to work, and had soon wrought
out his first complete bit of animal sculpture from
life.

This boy, Paul Bartlett, had not hit upon modeling by a happy accident; neither was he forced to
come upon the clay by a fortuitous route, or through
many obstacles. He was born—if we may be permitted to vary the old proverb—with a silver trowel
in his mouth. It was destined from birth that he
should be a sculptor. His father, Truman H. Bartlett, was a sculptor of note, as well as an art critic

[149]

and teacher. He did a considerable amount of decorative modeling for reproduction in terra-cotta. Probably his chief larger work is his statue of "Horace Wells," in the Capitol grounds at Hartford, Connecticut. The Bartletts were of Connecticut stock, and lived in New Haven at the time that Paul was born, in 1865, the year of the close of the Civil War.

The boy's first schooling was received at the public schools of New Haven and Boston, but at an early age his mother went to Paris to reside, as the sculptor's father was anxious that his son should have both art environment and training; so the boy was fortunate in growing up in a congenial atmosphere. At an age when most boys are skating or playing marbles, he found his chief delight in working with clay, and especially in modeling small animals. The little town in which they lived was also the residence of Fremiet, the famous sculptor, whose attention was finally attracted by this young American. The great man would pause in his rambles, and look over the hedge at some piece of work then in progress.

"*Bien!*" he would say; "you are coming along, my compatriot. But if you would look out for those legs—" Or, "What is it you would do, *mon ami?* That is not right." The boy may not have realized it at the time, but he was receiving individual instruction at the very time when it was of most value to

PAUL WAYLAND BARTLETT
In his Paris studio

him, and from one of the best men in his special line in all France.

However, Paul Bartlett treated sculpture from the start not as a mere pastime, but as a serious life-work. From boyhood on he worked soberly and faithfully; and the rewards which were to follow in after years were honestly earned, and no haphazard gifts of the gods. At fifteen he entered the École des Beaux Arts, and in addition to his work there he managed to attend his friend, M. Fremiet's class in animal sculpture and drawing, in the Jardin des Plantes. Here he had also the opportunity to observe the varied forms of bird, beast, and reptile life of the Jardin at close range. Within a few months, such was his application, he began to reveal a remarkable proficiency for such subjects.

The Bartlett home at this time was in a delightful side street leading off from the Rue de Vaurigard, as quiet and restful as though it were in the country. Here while still in school he opened up a small studio, and began work upon a composition which had engaged his fancy, a Lion, which was afterwards placed in the Porte St. Denis. This was followed by other animal pieces, culminating with "The Bohemian Bear-Tamer," his first important study, finished by the time he was twenty-one. At fourteen he had attracted attention as a "boy sculptor" by doing a portrait bust, that of his grandmother, which was accorded the honor of a place in the Salon. But in the Salon of 1887 his "Bear-Tamer" aroused more than friendly comment.

"This had been ready the year before," says Ellen Strong Bartlett,[1] "but it did not satisfy the requirements of the ambitious young sculptor, and thus had been subjected to reformation for another twelvemonth. It received a recompense at the time of exhibition, and it is unnecessary to say anything more about the merit of this youthful production than that the original cast is in the Chicago Institute of Art, while the bronze has one of the most distinguished places in the noble new Hall of Modern Sculpture, in the Metropolitan Museum. It is characteristic that this early work was not a reflection of a classic Hebe or Endymion, nor even a Fisher Boy or Indian Maiden, but was an interpretation in bronze through life to-day of a thought that enters every meditative mind. Here are two bear-cubs, 'delightfully clumsy,' as someone has said, gamboling with such grace as pertains to half-grown bruins, enjoying the moving of their newly-found muscles, too young to realize the full extent of their power,—cowed by the superior power of the man who looks down on them with the easy smile of conscious control."

[1] *New England Magazine,* December, 1905.

PAUL WAYLAND BARTLETT

Bartlett himself has told with quiet humor of this time when he was "animal crazy," and he and a friend, Gardet, a French student, used to go around "doing animals" for anybody and everybody who wanted animal subjects. He did the "fierce and terrible" creature for the Porte St. Denis above mentioned; and for an "Orpheus" in the Luxembourg which was by another hand, he did an attendant three-headed canine, Cerebus, of considerable merit. But his "Dying Lion" was his masterpiece among animals. On another occasion, he narrates, he manufactured a huge plastic elephant for an exposition at Amsterdam.

Two years after his first exhibit at the Salon he presented a work of totally different character, and, for that matter, unlike anything he has done since. It was entitled "The Ghost Dancer," and revealed the spare, nude outlines of an Indian warrior engaging in one of his tribal dances. This was later shown at the World's Columbian Exposition, at Chicago, in 1893, and is now the property of the Pennsylvania Academy of Fine Arts.

In recording these first triumphs of the young sculptor, such early recognition sounds easy—as though Fortune had indeed chosen young Bartlett for a favored son—but we must recall again the years of assiduous study since boyhood. Granted that there

[153]

was indubitably the natural gift, it would have been well-nigh valueless, had he not possessed also that inestimable gift of taking pains. This latter faculty was revealed strikingly in the next expression of his talent—experiments in bronze-casting, in the way of small animals, fishes, reptiles, crustaceans, beetles, and the like, all not only patterned with minute fidelity to life but also colored in the firing of the bronze. Says Lorado Taft:[1] "Mr. Bartlett made, in the Salon of 1895, an extraordinary display of small bronzes. In them his profound study of bronze-casting in its most difficult forms, and his skill with patinas (coloring of bronzes) shows to great advantage. His beetles and reptiles were tiny masses of modeled metal of such wealth of color, as one could scarcely believe possible outside of the realm of precious stones,—rich golden browns and greens, iridescent and brilliant in the light and intense and deep in their shadows, effects as of metallic jasper and beryl and agate and of vibrant blue, like azurite; the mimicry of the work of centuries."

This exhibit won honors at the Salon, and was afterwards shown at the World's Fair at St. Louis, where it was so much admired by the Japanese, who are themselves world-masters in the art of bronze casting, that they tried to buy a part if not all for

[1] "History of American Sculpture."

[154]

their Government. But the artist refused all offers, preferring to keep these examples of his early work in an untried field; and in succeeding years he added other pieces, making a considerable collection and one certainly unique among American artists.

It was apropos of this work that Jean Carries, a celebrated French sculptor and potter said: "He reminds me of one of those artisans of the Renaissance who had nothing but art in view and in mind—of those artists who, jealous of the perfection of their work, would not think of leaving anything of it, however menial, to be done by other hands; who were masters of a foundry as well as a studio, and to whom the smallest details to ennoble a work of art were as important as the conception. . . . Bartlett spends his days in his studio, in his foundry, not only giving life to his conceptions and modeling them in clay, but after the selection of the material it is he who cuts and chisels. He works like the ancient artisan who spent days locked up in his studio to discover an artistic effect, which to the casual observer may pass unnoticed; but which, to future connoisseurs, may establish not only the lasting reputation of the artist, but elevate national art. When his mind is fatigued with working at some grand piece of sculpture, he seeks relief in modeling curious reptiles, small objects of art, and he himself casts them *a cire perdue;* then

[155]

comes the most fascinating of his occupations, the making of patinas. Paul Bartlett's patinas vie with those of the old Japanese artists; they are simply most admirable."

The French were prompt and generous in their recognition of the young artist. In 1889, they made him a member of the Jury of Awards, at the Paris Exposition (he was then but twenty-four), and, in spite of that, a medal of honor was awarded to him. Since that was hardly in keeping with his place on the Jury, they considered making him a Chevalier of the Legion of Honor. But he was too young for that distinction, and had to wait to "the venerable age of thirty" to be thus decorated. It was in that year that he exhibited his small bronzes in the Salon, which made him *"hors concours"* or in a class by himself, as we would say. And he served again on the Jury at the Paris Exposition of 1900.

Meanwhile, another honor had come his way, which, however, was not all "beer and skittles." In 1898 the school children of the United States subscribed $50,000 for a monument to Lafayette, as a gift to France, which was to be set up in the garden of the Louvre. Mr. Bartlett received the commission to execute this statue, an equestrian one, partly because his long residence in France gave him a close understanding of the people. The committee in

THE BEAR-TAMER

By Paul Wayland Bartlett

charge also pointed out to him the desirability of finishing this work, if possible, in time to be unveiled during the Exposition of 1900. The interval was short, but the artist lost no time in getting to work. His preliminary sketches were approved, and he then rented a large barn in the village of St. Leu, about twenty-five miles from Paris, which he turned into a studio. With one assistant at first, and a beautiful horse which he used for a model, he went to work. He made no less than five miniature models or sketches, before he was satisfied, and although he had worked almost night and day, the months had slipped by and the time drew near when the committee had planned for the unveiling. The final sketch, which was only a few inches high, was then enlarged by careful calculations, until the life-size model was reached; then as there was not time enough to cast it, the committee decided to set up a temporary statue in plaster. This plan suited Bartlett, who was still not quite satisfied with the work.

In order to expedite the final process, the life-size model was sawed into sections and the sections sent to different plasterers. So skilled were these workmen that when the pieces came back they fitted perfectly. The completed plaster statue colored to represent bronze was unveiled on July 4 (Independence Day) 1900, with impressive ceremonies.

Both the American nation and the sculptor were honored in the choice of site. The beautiful little inner garden of the Louvre was especially designed with reference to having an equestrian statue in its center, and at one time it had been planned to set up one to Napoleon there; but the Franco-Prussian War had interfered. Now the committee unanimously gave it to Bartlett for his Lafayette. Says Charles N. Flagg:[1] "The Court of the Louvre is, in itself, exquisitely beautiful. And when one stops to consider that it is surrounded on three sides by the matchless architecture of the palace of the Louvre, in whose various buildings are stored choice works of art of multitudinous variety, the place becomes one of very huge importance. And when we realize that this Court with its fine gardens and entourage is but a part of the most successfully planned large civic center of modern times, it grows still greater in importance. . . . Bear in mind that no other country had been invited to figure conspicuously and permanently in this great civic plan until the American school children made their five-cent contributions for a memorial to Lafayette, and that the French commission having the matter in charge would have accepted no sculptor in whom it did not have entire con-

[1] *Scribner's Magazine*, March, 1909.

fidence, to place a statue in the choicest position in France for a monument of the kind."

This series of facts, while being a very pretty compliment to Paul Bartlett, left him by no means in a settled frame of mind. Now that the full-size statue was up on its pedestal and in its final setting, he found many details to criticize. He did not say much, even to the commission, but he went back to his studio and started all over again! He was afraid, for example, that the horse was too slender, so he bought a big Percheron, and made models of him. The sword in the General's hand also worried him, and he tried it in many poses. Meanwhile, more months went by. Plaster of Paris is not a durable medium for an outdoor statue, and soon the General who had been unveiled with so much ceremony began to peel, as though he had some contagious disease. Another coat of bronze paint only arrested his ailment temporarily. Complaints began to be heard concerning the shabby statue placed in so conspicuous a spot. But still the sculptor worked and experimented.

To make a long story short, in June, 1908, ten years after the first sketch had been submitted, and nearly eight years after the unveiling of the plaster statue, the bronze horse and rider were hoisted into place— a thing of beauty thoroughly satisfying to the eye, and let us hope—likewise satisfactory to the artist himself. As Mr. Flagg adds: "All these experiments took time—years of time—during which complaints came thick and fast. It was in the midst of this puzzlement inside and worriment from outside that Bartlett's saving sense of humor stood him in good stead. He determined to adopt an heraldic device; hence the little bronze turtle on the plinth of the monument, marching bravely beside the great horse!"

Naturally, Mr. Bartlett could not give his entire time during this long period to the Lafayette, although he returned to it again and again. Various commissions interposed, some of them highly important. He was asked to contribute a large fountain group for the Pan-American Exposition at Buffalo, one of those temporary effects in plaster which must be the secret despair of every sculptor—for he knows that they are created only for the day. His group, "The Genius of Man" was the result, chiefly important in being one of his first works of any size in America, but it was by no means satisfying to his admirers. For one thing, Bartlett was abroad, and could only send a small model to this country, which had to be enlarged and pointed up by other hands. For another, there was some difficulty in getting the pipe lines to his fountain, and it was finally left high and dry on the grassy sward. "The chariot and sea-horses rose proudly out of rippling waves of verdure," says Taft, "and the ruffled fishes and unruffled water-babies sported together in the hot sunlight, quite unaware that they were not afloat in their natural element."

Then came another American commission far more worth while, though not exclusively his own. The veteran artist, Ward, had been asked to execute a pediment for the splendid new structure housing the New York Stock Exchange. This pediment was in the shape of a huge, flat triangle over one hundred feet long, and nearly twenty feet high in the center. Ward drew the design for this large decorative area, but his failing health and advanced years prevented his undertaking the actual work; so he called in Bart-lett, who later worked out the design in detail and modeled the separate figures. The completed work is therefore as much the younger man's as the elder's, and reflects equal honor upon both. The group is commercial in theme and has been called "The Balance of Trade." The central figure, "Freedom," is about fifteen feet high. At each side are toilers in various fields of industry. This arduous work, for which another man was to receive a large share of the credit, was yet worth while in that it made the genius of Bartlett better known in his native land (for we must remember that he had lived practically his whole life abroad) and it also gave him a practical experience in this particular type of sculpture, which stood him in hand, a little later, in his work for the House of Representatives in Washington.

To this same period belong two memorial portraits, an equestrian "General McClellan," for Philadelphia, and a standing statue, in Boston, of "Doctor Warren," one of the first to give his life for American liberty, at the Battle of Bunker Hill. At the base of the Boston statue is a bas-relief, "The Death of Warren," one of the choicest things in this *métier* that the artist has ever done. Then came three other studies which, through the prominence of their setting as well as their mature technique, will always be associated with Bartlett's name. They are his allegorical figure of "Law" and his portraits of "Columbus" and "Michelangelo" for the rotunda of the Library of Congress, at Washington. The appointments of this spacious building, both inside and out, have a detailed sumptuousness peculiarly their own. It is a treasure-house of mural and sculptured art. The rotunda is a lofty vaulted chamber one hundred feet in diameter, guarded by eight heroic figures each over ten feet high, depicting "Religion," "Poetry," "Art," and so forth, and done by leading American sculptors. To Bartlett, as we have said, was given "Law." The other two studies are in bronze, slightly larger than life, and are a portion of a scattered array of sixteen such statues representing famous men. The "Columbus" is a sturdy figure standing with one foot advanced, and head thrown back, as though facing the inquisitors of Queen Isabella's court with the proof of his theories. The "Michelangelo" aroused much discussion when first put in place, because it showed the great master as an ordinary workman rather than some lofty and remote personage. It made him human, a toiler with chisel and mallet, as he undoubtedly was.

Bartlett's next "big" commission illustrated again his painstaking methods of work; it was for a pediment of the House of Representatives, at Washington. The committee in charge had asked the National Sculpture Society to submit a list of ten artists best qualified to undertake such a work. They did so, and the name at the head of the list was that of Bartlett. Accordingly, they summoned him to Washington, and, in February, 1909, he submitted a small preliminary model, or sketch, which they accepted. Taking this back to Paris with him, where he had larger equipment and better facilities, he set to work; but two disturbing factors arose. He became dissatisfied with many details, as the group progressed, and he received, about this time, an order

[163]

for six large figures for the newly-completed New York Public Library. He may have thought, like the distracted lover of the old saw, "How happy I could be with either, were t'other dear charmer away!"

For the next seven years he was chiefly occupied with these two tasks—Bartlett would never allow the element of time to influence him—designing, re-designing, casting, destroying,—at all times his own severest critic. When the House pediment was finally completed, the committee had some difficulty in recognizing the original design, yet they saw that in many ways it marked an advance. The central figure, "Peace Protecting Genius" is about nine feet high, while the figures on each side, somewhat larger than life, represent "Manufactures," "Navigation," "Husbandry," "Agriculture," and similar themes. These figures are done in Georgian marble, and stand out in bold relief from the background. They seem actually on the point of stepping out of their setting. The sculptured space which they fill is over sixty feet long, and about eleven feet high in the center. The depth of the tympanum was about three feet, which allowed the artist to complete the foremost figures almost in round. This was of advantage, as the work would be viewed from the sides as well as directly in front by persons going up the central flight of steps of the Capitol, some fifty feet below.

The homely nature of the entire group (using the adjective in its better sense) was in accord with the wishes of the committee, which wanted "something familiar, native, comprehensible, and not a more imaginative and decorative symbolism inspired by alien themes." The sculptor felt, with the committee, that a present-day treatment was quite as inspiring and far more understandable, than some Greek procession dating back to the fifth century, B. C. His theory of a suitable decoration for a legislative building was in line with that of President John Quincy Adams, who wrote to the original architect of the Capitol, many years before, that he "disclaimed the wish to exhibit triumphal cars and the emblems of victory, and all allusions to heathen mythology, and thought that the duties of the nation or its legislators should be expressed in an obvious and intelligent manner."

The pediment was unveiled with impressive ceremonies, August 2, 1916. Speaker Clark, of the House of Representatives, made an address, and Mr. Bartlett himself spoke—which again was an honor that committees of arrangements generally overlook; they are too prone to regard the artist as only a necessary workman. The sculptor began by saying:

"It is very unusual for an artist to be invited to speak at the unveiling of his own production. This ceremony, however, is unusual in so many ways, that I hope I may be for-given for having accepted the invitation. To be able to leave one's imprint in sculpture on the noblest building of this country is a great honor. To have the opportunity to add to its grandeur and beauty is, without doubt, a rare priv-ilege. It has also been a great responsibility—and you may well believe that the responsibility of this privilege has never been forgotten for a moment, during these long years of work and study.

"We thought," he continued, "because the House represents in its largest sense the people, that the people, the life and labors of the people should be portrayed on this building— this temple of Democracy. Hence this conception. An allegorical group consisting of two figures, 'Peace Protecting Genius,' fills the center of the pediment. 'Peace,' an armed 'Peace,' stands erect draped in a mantle which almost com-pletely hides her breast-plate and coat of mail. Her left arm rests on her buckler, which is supported by the altar at her side. In the background is the 'olive tree of peace.' Her right arm is extended in a gesture of protection over the youth-ful and winged figure of 'Genius,' who nestles confidingly at her feet, and holds in his right hand the torch of 'Immortal-ity.' The composition is completed by two other groups, symbolizing the two great fundamental powers of labor, the two great sources of wealth, agriculture and industry.

"The most modest of our farmers and laborers can find in these groups the symbol of his own self and of his endeavors. He may even find his own resemblance there, and he will see that his helpmate, his children, his cattle, and the harvest of his fields, have been exalted and carved in marble forms on the Capitol of the United States. The printer, the iron and steel

PEACE PROTECTING GENIUS

By Paul Bartlett; center of the House of Representatives Pediment,
Washington

worker, the founder, may do the same and enjoy the same profound satisfaction. The toiling factory girl, spinner or weaver of textiles, will observe that she has not been forgotten, and those who are devoted to the sea can discover a group which will remind them of the joys of their vocation.

"A wave terminates the sculpture at either end of the pediment; all its power and energy are comprised between the shores of two oceans, the Atlantic and the Pacific."

This description, or rather explanation, couched in the artist's own words sums up admirably the spirit of the work; and it does more than this—it conveys to the lay mind some faint conception of the immense study as well as labor which goes into the formation of some public monument. We passers-by of the street, intent upon our own affairs, glance upward for a moment but do not stop to grasp either the symbolism or the art which thus tries to tell to future generations the genius of America, in the twentieth century. Who knows? Perhaps in some far-distant epoch, it will be some such fragment, persisting like the ruins of the Parthenon, which will tell of "the beauty that was Greece and the grandeur that was Rome" in our own civilization.

Says Mr. Bartlett: "For a real artist, every new subject, every new undertaking, is a new problem and requires a new solution, adapted, of course, to the special characteristics of the case in hand. Any art

[167]

which is not based on this principle is not living art. Any effort to use an old solution for a new problem is the admission of artistic impotence; and the artist in so doing not only eludes the difficulties of his new problem, but also loses his opportunity to discover some new forms of beauty."

In other words, he considers art as a perpetual quest—a seeking after new forms of beauty and truth. It is not sufficient that persons in one epoch expressed themselves in so complete a fashion for their day that the term "classic" has been applied to their art; we of another time and under other conditions must seek our own medium of expression, and it must be ever new, as the conditions of life themselves are new. Under such a sane and searching philosophy as that—which I have found to be the creed of others also in this group of virile American sculptors—who shall say what bounds are to be placed upon its high output in the years to come?

With further reference to his work on the House pediment, Bartlett says: "It presented its own particular problems. The fact that this building has such a wide façade and three pediments, that it is generally approached by the sides, and that a person standing on the plaza has a slanting view of at least two pediments, changes entirely the ordinary scheme, and has necessitated a new principle of composition.

The means employed to meet this contingency are not very visible from the plaza; they were not meant to be visible; but great care has been used in the effort to make the side views equal in interest to the front view.

"There were other problems, such as the scale and grouping of the figures, the spacing of the groups, and so forth. Suffice it to say that with time and study they were solved to my satisfaction. The method of work was—first a small sketch was made, then a larger one, and then another. These were changed, figures were taken away, and others put in their places, so on and on, in a continual effort to improve the scheme until the final models were finished, ready to be carved in marble, erected, doweled, and cemented in place."

With his work for the New York Library the problems were not quite the same, but no less demanding. Here he had a cornice not much more than a foot broad, upon which to place six allegorical figures, each about twice the size of life. They must give the appearance of standing away from the wall of the building, and yet not appear to be in danger of toppling over into the street. How well he succeeded is still a matter of some debate among artists, but there is no question as to the beauty of the figures themselves. There are six large figures in classic drapery—two groups of two, with a single figure at

each end, this arrangement having been made necessary by the architectural lines of the portico below.
Two dignified male figures, "Philosophy" and "History" guard the northern and southern ends; and two
graceful feminine groups occupy the center,—
"Drama" and "Poetry" the northern, and "Romance"
and "Religion" the southern section.

As showing further the artist's attempt to find new
conceptions for well-known subjects, we may cite his
recent statue of Benjamin Franklin, for the town
Green, at Waterbury, Connecticut. Here is a seated
figure with both hands resting upon his staff, and looking thoughtfully off into space; it is Franklin the
philosopher. The artist has tried to show "the men-
tality" of the man, rather than to make any fixed life
portrait. "This curious and original presentation,"
says William Walton,[1] "an attempt to represent in art
that which by some of the schools would be considered unadvisable, so far removed is it from the
merely plastic and visual, may be compared with a
vastly different work, Rodin's 'Thinker.' Mr. Bartlett's statue, the more it is studied, will seem like a
very successful attempt to suggest the sudden arrest
of the merely physical in a concentration of intellect
and will."

And what of Bartlett himself? His moods, his

[1] *Scribner's Magazine,* October, 1913.

[170]

attitude toward life may be best discerned by a study of his works; for into them he has put and is putting his whole life and thought. For Bartlett there has been but one mistress—Art. Ever since his student days in Paris, he has lived a quiet and sedentary life. He still lives and works abroad, in a large studio near that city. He cares little for society and its distractions, and when engaged upon some big problem he draws himself entirely aloof.

"It is surprising to me," said a fellow-artist to the present writer, "that Bartlett has kept as close to American art as he has. All his life has been spent in France, with the exception of a few flying visits to this country; his friends are in France; and in looks he is much more the Frenchman than the American. He has acquired certain mannerisms of his own, due to his long residence abroad, but they are not affectations. No, I should not call him cosmopolitan—he is Gallic. For this reason his ability to grasp and project himself into American themes is all the more remarkable. He does not work from a detached viewpoint. Bartlett is distinctly a force in our art— or in any art—to be reckoned with."

It would indeed not be surprising that he won his first spurs abroad, or that the French still consider him one of themselves. A recent edition of one of their art monthlies, *La Peinture*, is devoted almost entirely to a discussion of his work. On the cover is the picture of a marble torso by him, with his name beneath, and in still larger letters the caption, "France-Amerique." Pierre Darius, in a lengthy estimate of Bartlett and his work, claims that although he is "American by birth" he is a "Frenchman of Paris." And further, "Paul Bartlett is American by birth, but his sculpture is the expression of Latin genius, and his heart unites an equal love of the country of Washington and that of Lafayette." He concludes: "Bartlett is a great sculptor. I add, he is more than a great sculptor; he vitalizes stone."

Mention has already been made of the honors accorded to him in the land of his adoption while still a very young man. Later he was made an Officer of the Legion of Honor. He was elected, on the first ballot, to the coveted honor of member of the Institut de France, there being only eight such foreign memberships to sculpture awarded at the time, and Saint Gaudens being the only other American. He is a member of the Royal Academy of Belgium, in which the only other American is the painter, John Singer Sargent. In 1913 he was appointed Director of Sculpture in the Glasgow School of Fine Arts. At home, in addition to being a member of the National Sculpture Society and other purely art organizations,

[172]

he has been elected to membership in the American Academy of Arts and Letters.

To those who know the man himself, however, the mention of honors received does not explain him. Bartlett has never worked for money or honor alone. He has frequently devoted ten times as much labor to a thing as the payment would justify. He views life as "one problem after another," and he feels that he can live his life satisfactorily only by endeavoring to solve them.

"I want to confide to you that I am very fond of fishing," he said one evening to some friends. "I like a shady spot and a quiet stream. I like carelessly to watch the slowly moving cork and see it bob up and down. I like to be able to survey the landscape and enjoy the changing moods of the passing day. All these charming and subtle influences of Nature help to clarify one's thoughts. Thus I have often been enabled to visualize and solve problems which proved obdurate under ordinary conditions."

Said a writer several years ago in the *Craftsman:* "Between the Cerberus of the Luxembourg and the Lafayette of the Louvre lies a period of something more than a quarter of a century, and it has been filled to overflowing with the products of the many phases of his inspiration. He is the craftsman as well as the artist—at home in the blouse and famil-

[173]

iar with the leather apron; he handles the chisel; he
works in his own foundry; he gives to the world those
seductive, iridescent patinas which compel the Japanese to acknowledge him a master in their art; he
revives after more than a century the 'lost wax' process of the ancients; he studies the minutiæ of costume
—in short, his is a vivid and restless mental activity
and a Puritan conscientiousness investigating to the
last detail the subject in hand. His more important
works show a steady advance in well-defined steps:
the firmer grasp on technique, the larger conception
of his art, the deeper insight into life; each unfold-
ing in turn new vistas before him. And at every
step in each creation there is real achievement."

He exemplifies in his own work the "infinite capacity of taking pains." We have already seen how in
the case of the "Lafayette" statue he devoted years
to certain details which baffled him—changing, re-
drawing, experimenting, until he himself should be
satisfied. He has the thoughtful, quiet air of a
dreamer, but also the determined look of one who,
having found his vision, will never cease following
it until it is realized.

Mr. Bartlett is of good height but slight of build,
with thin face coming down to a pointed chin which
is accentuated by the cut of his mustache, high cheek
bones, and lofty forehead. His eyes narrow into a

straight line when in a reflective mood—as he is very often discovered. In appearance he is more French than American, due to a lifetime spent abroad. We must remember that he went to France as a small boy.

The following pen picture of Bartlett as he is to-day, by a French interviewer, and sent by the artist to the present writer, is of interest:

"Mr. Bartlett who has lived most of his life in France, was born in New Haven, Conn., in 1867 [*sic*]; though seeing him it is hard to believe his age. His slender figure still suggests youth, as does his emphatic voice, so well blending the strength of America with the Latin charm. French is almost as much his mother tongue as English, which by the way he speaks with almost a foreign culture, and entirely devoid of Americanisms, and slang phrases, or nasal accent.

"On entering the vast atelier of the great American sculptor the first object that catches and holds the eye is the huge equestrian statue of Lafayette. Holds the eye, and more, for in the pose of the upraised hand holding so virilely the sword there is life and force. The head thrown back in an attitude of forceful abandon compels one to look into the eyes, sure that they are going to radiate light and color, and it is only the lack of that color that brings one back to earth, and the realization that the vital figure astride the enormous horse is merely a statue, and not a living, breathing human being.

"The entire atelier lives, palpitates. Nude figures, vigorous and somber; heads of animals that haunt one. Always, and everywhere the vital, classic line of beauty, unmarred by commonplace attempts at ultra-modernism."

[175]

"Mr. Bartlett," he was once asked, "can any artist who has 'arrived' have any further ambition?"

"Ambition?" he repeated. "A sculptor has ever the agony of doubt in his heart, for he is never sure of what he is going to be able to do in the future. He may have made a masterpiece, but will he ever make another? In any career outside of Art, when one has arrived at the top, he knows he can stay there, for the work is always within his power, within his capability. In Art there is no top to the ladder, for the ladder ends with life."

VI

GEORGE GREY BARNARD

THE SCULPTOR OF PROPHETIC VISION

GEORGE GREY BARNARD

THE SCULPTOR OF PROPHETIC VISION

"WHEN did I first determine to be a sculptor?" Mr. Barnard looked at the questioner in some surprise, and sat a moment as if pondering the question. "Why, I do not remember when I did not have some latent longing to mold or model things—but I did not know at first that it was sculpture that I wanted to do."

George Grey Barnard's father was a Presbyterian clergyman, whose pastorates required him to remove his family from place to place. At the time of the boy's birth, on May 24, 1863, they were living at Bellefonte, Pennsylvania. In a few years they moved from there to Chicago, and thence to Muscatine, Iowa. It was in the Middle West, therefore, that the boy received his first impressions, and to all intents and purposes he is a Westerner.

"As a boy," he told the writer one day recently in his studio up on Washington Heights, in New York City, "I had a passion for collecting things.

I remember yet the delight and surprise I felt at the mysteries of nature. Somehow I felt even then an integral part of it all. I did not understand why, then, but I know now. At eight years old, while rambling in the woods along the banks of the Mississippi, I began a collection of small birds and animals, and by the time I was twelve I had a hundred specimens for every year of my earthly existence. What was more, I painted in the backgrounds and arranged the foliage as naturally as I could.

"The first specimens were stuffed, as I had seen a few such mounts done, with tow or wool, but I soon discovered that this gave the specimen an unnatural appearance. A birdskin, as you may know, stretches; it has hollows under it and—what most people don't know—other spots on which there are no feathers. To stuff such a skin was bound to give the bird a distorted look. So I began modeling the bodies in clay or plaster or wax—whatever I had handy—and then pulling the skin back over that."

"But who taught you to model, Mr. Barnard?" I asked.

"No one; there was nobody out in that neck of the woods who could teach me. I simply followed the outlines of the little body that lay before me, and supposed that it would have been easy for anybody else to do the same. And even then I had not

GEORGE GREY BARNARD

From a photograph from life

given any thought to the idea of taking up sculpture as a life-work. It was simply a natural impulse, naturally followed. I recall the delight I used to feel when examining the marvelously overlapping feather armor, by which a bird is protected. I have sat up half the night studying a single birdskin, fascinated by the play of light and intricacy of movement.

"As I said, by the time I was twelve I had a museum of 1,200 specimens, which were housed in the barn and in the attic. I was fortunate in having sympathetic parents: a mother who was of emotional type, and a father who could enter into my aspirations and understand them. My little museum soon became the talk of the town as anything out-of-the-way in such small places will. Among others who saw it was a gentleman who was American Consul to Rome. When he found out how I had mounted my specimens, he exclaimed, 'Why this boy ought to be a sculptor!' I think this suggestion, at thirteen or fourteen was my first definite impulse—at least by name."

"This encouragement," writes a friend who knew him in those early days, "finally led him to attempt a more ambitious task in this new line of effort, a portrait of his small sister. The likeness which he obtained was so faithful that it aroused the admiration of the entire village. However, the good 'practical' people of the town felt that so great a skill of hand and eye should be turned into a means of gaining him a certain livelihood, and he entered the local jewelry store as an apprentice. In this trade, and particularly as an engraver and letterer, he soon became an expert. The longing for an art career was by this time thoroughly awakened in him, and he came to Chicago. This move was ostensibly to pursue his trade and to bring himself to a higher degree of proficiency therein —a plan which he took steps to carry out immediately upon his arrival.

"He had not, however, been long at work under one of the best engravers in the city when the desire to become a sculptor got the upper hand of him. For several months the boy waged a constant battle of deliberation between his art ambitions and his trade. By means of the latter he could earn what was then a very handsome salary for a young craftsman, as he was recognized as a workman of superior abilities. On the other hand, if he chose to learn how to model, it was practically certain that he could earn, for the time being at least, practically nothing. On the one hand he was assured comfort; on the other unknown privations."

It was the age-old struggle over again, of the fight

between ease and ambition—and fortunately for American art, ambition won.

Young Barnard's father encouraged him to follow his natural bent. In the father dwelt a large portion of the same artistic impulse, which had been held dormant through lack of opportunity, and it was a matter of pride with him to see his son giving form to the things which he himself had felt but could not express. He was fortunate also in this formative period in making friends with an old, retired sea captain who then lived in Chicago. The captain had amassed a wonderful collection of seashells and geological specimens, and noticing the boy's eager interest in them, he painstakingly told him all about them. It was not long before George could name any piece in the collection, thus giving himself a grounding in both science and art. Later, the collection was given to the University of Chicago.

This eager interest in shells and minerals and his own collecting of animal specimens, was prompted by a desire to study form and color. Barnard, indeed, would doubtless have become a great natural scientist, if the urge of art had not been stronger than the wish to study primal causes.

Like Saint Gaudens, he served an apprenticeship as an engraver, as already noted, and this was of great service to him later in the training of both hand and eye; but as he grew more proficient the impulse to study art for art's own sake was too strong to be resisted. Like many another struggling student he cast himself out upon the wave, determined to swim, or sink. Art history is full of such heroes and heroines, but we never hear of that great majority of unsung strugglers who go down!

At the age of seventeen young Barnard cut away his moorings and embarked. He entered as a student in the Chicago Art Institute, with only eighty-nine dollars upon which to live. He stretched out these precious dollars to last a whole year. How often in those months he went hungry, he himself will not now admit. Instead, he always says that it was one of the happiest years of his whole life. At last he was being given an opportunity to express himself. He knew now that he wanted to be a sculptor—and had always wanted to be one.

The sculpture department of the Institute was then a very meager place indeed. Work by contemporary American sculptors was almost totally lacking, and the teacher to whom he went had four casts of antique statues in reduced size. These Barnard drew in every possible position, meanwhile looking about him for other subjects. He was like Oliver Twist, asking for more. He chanced to hear of a collection of casts of Michelangelo's work, in a closed room of the Museum, and was all "on edge" to see it. But when he first went to the curator with his request, it was denied.

"We have been forced to lock this collection up," explained the curator. "Some students last year abused their privileges and committed some acts of vandalism; so we do not feel now that it would be safe to throw it open to the public."

"But I am not the public," persisted the young man. "I expect to devote my life to this work."

"I am sorry, but we can make no exceptions," said the curator, and he was turning away when again the student stopped him.

"But I *must* see them," he persisted. "Michelangelo lived and worked for me just as much as Jesus did. His works belong to me; I must see them!"

The official relented, and later gave Barnard the keys to the room allowing him to come and go as he pleased.

"If one could really know the boy's emotions," says Caffin,[1] "what a revelation it would be! To most of us, if we can recall our youth, the impressions that counted most came gradually, finding us often unprepared for them, and through circumstances or our own levity of soul unable to receive due profit at the

[1] "American Masters of Sculpture."

time. But to the young Barnard, with a seriousness beyond his years, peering into the mystery of life, feeling after expression in form, the revelation of Michelangelo's genius must have been like sudden light to a blind man, who, hitherto, had had but vague imaginings of light and form. There, in the quiet afternoons, until daylight faded into twilight, alone with these sublime beings, the boy would sit and sit. Tired on one occasion, he sat himself in the lap of the 'Moses'—for he was small and boyish-looking despite his seventeen years—and resting his curly head against the statue's beard fell fast asleep, his young, eager spirit wrapped around and absorbed by the influence of the mighty dead."

At the end of this year at the Art School, he received his first commission. It was to make a portrait bust of a child in marble. He was full of the joy of triumph when he first received this order, but presently the difficulties began to loom up. To make the clay model was easy enough; he had been modeling in clay in one way or another for nearly ten years; but the marble! He went to a marble yard in the city, where the kind-hearted proprietor gave him a small block of marble of sufficient size for his purpose; but there was no one at the School or in the city who could give him a word of advice. Here was the model—there the stone. It was his job to transfer

the one to the other—to find "the angel in the stone."
His only tools were a mallet and chisel; he seized
them and went to work! That he succeeded in this
first attempt, where nineteen out of twenty would
have failed, is evinced by the fact that the satisfied
patron paid him three hundred dollars for the completed work.

Three hundred dollars! What a fortune to one
who had lived a year on less than a third of that sum!
Barnard was now to prove that he was a still greater
financial genius. He went abroad and studied for
twelve years, living most of that time on next to
nothing. Of the struggles and privations of that long
period we need not dwell. The artist himself does
not talk about it; he seems to take it for granted that
all art students must pass through such a purgatory
to reach the paradise of their ambitions. We know
that he suffered from cold and hunger more often
than he would admit; that he subsisted for days at a
time on rice and milk; and that he often worked sixteen hours a day on such scanty nourishment. But
through it all and despite it all, he never wavered.
His force of will drove ahead his flagging body, while
ever before his eyes was the splendid vision of what
he himself might do—nay, felt driven to do.

The curse of poverty, nevertheless, made itself felt
in more ways than one. The first figure which he

completed in clay, he did not have the means to have cast, so it was destroyed. It was a "St. John," said by some of his fellow-students to have been one of his happiest inspirations, a thing of compelling beauty.

For a time Barnard studied under the Academician, Cuvelier, but his funds would not permit a long course. Then he opened a little studio of his own, and eked out his capital by small commissions. Meanwhile he took little or no part in the bohemian life of the Latin Quarter—partly because of lack of inclination, but mostly from lack of funds. Nor did he go in much for modern French art. The influence of his old ideal, Michelangelo, was still strong upon him, being shared by that of two other masters— Phidias and Rembrandt.

"They have always been an inspiration to me," he told the writer one day recently. "Who can approach the masterful molding of the human body, like Phidias? Who can bring out such lights and shadows as Rembrandt? He thought in terms of light and color—and ever since I fell under his spell, I have done the same."

As a result of his enforced manner of living he became more and more of a recluse, leaving his studio only at night, and walking the streets in company only with his thoughts. Always of a philosophical trend, he became introspective, even mystic, and this has colored all his succeeding work. It is a thoughtfulness and an originality of conception which are more nearly comparable to Rodin than to any other contemporary.

There came at last a day in this struggling student's life when there seemed no further way out. His funds were exhausted, and his clothing was in rags. The problem of actual existence must be met. At this critical moment it is pleasant to note that he found a friend in a fellow-countryman, Mr. Alfred Corning Clark. Hearing of Barnard and his difficulties, as well as his remarkable promise, he bought the young man's first art work, and thus relieved the pressure of want.

The story of this fortunate meeting is graphically told by Alexander B. Thaw,[1] who says: "This work, 'The Boy,' made when Barnard was little more than a boy himself, was modeled in his little bedroom, under a roof through which the rain and snow poured in, so that the sculptor was obliged to hang canvas over his iron bed; and the clay in its wet wrappings had to be covered with part of his bedclothes.

"One day after his four-mile walk from the Beaux Arts to his room near the Versailles Gate, he found a note asking him to call at the hotel at which Mr. Clark was stopping. The next evening at dusk in clothes

[1] *World's Work,* December, 1902.

[189]

that were mere rags, he reached the door of one of the great hotels near the Opera, only to be stopped by the doorkeeper. But upon Barnard's quiet insistence that a gentleman wished to see him, inquiries were made, and it was found that 'the boy' should be admitted. And these two Americans met in the private parlor, and the boy sat down just as he was to a Parisian dinner, his first dinner in many months.

"They sat and talked for awhile—and each understood the other. But when they parted who shall say which was the happier or the more deeply moved, the man who had found that boy, or the boy who had found a friend. With the fabulous sum of fifteen hundred francs as partial payment for his first statue wrapped up in his new friend's handkerchief and put in his hat for safe keeping (for there was not a safe or secure pocket in his rags) Barnard ran, through the night, all the way to the studio of an American acquaintance (for he dared not return to his home near the haunts of thieves and murderers), and there he lay on a couch, dreaming all night of the great work that he was to do."

The charming figure of "The Boy," which was afterwards added to Mr. Clark's New York collection, was no "promising" work of an amateur or beginner; it revealed the mature artist—one who awaited only the opportunity to pour forth a rich measure of accomplishment. The long days and nights of brooding and labor were to produce their ripe fruitage.

Barnard's next commission of importance was a symbolical group for the tomb of a Norwegian philanthropist, a man who had spent his whole life in service for others. The artist chose for his theme, "Brotherly Love." It is the figures of two young men, who are only partially revealed from the block of marble out of which they are hewn. Their heads are partly buried in the stone, but they seem to be seeking each other, to stretch out their hands each to the other. "I remember," says a writer in the *Studio*, "when first seeing this striking monument in the old cemetery of the little seacoast town in Norway, that it seemed to epitomize Emerson's idea of friendship: the man whom we are all seeking and whom we so seldom find."

An interesting feature of Barnard's method of working at that period is that he actually handled the mallet and chisel himself. Many sculptors prefer to turn over this laborious detail to workmen, who carve under their direction; but Barnard delighted in making the chips fly from under his own blows. The years of privation in Paris had not permanently weakened his naturally rugged physique. His forearm soon acquired skill and power, which have never forsaken him; and in doing his own carving he but harked back to the methods of the ancient masters.

During this period of awaiting his larger recognition in Paris he turned his hand to wood carving, and produced a single example which at once placed him with the best of the Swiss masters in this rare art. His subject was an immense clock, its entire surface covered with wonderful figures taken from Scandinavian mythology. The artist himself thus explains it: "Every child in our day inherits the precious 'Life of the Past' in a wealth of detail and sense of growth of the world that could not belong to Homer or Phidias. From reading our histories of 'Man and Earth,' a vision in its ensemble, taking the form of an evolution, becomes an ever-present consciousness. This consciousness and relation of earth, its elements, wind, water, roots, and unseen powers, with man struggling out from it all like a spirit on the waters, is what I have feebly expressed in my carving of oak. Struggling against and out from the water and roots gleams here and there a serpent form typifying unseen power, Man. This struggle between the elements and man goes on up to the foot of the dial, where the water ends and roots first take bud and leaf. The two sources of nature in the form of man and woman holding urns from which water flows in the depths below, the maiden at the top typifying peace and simplicity, the true rulers over all."

GEORGE GREY BARNARD

We who have been privileged to see this unique example of oak carving (unique in more than one sense) which Mr. Barnard still keeps in his Washington Heights studio, have recognized that the workman is indeed a mystic, and that poems are not written merely in flowing lines on paper, but assume myriad manifestations.

Consider, as another evidence of this truism, a further experiment of this period, on the part of the artist, who, as we have said before, was a born experimenter. It was a Norwegian stove. The reader may lift his eyes in surprise. A stove? But anyone who has read "The Nuremberg Stove," or who has seen some of these fearful and wonderful creations of the northern lands, will not be surprised. Barnard's stove was a worthy companion of the tribe, big in size and design and, like the clock, illustrating in bold relief man's struggle with the elements.

"Struggle" was, indeed, the keynote of the young sculptor himself during this period of preparation. It is to this time that we must date his first masterpiece of sculpture, "I Feel Two Natures Struggling Within Me." This work, which was later purchased by the Metropolitan Museum of Art, was not, however, so much an evidence of the artist's physical as of his spiritual, struggle.

"I was only twenty-one or twenty-two when I did

that," he says. "I simply expressed my mood at the time. The young man just facing life has no conception of his higher self, his oneness with the Divine. But as soon as he realizes his larger part in the universe, as soon as his sense of immortality is born, then he begins to cast off the earthly and reach up toward the stars."

The work depicts two nude male figures, with similar forms and features, engaged in a contest for the mastery. One is recumbent, while the other is slowly rising, and as though with an effort, to his full height, his face turned upward. The group is considerably larger than life-size.

Another early work which has remained a favorite, and which is of totally different type, is the exquisite nude female figure, "Maidenhood." It represents a young girl seated upon the ground and half supporting herself by one arm. The pose is unstudied and graceful. It was, in fact, hit upon by accident. While awaiting the call of the artist, the model had assumed this careless position. "Hold that!" cried Barnard, the moment he saw it, and immediately seized clay and went to work. This figure, unlike most of his conceptions, was not done primarily to express some thought or spiritual truth, but to reveal the harmony of light and form. It is a poem in stone, recalling to us the words of Keats: "Beauty is truth, truth

[194]

beauty—that is all ye know and all ye need to know."

It was not until Barnard was thirty-one that his long period of preparation and waiting for recognition came to an end. The year was 1894, when he exhibited several of his works in the Salon of the Champs de Mars. That it should be, in name at least, a "battle-field," was peculiarly appropriate in this instance.

The result of this exhibit—set up with who knows how much of anxiety—was a striking personal triumph. Barnard became overnight one of the most talked-of artists in the city. The critics and fellow-artists united in their praise. Certain reviews of the Parisian papers may still be read with interest. The *Figaro* said: "Mr. Barnard is possessed of very great qualities, the first of which is the freshness of eternal youth." The *Temps* said: "We have a newcomer who possesses all the qualities of a great master. He belongs to that young and virile America." (Note how both reviewers stress the note of youth, which has always remained a keynote of Barnard's work.) The latter paper continues: "Mr. Barnard's efforts are manifested in various forms, for the most part unexpected. He demonstrates with a singular power his contempt for conventional methods. . . . If the artist has started from principles found in the French masters, he has developed all that is essentially his own, and that with an extraordinary power. Unless I am greatly mistaken, Mr. Barnard is destined to make no small stir in the world."

The artist was at once elected an associate member of the Society of the Beaux Arts, and a career opened itself to him in this great art center, and among congenial surroundings. But, like Ward of a quarter of a century earlier, Barnard had faith in the future of American Art, and wanted to do his bit to achieve it. He believed that the place for American sculptors was in America; and against the advice of his friends he came back home to work out his creed.

It was not an altogether easy thing to do. While his fellow-craftsmen might be friendly, the public at large did not understand Barnard at first (some of them never have understood him!). He did not work along accepted lines; he persisted in striking out into pastures new. This trait was seen in his first commission done in New York, the "Great God Pan," destined for Central Park. This fantastic, reclining figure at once challenges the attention of the passerby. There is a quiet sardonic humor in the god's attitude, a whimsicality which suggests the moods of eternal Spring. That the artist had again struck a new and compelling note in this finely-executed bit of bronze was reluctantly admitted even by those who shook their heads and "didn't understand him."

And yet the man himself has never made any mystery of himself or his intentions. He talks freely of his art, but always as a thing apart from himself. "I am not an artist for art's sake," he states simply; "but I am merely trying to express a little of the universal truth." He evidently believes, like Shakespeare, in "sermons in stones and good in everything."

Mr. Barnard's first "big" commission in America, and one of the largest which, up to that time, had ever been given in this country, was for two sculptural groups for the Pennsylvania State Capitol, at Harrisburg. "In July of 1903," he says, "I was asked to go to Harrisburg to consult with the commission that had been appointed to have charge of the building of the State Capitol. They sent for me because some of my work had attracted attention, and because I was a native of Pennsylvania.

"They had a magnificent set of plans. There was a generous allowance for art. They had filled in the plans with a lot of stock figures that may be found everywhere. They said they wanted me to do the sculpture work. Within ten minutes I had sketched out a plan of work that met with hearty approval. It wasn't so impromptu, though, for in that plan I concentrated a lifetime of study and thought. I was glad to put together what I had been thinking and studying about for years. Michelangelo did only

[197]

nineteen figures in all his life. The big plan that we agreed upon had in it sixty-seven."

The way was beset with many difficulties, however, before the artist carried out his project—and then in curtailed form. It was the old story of graft and incompetency in high places, as he was to discover. Armed with his contract, he went back to France, where he could get an abundance of skilled labor, and set up a huge workshop in Moret, a suburb of Paris. He engaged fifteen workmen and pushed forward his studies. It was not long, however, before his personal funds gave out, and no money was forthcoming from the Pennsylvania commission. The first sum agreed upon for the great undertaking was $700,000, but later the commissioners told him that $300,000 was all that could be spared. Later still, they pared this down to $100,000, to be spread over three years of labor.

The artist was discouraged almost to the point of despair. He had followed their first instructions in good faith, with the result that much of his first work was wasted; and, what was still worse, he found that he could not collect any of the final sum promised him! Calling his workmen to him, he explained the situation and told them he would have to close his studio. They announced, however, that they would not leave, if there was any possible way of completing the work; their hearts were in it. Barnard racked his brain for an idea, and at last one came. He had long made a special study of medieval art, and he now set forth on a bicycle to ferret out fragments such as might be found in ruined monasteries, churches, or farmhouses. His search was successful, and he realized some $20,000 in selling them to Parisian art dealers. This kept his studio going for a few months longer, and by this time a committee of prominent Americans, hearing of his plucky struggle, came to his rescue, supplying needed funds and bringing such pressure to bear that the Pennsylvania officials were forced to "come across."

Thus at last the two great groups, "Work and Fraternity" and "The Burden of Life," were completed, and were placed on preliminary view in Paris, where they created a considerable sensation. Rodin, Boucher, Lefebre, and other noted French sculptors, were enthusiastic in their commendation. Boucher stated that he felt it would take rank with the greatest examples of all sculptured art, and that one would have to go back to Greek art in order to find anything comparable with it. Barnard himself still feels that this work is as typical of his creed, his aspirations, as anything he has ever done. In the two great groups, heroic-size, which were finally placed in the State Capitol, there are thirty-one different figures.

His turning aside of necessity to collect medieval
art treasures has had another happy and unexpected
turn. He began garnering these bits of shrines, im-
ages, furniture, and even columns and ruined arches,
for his own possession—and gradually as his collection grew in importance, a unique idea was born in his
brain. Most of his treasures he found in Languedoc,
in the ruined monastery of Saint Guilhem. He
would build another monastery of his own, back in
America, where these old saints in plaster and wood
and stone could again fraternize. Bringing them
back to New York, he purchased a large tract of land
adjoining his studio on Washington Heights, set on
the brink of a hill with a sharp valley beneath and
the Harlem River beyond, and there he erected a
structure called "The Cloisters," and dedicated it to
France. This was first opened to the public in 1914,
and it has remained one of the choicest bits of the
Old World to be found in the New. Mr. Barnard
relates many amusing stories of his quest for these
interesting old relics; and their adequate housing was
a labor of love. The sculptor turned architect for the
nonce, and built almost with his own hands a structure with outer and inner courts, crypts, recesses,
shrines, arches, and galleries, so quaint and medieval
as to defy any brief description.

To illustrate how the architects themselves viewed

"I FEEL TWO NATURES STRUGGLING WITHIN ME"

By George Grey Barnard

this performance, I quote from a richly illustrated article in *Architecture*:[1] "I do not know of any other one thing in this country that should be of such pertinent interest to all architects as is this extraordinary building, because, besides the keen delight it affords by the wealth of beauty of its rare objects, and the charm of their setting, it also has an important lesson to teach, hidden in the subtle irregularities of its graceful arches, and its endless variety of simple detail,—and that is, it shows the true relation of a drawing or plan to the actual building. Here no working drawings were prepared at all, except right at the building in the presence of the workmen, and they were made by Mr. Barnard in full size, marked out on the floor with a pointed stick. Every arch was outlined in this way, in free hand, each with a separate centering, because every column and capital upon which the arches rested were different in design. Some of these arches were put up and torn down a great many times, in order to obtain the effect which seemed best to Mr. Barnard, and which now seems so exquisite to the beholder. It was infinite perseverance, together with a keen sense of proportion, that has produced this wonderful result, this unified expression."

This result has been achieved by a general design

[1] By Jerauld Dahler, March, 1916.

by no means symmetrical, but following the lines of a square. One enters a sunken yard "dedicated to the dead soldiers of France" and approaches a red brick structure flanked by a ruined court—the whole giving the aspect of great age. Two entrance doors of massive oak heavily studded with iron bolts preserve this illusion—for they are a relic of the twelfth century. You ring an ancient bell from which a rope depends, and are admitted to a little outer foyer which leads around the sides of the cloister, and against which are arranged bits of shrines, saints, crusaders, Virgin Marys, and tall lanthorns. The inner cloister or nave is separated from the outer by a low, irregular brick wall supporting quaint old arches, with an upper balcony running along the two sides, the eastern wall opening into a splendid crypt, with smaller recessed arches overhead; while here, there, and everywhere are scattered these relics of the Middle Ages. The illusion by now is so perfect, that one fancies they have always been just here, and that the sleeping Crusader in the center will one day come to life.

The studio of the creator of all this beauty is a hundred yards away, and here the visitor may perhaps meet the artist face to face. Mr. Barnard, now just turning sixty, still gives the impression of youth and tremendous vigor, despite his iron gray hair. His

skin is clear, his eye alert, his step springy. He says
that he frequently stands all day at his work, and his
leg muscles attest this, for they are as taut as piano
wires. He is of medium height, but compactly built,
with long arms and powerful forearms. His hands
are wonderfully expressive as he talks. His eyes are
dark and searching, his look that of a thinker. When
following some favorite line of thought his face lights
up, like that of a seer or mystic. He is not merely
an artist for the nonce but a prophet—a preacher.

He is, in fact, a preacher in stone and bronze.
His work he regards as not alone form and color, but
as a definite message, however imperfect, of the great
truths of life. Had he not been a sculptor, he would
doubtless have been a minister, like his father before
him. We are not surprised to find that he occupied
the pulpit of St. Marks, one Sunday evening recently,
at Dr. Guthrie's invitation, and I have no doubt that
he gave his listeners an inspiring sermon.

"I have evolved my own creed," he told me, as we
sat in his studio one evening. "It may not follow that
of any particular church, but it is wonderfully satisfying to me. It is in part this: Life and light are one
and the same thing. We reach upward to the light,
just as the plant does, because in this way only can
we reach life. All my life I have been a worshiper
of light; I work by light effects, rather than by form.

Perhaps I can show you what I mean, by this head of Lincoln."

He turned to a marble placed on a pedestal and facing a window. It was a replica for the head only, of the famous full-length portrait which aroused so much discussion, a few years ago, and at least four copies of which have been placed abroad.

"Now watch the eyes especially, as I slowly draw this window-shade back," he invited. I did so, and the features lighted up with a startling semblance of life, while the eyes seemed actually to open and look at me! It was uncanny in its realism.

"All done by planes of light," he explained. "There are certain contours behind every composition which, if once discovered, will catch and hold the light rays. And this after all is the secret of every painting, every carving—the catching and imprisoning of the proper rays of light. Why, we are all creatures of the light from birth to the grave. We swim in it, just as the fishes swim in water. It is our natural element. The human eye is its own spectrum. Close your eyes in the bright sunlight, and what do you see? You perceive color, which is only the breaking up of the light ray into its component parts. Keep your eyes closed, and you can discern each of the primary colors, and perhaps many others. Further you can see countless tiny light rays. They fill the entire universe—they are all about you—they reach back to the stars.

"And this proves another truth, and perhaps the biggest truth of all: We are parts of the great ensemble of the universe, and as such can never be lost or destroyed; for nothing in nature can be lost or destroyed. This proves immortality, does it not? We are given a definite part to play in the cosmic scheme. We cannot evade it. We can only strive to measure up to the tremendous responsibility that this implies. All life is a continual reaching out.

"This thought brought me to another—and I gave a great shout of surprise not long ago when I discovered this—felt like some old Greek philosopher. It is that I myself am the center of the universe! Each one of us is in the exact center of the universe. In every direction from you, equidistant, stretches out this great world of space. You have equal opportunities with the greatest man that ever lived, because you, like him, are in the center of all life, all light. What endless possibilities this suggests, when you stop to study it out! Since I discovered it for myself, it has changed and colored every consideration; for now when I discuss a thing, it is from the standpoint of the thing itself—since it also is in the center. Take the flower growing by the roadside. If you can follow that flower back, you reach one after the other every primal force in nature. Every element which enters into it is eternal, indestructible."

Standing in the center of the studio, on this particular evening, was a draped female figure, unfinished, in heroic size. The statue stood erect with head uplifted and arms upraised as if in invocation. The expression was that of benignity and peace. The artist explained that the statue was being done at the request of a committee of Jewish citizens.

"They desired a symbolical figure, not necessarily religious, which would typify Jewish thought, and they left the concept with me. I countered by asking them, what is the universal desire in every human breast? And when they hesitated, I answered for them, 'Let There Be Light.' That is the title of the work: it represents the universal cry from the dawn of time; and in the case of the Jews, one of the races of antiquity, it seems peculiarly appropriate."

"And what of America and the future of art, especially sculpture?" The questioner reluctantly turned aside from this engrossing subject.

"America is destined to be the center of the world of art. Our sculpture which has made marvelous strides in the last fifty years is only at the threshold. Partly as the result of the War, the old countries are pouring in upon us their life-blood of art, particularly Russia and the countries of Central Europe."

"But that is not strictly *American*," I ventured.

"Not now, but it will be in another fifty years, after a generation or two; for America is the great melting-pot of the world, in art as in civilization. It is good to be an American—to have a part in this great formative era."

Then for an hour or more, the artist enlarged upon his favorite theme of art existing merely as an expression of universal truth; while the listener followed unwearied. It was metaphysical, almost occult at times, but as the man explained it, it seemed simple and, better still, *workable*. The world would be a better place in which to live, if each one of us could get the sense of responsibility, of understanding, which such a truth implies.

Of his own art Mr. Barnard said little in this talk, so engrossed was he in this philosophical strain, and then only when brought back to it, by some question regarding an unfinished piece of work in the studio. One such piece is an enormous head of Lincoln, a congenial subject with him, which has been done in plaster and is nearly fifteen feet high.

"Will that be the size of the completed portrait?" he was asked.

"By no means," he answered. "The final work

will probably be four or five times larger than that. The plan now is to place it out on some scenic spot of the Lincoln Highway in the West; to take some natural promontory of granite, and carve it out not merely for the features but for the complete head. That is one suggestion. Another is, that the Negroes of America set it up as a great memorial of their emancipation. You know, they have no such monument of their own as yet."

The subject of a War Memorial to be erected in or near New York now interests Mr. Barnard more deeply than anything else. He regards all his past work as only a preparation for this. To it he has devoted much time and thought during the past four years. He has lectured upon it in several cities, by invitation of the general committee, and if they had their way he would lecture in every city in the land. But he cannot do this and plot out the art work also.

The conception is so vast that it will require many assisting sculptors and architects. It is no mere "Arch of Triumph," celebrating the glory of war, such as has been done in the past. The world has moved forward during and since the last world cataclysm. We no longer talk of the "glory" of such a struggle. Instead, this is to be a "Monument to Democracy" or "Peace," and in its project seventy nations are joining. It will glorify Labor in a series of groups show-

[208]

ing our farmers, miners, and industrial workers.
Then by swift contrast it will show forth for all time
the horror and uselessness of War, its bitter struggle
and sacrifice, on the part of both Manhood and
Womanhood, and point the way to the highest expression of the race—the Brotherhood of Man.

As the sculptor now visualizes it, the memorial will
take the form of a gigantic amphitheater, or acropolis,
one thousand feet square, perched upon the northern
spur of Washington Heights, looking toward the
Hudson River. The land would be given by Mr.
John D. Rockefeller. It would be laid out in a
series of gardens or quadrangles, each hedged about by
masses of sculptured stone or bronze done in allegorical figures. In the center of the inner garden—the
"Garden of Peace"—would be a great bronze tree,
forty feet high, the "Tree of Life."

Mr. Barnard has already done many small figures
for this work, which are housed in a larger studio out
near the proposed site of the Memorial. "Night
after night the visions come to me," he confesses.
"Often I arise at three and work until five, giving
form to these pictures in my subconscious brain. I
work rapidly, almost with feverish haste, and entirely
without models. Here is one such figure."

He showed a statuette like that of Ariel or Mer-
cury, a lithe figure poised on tiptoe and reaching up-

ward—every muscle tense and alive with emotion. It seemed more like the long and careful study of a living model, than the freehand creation of the vision of a night.

But space does not permit here anything more than a general idea of this, one of the most stupendous conceptions in the history of art. Mr. Barnard freely admits that it expands so continually as to have long since outgrown his individual grasp and control. He asks us to banish the "one man idea" at the outset. "Why, if it is properly carried out," he exclaims, "this great memorial of love, meant to incorporate the triumph of right over wrong, would absorb for a decade the toil of fifty sculptors. America must give this message to the world, as an antidote for War. It matters not whether you or I will live to see its completion. Others will take it up—and still others—until it is finished!"

Such is the grandiose dream of a man who views any individual effort only as a part of the grand mass. The sculptor who has given the world such noble conceptions as "Two Natures," "The Hewer," "Adam and Eve," "Rising Woman," and many another, looks upon them only as preparation for the greater things to come.

"Do not credit me with anything done as yet," he says; "the message lies yet in the future."

VII
GUTZON BORGLUM

THE SCULPTOR WHO "RODE TO FAME ON HORSEBACK"

VII

GUTZON BORGLUM

A FEW years ago, a famous general stood looking moodily out of a window in Washington at the statue of another famous general decorating a public square. The sculptured leader sat comfortably astride a stolid beast which seemed to be suffering from overfeeding.

"Whatever you do after I am gone," said the living soldier, "don't put me on a horse like that!"

It was General Sheridan who spoke, and the sculptured general was—well, never mind, he is still there, and there are others like him in these United States! What lends more point to the story is that, some months later, when Sheridan had passed away, they did in fact try to put him on just such a steed. But Mrs. Sheridan carried out the wishes of her husband in refusing point-blank to accept the sculptor's design. The Washington Art Commission argued with her. They said that the artist had labored over the sketch for several months, and that it was of generally accepted type—both of which statements were indeed

[213]

true. But Mrs. Sheridan was adamant; her husband had never ridden twenty miles to rally his troops on any horse like that.

At this juncture, President Roosevelt, himself a keen horseman, intervened. He persuaded the Commission to junk the sketches and start afresh; and he recommended another sculptor with a queer name, who was rapidly winning a reputation as a depicter of horses in action. The new man was called in, and his original models found favor at once. His predecessor had been at work, off and on, for seven years, and had achieved only a plaster model. Nine months after the sculptor with the queer name, who "knew horses," took hold, the completed monument was unveiled in Sheridan Circle.

Gutzon Borglum has done many things since then, but he will always be known as the man who knows horses. Still earlier in his career, while making some of his first studies out West, a lady predicted that he would "ride to fame on horseback." She was the wife of General Fremont, and whether she had in mind his skill in horsemanship, or his artistic ability, history does not state; for just then he was hobnobbing with cowboys and having a royal time of it.

Despite his foreign-sounding name, Gutzon Borglum is of native birth and American to the core. His father, Dr. James de la Mothe Borglum, was a Danish

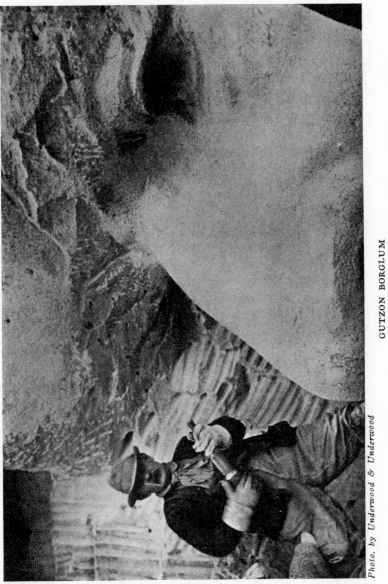

GUTZON BORGLUM

At work upon the head of General Lee, at Stone Mountain, Georgia

pioneer who in youth had been a woodcarver, but who had turned from that to the more practical and lucrative profession, in the New World, of medicine. Gutzon was born near the border of Idaho and Nevada, then frontier country, March 25, 1867; and it was originally intended that he should carry the full family name; but when he later got out into the world he shortened it to the two words.

Towards the end of the following year, another son was born into the Borglum home, and was christened Solon. He likewise rose to fame as a sculptor, particularly of frontier types. When Solon Borglum passed away, only a few years ago, American art lost one of its strong men. The emergence from this one pioneer family of two such artists, and the father's skill in carving, indicate a family strain which must have had its origin in some forgotten ancestor in Denmark.

As a boy, Gutzon showed an aptitude for both drawing and modeling. He loved paints and would make up fearful and wonderful concoctions with the limited materials at his disposal. Modeling stuffs were no less scanty, in the little Western town, and so he and his brother had to rely on their own resources. He has been doing that, in fact, ever since.

"From his father, undoubtedly, he inherited an inclination for art, with large-mindedness and independence of conviction. Independent he has been, in all truth, since the beginning. When he was seven years of age he ran away from home, and, figuratively speaking, he has been running away ever since from the restraint of traditional convention. He has not been willing to be bound by accepted rules, or to follow in the paths others have trodden. He has insisted upon thinking for himself, and finding his own way, unguided. With wise self-direction and sufficient latent ability, this in the end produces the most valuable results, but it makes a rough road for the traveler." [1]

His father recognized his talent from the outset, and wished to give him any possible help which was then to be found in the West. The family were devout Catholics, so the boy was sent to a Catholic boarding school—St. Mary's College—managed by monks, in Kansas. There he was set to work copying madonnas, saints, and cherubs. We can imagine how congenial such subjects must have been to him. One day, the priest coming in suddenly discovered that he had covered his sketch-book with Indians and wild horses. He was given a sound scolding, and a double portion of the saints to do, for his next lesson; but there wasn't any next lesson. He "turned up missing," and when later heard from, he had made his way

[1] *Studio*, April, 1906.

back by stage and pony express to the Far West.

He himself describes this formative period as follows: "I was born in the Golden West, reared in the arms of the Church, deluged with 'saints to draw from,' and suckled on Italian art: my slates were covered from end to end with portraits of Savonarola, Fra Angelico, and Wild Bill and Sitting Bull; I knew all equally well and admired them about alike. Dante, Angelo, and Petrarch were my intimate friends, with Crow and Sioux raiding all about. Into this were injected the legends of the Danes, poured into my ears by a Danish mother, while a father talked Socrates till the candles went out. I grew into manhood with this variety of ideals and of life from all the corners of the Old and New Worlds.

"Over it all, goodness and beauty and the emotions seemed to hover. And I remember very distinctly that beauty and form and the making of things all seemed to be a very idle kind of pastime, until I myself formed some definite ideals from my own life, quite apart from my own work, and then the work shaped itself to fulfill that life."

This process of finding himself, however, was to take some years. Fortunately there was in San Francisco, as early as the eighties, an artistic colony, and thither young Borglum went. At the Art Association there he studied under Virgil Williams, to whom he acknowledges much indebtedness, but it was William Keith, a landscape painter, who most strongly influenced him at this time. Always, however, he liked to experiment, and he had not yet decided whether to go in for painting or for sculpture—a problem which "bobbed up" at recurring intervals all through his life. He worked a great deal out-of-doors, and thoroughly absorbed the Western atmosphere in this formative period. Better still, he found himself. By the time he had attained his majority, his art had become grounded upon native traditions.

This is shown by the fact that when he sent two pieces of work to the Paris salons, on the advice of his friends, neither was a copy of any classic subject; they were just bits of life that he best knew. "The little painting which found admission to the old Salon was a picture of a mare protecting a colt; and the small piece of sculpture which won him membership in the new Salon represented a horse standing over a dead Indian. In both instances his subjects were chosen from the life he knew, and were set forth with unaffected sincerity. Because they were to him so commonplace in theme, their worth was underestimated, and when the young sculptor received from the Société Nationale des Beaux Arts the notification of his election to membership he was so sure it was a mistake, that he dared not make acknowledgment. The following year, however, he received the benefits of his privilege, and exhibited again both in sculpture and painting." [1]

For the artistic life of Paris he did not much care. The loose conventions of the Latin Quarter did not appeal to him; nor did the endless prattle about the various foreign masters. If he liked a thing, it was for its own sake, and not because so-and-so had done it. His sturdy Americanism survived three years of student life in Paris; and while the stay may have improved his technique, it changed in no whit his ideals. Then, turning his back upon the Latin Quarter without regret, he wandered down into Spain. The stories of the Spanish conquests in America had always fascinated him, perhaps because of the Spanish settlement of California, and he dug up tales of Columbus, Cortez, De Leon, Pizarro, and the rest, with much gusto. As a boy of sixteen he had conceived the idea of a large canvas to be entitled "The Conquest of Mexico," and for two years he worked upon it in Spain, but without completing it.

Now at twenty-five he returned home to his beloved West. There was a restlessness in his blood that no indoor studio could quell. He went straight back to California and hunted up his brother, Solon.

[1] *Studio*, April, 1906.

"I'm tired of it all," he said. "Come on, let's hit the trail."

And Solon, nothing loath, agreed. They packed upon burros their easels, brushes, modeling tools, and the necessities of life, and sallied forth on a glorious camping expedition into the heart of the Sierra Madre Mountains. Those months of roughing it, in 1893 and 1894, were rich in experience. They studied wild life at close range; they absorbed local color so thoroughly that henceforth they were never able to get it out of their systems; and, best of all, they discovered that true art is not the product of any one locality or of any one school under the sun. Wherever there is life, there is art.

Solon Borglum has given us some upstanding records of this frontier West in such unforgettable pieces as "The Last Round-up," "On the Border of White Man's Land," and his large group, "Stampede of Wild Horses," which won a medal at the Paris Exposition of 1900.

The tangible result of these months in the wilderness, for Gutzon Borglum, was a modest array of canvases, and a few small pieces of sculpture. Again he went abroad, but this time it was to London, where he put his Western works on exhibition. He had been told that London was "keener" for this sort of thing, than Paris, and it proved true. The English by reason of their Canadian interests and their kinship have always been interested in Western themes, and this exhibition in the Hanover Galleries caught their fancy. Court circles took it up, and Queen Victoria commanded that some of his canvases be brought to her for private exhibition. With the royal seal of approval, the California artist became popular overnight.

The success of his London exhibition set him on a more sure footing, and orders for portraits and busts began to come in with flattering rapidity. For a time he did "pot-boilers," then turned from the beaten track and tried his hand at illustrating. During the Boer War he made sketches, for newspapers and magazines, of many of the leading incidents of that conflict, and produced independently in bronze a small equestrian figure, "The Boer," which excited favorable comment. Not until 1898, however, when he was commissioned to make the decorations for the Queen's Hotel, at Leeds, and chose as his subject the story of Pan, did his real personality show itself, or his special genius come into play. This showed the laughing god taken captive by a group of dancing maidens, and is a thoroughly modern conception of the classic theme.

To this period also belongs the first of his better-known equine studies, "Pursued." It is a bronze statuette of two leaping horses, bestridden by naked Indians. The danger from which they flee is not indicated; but the terror which spurs riders and steeds into wild action, and the straining leap forward, is wonderfully depicted. This group was purchased by the German Emperor, for his private collection.

This little group at once calls to mind his "Mares of Diomedes," which, at one stroke, placed him in the forefront of American sculptors. It is a spirited bronze group—now the property of the Metropolitan Museum—alive with leaping, surging steeds. They are the man-eating mares which Hercules, according to tradition, was to capture and bring from Thrace. So much for the classic title and the classic story behind it; but the hero-rider himself is naked and might belong to any land and time; as also the horses. Knowing the sculptor's Western experience, we are not surprised to hear him say:

"That title, 'Mares of Diomedes,' was found long after the group was made. I have utilized a subject from the West—the stealing of horses. The method is, mounting a tractable horse, entering the band, and riding about quietly until the band follows—then leading them away. I stripped the horseman of garments, both to delocalize him and also to show the play of a fine nude figure on a nude horse. The name is a convenience—the motive of the group, mainly intense controlled action."

Horse studies, however, were by no means all of his interests. Following his London success he had returned to America, this time to New York, that center of American sculptors, and, in 1902, established himself in a roomy studio devoted to both sculpture and painting. He had brought back with him a commission to paint a large mural decoration for the Midland Concert Hall, in Manchester, England. There was to be a single canvas, thirteen by twenty-six feet, and twelve narrow panels. His subjects were, for the large canvas, the Arthurian legend, "The Coming of Guinevere," and for the panels, scenes from "A Midsummer Night's Dream."

Two pieces of work diametrically opposed to these and to each other, belonging to this same period, are the heroic figures of the twelve Apostles and the sculptured angels for the Cathedral of St. John the Divine, in New York; and the gargoyles for a Princeton University building. In view of his previous work and interests, it is hard to see the reason why he was selected from among the sculptors to do the church decoration. However, we remember that he came of religious stock and studied for a time in a Catholic school. In any event, he carved a series of angels which attracted much attention by their strength and originality. An interesting side discussion which waxed warm for a time was as to the sex of angels—whether or not an artist had any right to assume that they were either male or female.

As to the Princeton gargoyles, they are masterpieces of ugliness—which is, of course, a high compliment to pay to a gargoyle. The artist has shown his ability to create grotesque and horrible shapes quite comparable with the best of those on Notre Dame. And better still, he has been able to deduce a philosophy of life out of it. He says:

"When I was first asked to make some gargoyles, I confess I was somewhat at sea as to how to begin. I could hardly comprehend the nature of the motive. Nothing in life is without cause and effect. Nothing is merely a shell. Everything has some motive. I at length discovered that the gargoyle was the expression of an ignorant, superstitious artisan who imagined the projections of buildings to be the spirits he feared, and who fashioned them accordingly. The original idea of the gargoyle is a stick that carries water; but the ignorant peasant—the gargoyle was created in a most superstitious age—turned them into distortions of natural things. There you have the key to the creation.

"I went to work with this precedent, and made my North Wind, a creature of distended nostril, a wild-eyed thing with mouth hideously curved, in the act of emitting the fury of the sometimes death-dealing blast in the North and the West. I created my gargoyle, Snout, my gargoyle, Bottom (a distortion of Shakespeare's), my Half-equipped, the bird with one

[224]

arm, one leg, one foot, but, in spite of all, happy, for the reason that the half-equipped are always happy.

"Take every sentiment of virtue and vice, or of fear, and symbolize it, and you have the possibility of a gargoyle. Take the distorted face, the mouth awry, the crooked nose, the chin pushed sidewise, the hair blown wildly about, the eyes half insane, and you have the face one fears might peer suddenly out of the darkness—in other words, the gargoyle. Take the face of a friend suddenly converted by temper, by fury, by passion, into the face of a foe, and there once more you have your gargoyle."

His idea of the terrible is still further revealed in his "Nero," which was created about the same time. It is a conception of the Roman Emperor entirely different from history, or fiction (as instanced in Sienkiewicz's "Quo Vadis," where Nero is pictured as a man who aspired to be both poet and actor, despite his cruelty). Borglum's "Nero" emphasizes the beast that lurks in human form—a great, pudgy hulk of a man with outspread arms and clutching talons, reminding one of a gorilla. The sculptor later said of it:

"Each of us puts something of his life in his work. Something in my life made my Nero possible. It has passed; it has gone out of my life. It would be impossible for me to create another Nero or to shape a being at all like him. There are some days when, absorbed in my angels, my saints, I hate my Nero; but

[225]

if art is worth anything at all it must be real, and he was real at the time. As a matter of fact, I found the firebrand reincarnated in a man here in New York who had once been my friend."

Side by side with this fearsome being at an exhibition, was once placed a little seated figure of John Ruskin, the English critic and essayist, and a man of singularly lofty ideals. The contrast was indeed striking. Here one seemed to sound the heights and depths of human nature, as the artist then conceived them.

"When I saw Ruskin at Windermere," said Borglum in explanation, "he had drawn into himself. He knew his worth. He had full confidence in his own strength, but he was sad. The most marvelous, magnificent, unappreciated genius the world has ever known."

In a romantic mood was carved another figure which is frequently mentioned among his earlier works, "I Piped to You, and Ye have not Danced." It is the figure of a woman who stands in the attitude of resigned grief, looking down at the man who has been lying unheeding at her feet. In it is the poetic expression that too often our lives are wasted on the unappreciative, and if success comes at all, it is too late to compensate us for the sacrifice. The subject, however, is elusive, and does not deliver its message

[226]

©*Ernest L. Crandall*

GENERAL SHERIDAN

By Gutzon Borglum; at Washington, D. C.

unless the beholder pauses to ponder its meaning.

Then came his opportunity to make the Sheridan monument, in Washington, already referred to. Roosevelt had become familiar with his work through his "Mares of Diomedes," and possibly through his own sojourns in the West. "If Phil Sheridan could see that colossal image of himself he would rest content," says a writer in *World's Work*. "For he is riding down to posterity on a real horse, his own horse, which brought him from 'twenty miles away' to turn defeat into victory at Cedar Creek.

"When he began to model the 'Sheridan,'" the same writer continues, "he had young Captain Philip Sheridan of the Fifth Cavalry, at the same time of life and much the same figure as his father was during the Civil War, come up to his farm at Stamford, Connecticut, and ride for him. Time after time Captain Sheridan reined back Mr. Borglum's full-blooded Arab model to its haunches at the end of a sharp gallop until the sculptor-horseman's keen eye had caught all the details of suddenly arrested motion. So in place of the automatons other generals dead and gone are riding lifelessly in many a public place, Mr. Borglum has made one general live at the most dramatic moment of his life, on the back of a living horse."

As one looks at this spirited horse and rider, both so vibrant with life, one seems to hear again the leader shouting to his men: "Turn, boys! We're going back!"

It was in reference to this work that the sculptor wrote reminiscently as follows: [1] "When I was very much younger I was asked to join a competition, as all artists are asked to,—a very bad thing, which all artists should refuse. This competition was to make a monument for one of our great generals. I made a sketch, worked some weeks on it, left it, returned to it, and found that unless I turned to the face and name on the base, there was nothing in the monument that reminded me of the general. I am inclined to think along original lines,—that is, I feel things naturally, and perhaps in a sort of primitive way,— and I was shocked at my own production. I covered it up and started again, made another sketch, left it, returned to it, and found that I had made the same conventional 'monument.' It still looked to me like all other monuments.

"That was a very great turning-point in my own artistic development, because it compelled me to go into the cause of things in a way that I never had before, *consciously*. And I spent a great many days and a great many nights trying to get 'into my subject,' trying to get a point of view that would make it possible for me to create something belonging

[1] *Craftsman*, April, 1912.

to that general. As a result, I finally came to the very natural and simple conclusion that all I had to do was to write the story of the general in the monument. This I did. And I learned then that a monument to a man has no business to have anything upon it, not a stone or a mark that does not directly apply to the reasons for memorializing.

"I am telling that little story just as an incident, and it will apply to my later argument.

"Some years before that, I was sketching in California. A man wandered by me and watched me a little while. Then he said: 'Why do you do that?' I supposed he referred to the particular landscape, mountain, or tree, that I was drawing, and I made the conventional answer, trying to explain the beauty of the subject. But he said: 'That's not it; what I mean is, why do you do it *at all?*'

"That is the most astute question that I have ever heard put, applying to art. *Why do we do it at all?* And I hope those of you who care anything about art will never forget it. That question ought to be put to you in the making of everything you undertake in art, and it ought to guide you in the work.

"Another incident,—I am giving you three, these particular three, because they have enabled me to get a grip upon art expression. I was visiting a bachelor friend in New York, a very wealthy man, and he was fiddling away for all he was worth. After listening a little while, I put the question: 'Why do you do it at all?' He stopped fiddling for a moment. 'Well,' he said, 'there is no other way for me to use up my temperament. I can't paint; I can't model; this is the only way that I can express myself.' In other words, it was the only outlet that an over-full, stored-up, emotional heart had of getting relief!

"That is why we do it at all—all of the time."

The above anecdotes, which reveal a cross-section of the artist's own personality, are in key with much that he has said and written on the meaning and purpose of art. He has always been independent in his way of thinking, and courageous in expressing his thought. Consequently he has had more than one tilt with the critics. The writer has before him five or six lively magazine essays from the sculptor's pen, which show that he can carve as incisively with it as with his chisel. One paper is entitled, "The Betrayal of the People by a False Democracy," and in it is this pregnant paragraph:

"Democracy has betrayed the race, because education has not served man as was expected. Our crafts have suffered in proportion. They have lost the solicitous touch of man; are ripped, burnt, or driven into shape by steel and steam; and in man's æsthetic world the water-color has fallen to the lithograph, the drawing to the kodak, and so on, up and down

GUTZON BORGLUM

through life, man is suffering terribly from the idleness entailed by Democracy's false exploitation of higher education. Man no longer sees; his eyes no longer search the form, line, and color of any piece of work; his fingers no longer test the art and finish found on old and cherished master crafts. Democracy, 'education,' gentle breeding, academic training, have made a social doll of the immature, and taken from him the opportunity for him still to be something—know himself, record himself, in the great and simple emotions, the sense of æsthetic expression."

In the same article he relates a conversation held with Speaker "Joe" Cannon, on the necessity of divorcing ourselves from classic models, in our public buildings and monuments. In particular, Borglum deprecated the spending of two millions of dollars to build a Greek temple on the shores of the Potomac, and label it "Lincoln Memorial."

Mr. Cannon listened awhile, and then walked to the window and said, as he glanced at the stately Washington Monument: "The more I look at that obelisk, the more I am impressed with the beauty of it."

"Well," replied Borglum, "I agree with you entirely in so far as its beauty goes. But suppose you came from Timbuctoo, and you were wrecked on the shores of the Potomac, and you saw that obelisk,—is there any evidence on it, or anything about it that would give you any idea—if there wasn't a policeman to tell you—that the monument was placed there to record the work and life of a man who built this great nation after eight years of one of the most trying wars that a little people ever had?"

"No," Cannon answered; "you're right."

And Mr. Borglum concludes: "Why it is—and I always come back to that—that we do not think about our own story? There was never a better one lived. We have had all the emotions any people on the earth ever had. We have made sacrifices that the world outside of America knows nothing of, and which have not yet found their way into our art or crafts at all. There is practically no art produced in relation to it, and yet for subject-matter there is nothing better."

Again, in the *World's Work*, he voices the same appeal, in an essay on "Art that is Real and American": "Art in America should be American, drawn from American sources, memorializing American achievement." Here among other things he discusses some of his own native subjects, such as his two studies of Lincoln,—the seated figure in the Court House Grounds, at Newark, New Jersey, and his colossal head of Lincoln, in the Capitol at Washington.

"My seated Lincoln represents Lincoln as we might see him in his garden alone—as he would appear

[232]

alone, as he would sit and think and look, were he really alone. The placing of the figure at the end of the bench—the whole arrangement of the figure—is to get away from wholly false and artificial attitudes of the conventional commercial monument. The greatest compliment was paid to it by one of my antagonists, 'a very prominent New York critic,' who said, 'It did not look like a monument.' Another original characteristic of it is that it is placed practically on a level with the eye. This shock the art world quickly recovered from and is now adopting."

However, it is neither the art world nor the critics who are the beneficiaries of this fine statue. It is a pleasant sight, any sunny afternoon, to pause here in Newark and see the gaunt, kindly form of Lincoln seated at the end of a plain bench with, as likely as not, a group of children playing about him. No forbidding fence hedges him about. He is one of them. They are on the bench beside him, or clambering over him, as a beloved comrade. The writer once saw a little child seated upon his lap and leaning her head against his shoulder as if asleep. If the spirit of the great-hearted President ever wanders this way, he must be well content with such a memorial; for it is essentially human, just as he was.

Mr. Borglum in his studies for this statue and the great head of Lincoln accumulated a large mass of data. He made a close research not only of portraits but also of Lincoln's writings, in the endeavor to understand his character. He traveled in the Middle West, in the haunts of the rail-splitter and lawyer. To-day he is probably one of our foremost authorities on Lincoln.

"Do you know who was our greatest Northern general, during the Civil War?" he remarked one day. When Grant and others were mentioned he shook his head. "I have found private memoranda belonging to the President," he said, "such as plans of campaign scribbled on the backs of envelopes, and in his handwriting. They prove that he was the guiding genius of the War; and if he had not been in the President's chair, he would have been a brilliant commander in the field.

"The colossal head of Lincoln," he continued, "in the rotunda of the Capitol at Washington, is a portrait made from observation of the many splendid pictures and the life-mask by Volk. It was originally intended simply as a study. In fact, I used the huge fragment of stone much as a boy would use a slate. It is a head in scale to a standing figure twenty-eight feet high. The forehead has been cut and re-cut a dozen times; grief, pleasure, anger, surprise, and mixture of these moods were studied—drawn in the stone and in turn cut away. The structure of his skull is

Greek, the nose was meant to be Roman before it was injured, the cheek bones were not high, though they seem so; his eye sunken; his mouth, when not set in sadness, was responding to his roguish sense of humor."

The features of the martyred war president, in fact, have always held a fascination for Mr. Borglum. He wrote a paper on "The Beauty of Lincoln," in which he analyzed minutely every detail of the face, which he finds artistically harmonious.

It is in his deep love of American subjects and burning desire to perpetuate our own history in our art, that we find the explanation of the gigantic undertaking with which his name is now associated in the public mind. Columns of newspaper space and pages of magazines have been filled with the details of this epoch-marking project—the Memorial to the Southern Confederacy, on Stone Mountain, Georgia. For here is no mere shaft or sculptured group; a whole mountain is being converted into a story of the past.

Sixteen miles from Atlanta is a huge natural monolith, a rounded bowlder of granite three thousand feet long and rising nine hundred feet from the surrounding plain. Its smooth, sloping sides are devoid of verdure and present an unbroken surface. Standing out as it does from a verdant landscape, this mighty rock seems to have been placed there by some geni, to tempt mankind to write upon it their message for the coming ages.

Some such idea came to Gutzon Borglum, on his first visit there, about the year 1916. The Daughters of the Confederacy desired to erect a monument to General Robert E. Lee, the Commander of the Southern forces, and asked a group of sculptors to consult with them on the subject. Among the number was Mr. Borglum. Their original plan was for a bas-relief head of Lee to be cut in the base of Stone Mountain. As they outlined their idea, and Borglum gazed at the upreaching slope of stone, he felt that such a monument would be utterly inadequate, and he told them so. It would be dwarfed by the very size of its background—something like pasting a postage stamp on a barn door.

"If you take our idea away from us, you must replace it with something better," challenged the Southern women.

"There was nothing to do but try," said Borglum. "I had had in mind a design that would depict the whole South, that would be a portrayal of the mobilization of its mental and physical energy, and there as I thought it out in the sunset I could almost see the thing alive, crossing the face of the mountain.

"I made a design to illustrate my idea. It was

[236]

STONE MOUNTAIN

Near Atlanta, Ga.; showing the first of the line of gigantic figures. Gutzon Borglum in the foreground is 1500 feet from the mountain

immediately adopted, and we have not departed a great deal from the original. The design includes all branches of the Confederate Army on the march, with a central group of such leaders as Lee, Davis, Jackson, Johnston, Forrest and Stuart. The march flows in an undulating line across the mountain from southwest to northeast. At this angle light from the setting sun leaves the lower groups and with its last lingering rays touches the central and most elevated figures.

"After the design was accepted I prepared a careful estimate of the labor, cost of removing the stone and the necessary time for making the models. I estimated the cost at about $2,000,000. Since then I have increased the estimate to about $4,000,000, on account of greater cost of materials and labor. The committee had no money then to undertake such a work, but $2,000 was appropriated to make surveys to confirm the feasibility of the project. We labored for months against skepticism, but finally money was raised, and the site was dedicated in May, 1916. Work was suspended during the war and was not resumed until the fall of 1922. I want to finish the central group, which is about one-fifth of the whole, in three years. Next year we shall enlarge our staff and begin upon the rest of the design. I have promised to complete the whole memorial in eight years, but it should take ten or twelve."

[237]

FAMOUS SCULPTORS OF AMERICA

The ultimate dimensions of this granite panorama will be 200 by 1,300 feet—a quarter of a mile of marching figures. The figures are necessarily gigantic. The distance from the knee of Lee's horse to the General's hat is 120 feet. A man working on this hat looks like a fly. The depth of the relief at the extreme point is twenty feet, but four feet is about the average depth. All of this must be gouged out by pneumatic drills, by men in slings suspended by cables from the mountain top or on scaffolding hung in a similar manner. Blasting is impossible, for fear of injuring the bas-relief. At one time the question was raised whether the figures so laboriously carved would not be destroyed by erosion, but the State Geologist, summoned to decide the matter, estimated that the elements would eat away one inch every 100,000 years.

"The first problem to solve was how the design could be outlined on the mountain at the proper place," the sculptor continued.

"I had a large stereopticon made which would throw a picture 1,300 feet, covering 50,000 square feet of the mountain. From this picture men let down over the face of the precipice traced the outline in white paint. These designs were shown only for the purpose of locating the groups and chief characters. I make large and small models of the groups, then photograph them for the drillers who will block the entire surface to be carved. The lantern can be used only at night. The men go up and come down at night, and it is hazardous work, but since the work began seven years ago we have had no accident. I believe I can finish the work without losing a man or having any serious accident, for I take every precaution. If the windlass letting down the cables breaks, there is a safety clutch, and if that breaks the riders can stop it quickly by using a second brake always at hand. The cables are tested to 4,000 pounds and should easily hold 200 pounds.

"Lee's head was unveiled January 19, 1924. The State made quite a celebration of it. To reach the head the unveiling party had to ascend the mountain by the road and then descend 400 feet to the enclosure. A table was prepared on the shoulder of Lee, and about thirty guests sat down to luncheon. Even my little girl of seven came down the long steps. You cannot get off the passage unless you climb out, but you cannot see anything below for 600 feet, and it rather frightened some of the guests."

After discussing other interesting mechanical details of this colossal project which, some engineers say, presents more difficulties than the digging of the Panama Canal, Mr. Borglum continued:

"The thought in the minds of many of my Northern friends is, 'Why do I make so much of this memorial and lend myself to awakening something that should be forgotten?' That is a natural thought, but as I came to know the South I do not agree with it. In the first place, the South will not forget the war between the States. If it has some real opportunity to remember properly the six or seven hundred thousand men who gave their lives for the Southern cause, it will feel, as the world agrees it should feel, that the struggle was for a principle held and maintained by a great body of the founders of the Federation, and that the battle for States' rights can in no sense be considered rebellion. The struggle resulted by the character of its conclusion in the building and the completion of our nation.

"We must help them to honor the principles and sentiments of Lee and his associates, and I want to suggest this—that when the South has built the Confederate Memorial on Stone Mountain and has had a chance to express its real feelings toward that great leader, the last page will have been written of that great tragedy.

"The nature of this memorial has awakened the interest not only of the North but of the world. The South cannot be insensible to that, and you will find that the North no less than the South will claim this memorial as an American creation honoring great Americans."

GUTZON BORGLUM

The United States Government has given its seal of approval by the coinage of a "Stone Mountain" half-dollar. Five million are to be coined, and will be sold as souvenirs for one dollar each, thus adding $2,500,000 to the needed fund.

Not long ago at a meeting of business men in Atlanta, the presiding officer made the startling announcement: "This project will cost the city of Atlanta fifty million dollars." There was a chorus of exclamations and questions, until the speaker went on: "It will cost the city as much as that to build new roads and erect hotels, to care for the tourists who will come to see Stone Mountain."

For the preliminary work on this huge undertaking, Borglum erected a studio on his estate at Stamford, Connecticut, of ample dimensions. One could not only swing the fabled cat by the tail in this big workshop, but would also have had room to swing the ancient plesiosaurus. Here were made the first molds and casts of gigantic size. Here also were carved in stone—in small—complete working figures of horses and men. The stone was quarried near by on Borglum's "back lot."

One of his personal sacrifices to this herculean undertaking in the South is that for weeks at a time he is denied the home life which he so much desires, at "Borgland." This estate of two hundred and forty acres gives him, within his own borders, the delights of woodland trail, winding road, and flowing stream. He has left a great part of it in a natural condition, obtaining the quiet charm and restfulness such as only Nature affords. Other parts are highly cultivated, for he knows farming. Here also he can indulge in his favorite exercise of horseback riding to his heart's content—and, it may be mentioned in passing, that his blooded mounts would be the envy of any horse-breeder; for Borglum knows and loves fine horses.

He is by no means a recluse, however. At home, he is one of the townsmen keenly alive to local questions. He has worked like a Trojan for the cause of good roads in his county, and after they were obtained he was active in promoting a line of motor-busses to ply them. He designed the bodies of the busses in order to improve the looks of these lumbering vehicles, and is quite as proud of his roads and cars as of any of his paintings or marbles. He has been no less active in local and national politics, serving on State Committees, and going on the stump with the best of them. He believes that no amount of private or purely personal work can relieve a man of such obligation.

"The man of position or wealth, who remains passive in the public life going on about him, is in the same class with the man who feigns sleep with a burglar in the room," is his terse way of putting it.

Because of the fact that he is so keenly alive, and that he has pronounced and original opinions on a wide variety of topics, Mr. Borglum is a highly interesting man to meet. A chat with him is wonderfully stimulating. He is a "man's man" through and through. A fellow-sculptor remarked not long ago, "There's a man for you!" And another remarked to me only a day or two later: "Whether you agree with him or not, you've got to listen. He is one of the most impelling men to talk with that I have ever met."

Mr. Borglum is indeed a man of conviction, who manages to get his convictions across to his listener. He looks you squarely in the face and talks rapidly but earnestly. He has a muscular frame and stout legs betraying the bend of a good horseman. He is of medium height, sturdy, and active, a lover of the out-of-doors. The top of his head is devoid of hair, and the contour of head and face betray the man of intense energy and fixity of purpose—a Roosevelt type. He recognizes art, not as a thing apart from the life of the common people, but merely as a medium of expression.

"The reason for building any work of art," he says, "can only be for the purpose of fixing in some durable form a great emotion, or a great idea, of the individual or the people."

To him might well be applied the words of the poet:

> "Greatly begin. Though thou have time
> But for a line, be that sublime;
> Not failure but low aim is crime."

VIII

JOHN MASSEY RHIND

THE ARCHITECT-SCULPTOR

VIII

JOHN MASSEY RHIND

THE ARCHITECT-SCULPTOR

"COME right in!" A ruddy-faced, sturdy, well-set-up man with a friendly smile and a burr in his voice which proclaimed him at once as from the land of the heather, held open the door for me to enter. But it was not as a stranger that I greeted Massey Rhind, as he is known in the artistic colony of New York; for he is a familiar and congenial figure. In the Players' Club and National Arts Club, on Gramercy Park, and down on lower Fifth Avenue at the Salmagundi (of which he was president at one time) he is regarded as an essential part of the evening's entertainment.

To witness him carefree and beaming, retailing his apparently inexhaustible fund of Scotch stories to a group of listeners, one would not dream that here was one of the hardest-working men in the community. It requires a visit to his workshop, out on East Twentieth Street, to expel the idea that he is a dilettante.

His studio, such a visitor will discover, is in three sections. The first is a sort of study and reception room combined—a square room with two desks, one for himself and the other for a very efficient secretary. There is a cabinet filled with papers, also casts of completed studies in this room, not to mention a huge, pot-bellied stove. Next comes a smaller workroom taken up with odds and ends, and one or two incomplete studies of small size. This leads on to the big workshop at the back which is chock-a-block with work in all stages of completion. In the front room, on the afternoon in question, were two boxes, each about three feet high, protecting clay statuettes of male figures. The medium employed at once caught my eye, and I remarked upon it. It was of a rich terra-cotta color, with a soft gloss like cream.

"Yes, that is a fine clay," said the artist patting a little lump of it lovingly. "I get it a ton or more at a time from a place near Redding, England. You see, it is just like wax; you can knead it and it will hold any shape. It is the sort of clay I was brought up on, in the old country. And it always has this same peculiar color."

From a discussion of the clay—always a favorite topic with sculptors—we embarked upon the progress and technique of the various pieces of work in hand; and incidentally I obtained many interesting sidelights upon the sculptor himself.

America can claim Massey Rhind only by adoption;

J. MASSEY RHIND

From a recent photograph

but he came here as a young man, about the same time with Karl Bitter, and his life-work has been done here. To-day he is as much American in outlook and achievement as the best of us—despite that persistent "bur-r-r." He came of artistic folk, back in old Edinburgh, being born in 1860. His father, John Rhind, R.S.A., was one of the foremost sculptors in that ancient capital, and his father's father as well. His brothers were all sculptors except one, who was an architect. Young Massey, therefore, heard, saw, smelt, tasted, and touched art from his youth up; he does not remember a time when it did not loom ahead of him as a career. He learned to use modeling tools before he was old enough to consider them as anything other than playthings.

When still a boy in his teens, his father sent him to an art school at Lambeth, where he became the pupil of Delau, a well-known French sculptor. Delau was an expatriate who had been forced to leave Paris because of a communistic plot. Later the ban was lifted and he returned home; and Rhind had the privilege of studying with him also in Paris. His next schooling after Lambeth, however, was at South Kensington. He had been fortunate in winning a scholarship, which gave him an income of two pounds a week.

"I lived on it, too," he says with a chuckle. "I would work in South Kensington in the daytime, and

I had the privilege of attending the life classes at night, at the Royal Academy. I was at it for seven years altogether; then I was lucky enough to win another scholarship which sent me to Paris."

A biographer of Mr. Rhind, in *Munsey's Magazine*,[1] says: "Every student at the Royal Academy receives, at his entrance, a little ivory disk which bears his name. This disk is his 'open sesame' to all that is artistic in the British metropolis. It admits him to the receptions where artistic London meets, and where he has an opportunity to come in direct contact with the great craftsmen. As he wins honors—if he wins them—these are engraved upon his disk, until it becomes his history. Mr. Rhind took three gold medals in one year at South Kensington, being the first student who ever scored such a success. One day Sir Frederick Leighton, who had become his friend, came and stood before a piece of young Rhind's work. Sir Frederick, as President of the Royal Academy, took a particular interest in its most promising student.

" 'Where did you learn that style?' he asked. 'You had it when you came here.'

" 'From Delau,' Rhind replied.

" 'Then,' said Sir Frederick, 'you had better pack up and go over to Paris, and let him teach you the rest he knows.' "

[1] March, 1896.

[250]

JOHN MASSEY RHIND

Mr. Rhind spent two years in Paris, under several instructors, and when he returned to England the orders began to come in promisingly. Even at that early period he was interested in architecture as an allied art, and one of his first commissions was the modeling of a series of figures for a large building in Glasgow. While at work there, he was the guest of the architect, and as a result, he fell in love with and married the architect's daughter. Now, in the year 1889, his eye turned longingly toward America; he felt that here was the land of greater opportunity. The rapid growth of its large cities presaged work along architectural lines.

"There is no sculptural art in America," said his father, sententiously; "you'll starve."

But the younger man was more optimistic, and with his bride he landed on our shores almost a total stranger to both the country and its people. One of the first things he observed was that, in most cases where sculptural decoration had been attempted in our public buildings, they formed no integral part of the architectural design.

"Most of the sculptural decorations," said Mr. Rhind,[1] "conveyed to the trained eye an impression of being stuck on the edifice like a postscript to a letter, destroying whatever beauty or merit they may have

[1] *New York Tribune*, June 7, 1903.

had in themselves, considered apart from the structure from whose warp and woof they should have been inseparable."

The attempt to bring about a new order of things, to labor to make sculpture take its place in the public buildings of the New World as it does in the buildings of the Old World, became the young Scotchman's ambition. In a Fourteenth Street studio he set up his lares and penates.

"Alone and unknown in an inartistic country? A hard road! But if you can hold out two years, I believe there is a future." The speaker was an old painter who had strolled in from a neighboring studio. With an approving pull at his brier pipe, he turned from a critical survey of a few bronzes and several plaster casts, the only visible capital of the merry-eyed, soft-voiced young Scotchman.

"And I came just in the nick of time," mused Rhind long afterwards. "For, three years later, was the World's Fair, that great object lesson that quickened the national sense to form and color, and which was largely responsible for the present activity among the sculptors throughout the country."

Mr. Rhind's first work here was given him by Dean Hoffman, in the decoration of the chapel of the Episcopal Seminary on Twenty-first Street. The design was so beautiful and original that it showed his talents immediately to the little band of acquaintances he had made since coming here. Then came a still bigger opportunity to show the stuff that was in him. Mr. John Jacob Astor desired to present to Trinity Church some bronze doors, in memory of his family, and announced a competition for their designs. Rhind won the competition for one of the three portals, the other two being awarded to Bitter and Niehaus. His prize-winning design was a finely-chiseled panel depicting the expulsion of Adam and Eve from Eden. Mr. Astor had specified that the doors were to be completed within one year. By dint of great labor—and Rhind is a rapid worker—he completed his in two years. Ghiberti, he remarks, was forty years in finishing the bronze doors that made his fame.

It was about this time that the city of Albany was trying to find a design and a sculptor for a large memorial fountain to Senator Rufus King. They had held competitions on four separate occasions, but without obtaining anything to suit them. In despair they turned to the veteran, Ward, and asked him to submit the names of four men for a final trial. Ward did so, and one of these was Rhind, who finally made a fountain which remains one of the most successful examples of its type, in America. Says one critic: "For originality and dramatic effect, there is nothing in America to surpass it."

One of his first noteworthy examples of harmony between sculpture and architecture was his work on Alexander Memorial Hall, at Princeton. Here the scheme of the architect, William A. Potter, provided for an elaborate series of figures on the front façade. These, being numerous, could easily have been overdone either by boldness of treatment or too great depth of line. He, however, worked with constantly restrained chisel, and the resulting harmony of line and figure highly delighted the architect. It was but the forerunner of many such collaborations.

"The architects, with whom Mr. Rhind is deservedly popular," says Taft, "assert that no one knows better than he how to make sculpture an integral part of the whole design. Mr. Rhind has given this problem particular study, realizing that his own work gains by the harmony. An example of such felicitous union of structure and embellishment is found in the elaborate front of the Alexander Commencement Hall at Princeton, a work which occupied the sculptor some three years."

In commenting on this principle of his life-work, the sculptor said to me: "I think that I struck America at a particularly happy time. In the early nineties there were few examples of public sculpture beyond the occasional statue one saw in a city square. Our buildings either lacked ornamentation entirely, or else it was executed without reference to the idea that was in the back of the architect's head. Then came a sudden renaissance of building in this country—if such it may be called. Public buildings began to spring up all over America—not merely in one or two communities, but everywhere—in which the desire for a fitting ornamentation was apparent. And suddenly the group of sculptors who went out after such things found all that they could do. It was marvelous. I wrote back to my father that I had never seen anything like it—this universal impulse to civic beauty— and he himself could never understand it."

"Have you yourself any explanation for it?" I asked.

"Yes, I have a theory, and I believe it is the true one. As I have said before, I think that the World's Fair at Chicago gave the country at large its first big impulse to better things in this respect. At any rate, here I was on the ground and ready to work. As I viewed the problem, and still view it, the tasks set before the architect and the sculptor are one and the same. Too often, even to-day, we see fine examples of sculpture which do not fit the structure back of them. The sculptor has played a 'solo part'; he has been so keen for his own idea that he has lost sight of the ensemble. His sense of proportion may be at fault, or he indulges in over-ornamentation. Sir

Frederick Leighton said to me once, when I was a student: 'If a bit of sculpture is too picturesque, it is not good sculpture.' Here—I will try to show you what I mean."

Mr. Rhind opened a portfolio on his desk to the picture of an elaborate bas-relief by another artist, in position on the side of a building.

"That is undeniably a fine piece of work," he continued. "Just notice the sweep of those lines, and how the whole thing stands out in bold relief. But that is just the trouble: it is too bold—too much of a detailed picture. That sort of thing might be all right for a museum piece, but is out of place as an exterior decoration.

"The subduing of such relief work is by no means all our problem," he went on, turning the pages of the portfolio as he talked. "Take this picture of the front of the American Surety Company Building, in New York, as another example. The entrance on the street level is flanked, as you see, by straight columns of severely-classic design. Continuing above them in a straight line and resting on this cornice are my symbolical figures. You will note that I have purposely given them a restrained treatment. They are symbols, not portraits, and treated quite simply. They had to be treated thus in order to carry out the lines of the severe columns below. Probably the

passer-by in the street will not stop to give them a
second glance—but Mr. Price, the architect, has been
often complimented for erecting here one of the hand-
somest buildings in the financial center—and I am
quite content.

"Again—here are some figures which were placed
on the top of the Court House at Memphis." He
turned the pages to some views of the imposing and
beautiful county structure now standing in the
Tennessee city. "In modeling these figures, I had
to stop and consider how they would be viewed. In
the first place, they would only be seen at a considerable height—nearly a hundred feet; and secondly,
they would be viewed at an angle. Consequently,
the figures had to be made out of drawing—fore-
shortened here, elongated there. This drapery had to
be modeled in heavy, accentuated lines, instead of
light and airy, and the figure had to be made actually
to lean out from the perpendicular, in order to avoid
the appearance of falling over backwards. You
have seen some of the odd effects that amateur
photographers get, by having a foot or a leg too
prominent; well that is the sort of thing that we must
always guard against in groups designed to be set at
a height.

"And still another problem is that of proportion.
I don't mind telling you that I have won more than

one competition, because I have kept that one element in mind; when perhaps some other fellow drew a prettier picture. Take, as an example, these tympanums for the new Agriculture Building at Washington. You will note that I have inserted only one figure on each side of the central scroll, and that figure sets back in and fuses with the supporting architectural lines both above and below. That is why—the architect told me—they preferred my design to any other submitted."

He stopped and laughed apologetically. "Please don't think I am egotistical in thus describing what I am trying to do," he said; "because it is the principle that is being illustrated, and not my work. That, like any other work, must stand or fall of itself."

The writer nodded, unwilling to interrupt this most interesting discussion. However, at this period of Massey Rhind's career he could hardly be accused of blowing his own horn. His output along architectural lines during the last thirty-five years is probably far greater than that of any other one man, and the quality of that output has remained uniformly sincere.

Mr. Rhind worked for more than two years upon the four figures that adorn the Exchange Court Building in New York, but the result justified the time spent. They are placed over the porticos in such a way as to form a component part of the structure. They are each ten feet high, done in bronze, and are idealized portraits of men who had an important part in the historic development of the city—Hudson, Stuyvesant, Wolfe, and Clinton. Stuyvesant with his wooden leg is the most popular figure in the quartette, and has been often pictured. At a later period, Rhind made another Stuyvesant for Jersey City—a fine and spirited conception.

That, however, was twenty years ago, and the record since reveals an amazing total, without any slackening in his early ideals. Many of our public and commercial structures have been embellished with his chisel, but so subordinated and harmonized with the whole, that he does not get the popular credit he deserves. For example, Macy's great store in New York has four charming female figures, done in pink Tennessee marble, over the entrance. And for the Farmer's Bank of Pittsburgh, a costly structure of the skyscraper class done in early Renaissance style, he carved eighteen figures, each ten feet high, and chiseled out of solid blocks of marble. Says one observer: "So harmoniously, so naturally do the figures take their place in the architectural scheme, that the impression of the whole is not unlike that of the woman of whom the French wit said he was sure she was perfectly dressed, since he had no recollection of what she had on."

The work upon the Court House at Memphis has already been mentioned. One also calls to mind the elaborate bronze figures which decorate the Carnegie Institute at Pittsburgh, the work done on the Providence Court House, the New Haven Court House,—and many another artistic aid to the architect's problems.

Such work by no means represents his entire product, however. In the beautiful memorial recently erected to William McKinley, at his birthplace, Niles, Ohio, the exquisitely classic building designed by McKim, Mead and White, surrounds an inner court. Here flanked by a semicircle of white columns stands the portrait statue of the martyred president, modeled by Mr. Rhind. It is treated quietly; there is nothing heroic about this man who has apparently just risen from his chair; but the severe simplicity of the portrait set against these stately columns as in a shrine strikes a new and enduring note in American memorial art. And it is satisfying, we hasten to add, because again it marks a fine harmony between architecture and sculpture.

Another portrait statue, which has aroused favorable comment, is that of John Wanamaker, lately unveiled in City Hall Square, Philadelphia. It is

WILLIAM MCKINLEY

By J. Massey Rhind; in the Memorial at Niles, Ohio

strictly a character study. The merchant prince stands there in everyday pose, just as he must often have stood in life—his hat and coat over one arm, and the other hand resting by its thumb in a trouser pocket. "Mr. Wanamaker often stood that way," said the sculptor. "I couldn't do a 'stagey' portrait of such a man, even if I wanted to. As he stands there, he is both at rest and in action. I have tried to show him just ready to walk out of his office and stopping to say, 'Well, how big an order shall we place for those goods to-day?' "

One of Rhind's most original conceptions, however, is his "Washington" and his horse, which stands in a public square on busy Broad Street, in Newark, New Jersey. It is an equestrian statue, but unlike other such statues, the General is not mounted on his steed or brandishing his sword, but is standing quietly by the side of his horse, one hand resting lightly on its mane. The treatment is so unusual that it at once challenges the attention. As a matter of record, there is only one other such treatment of horse and rider in America—the high-relief bronze of "Lafayette" done by French for Prospect Park, Brooklyn. When the coincidence was called to his attention, in a recent chat, French laughingly apologized for "stealing Rhind's thunder."

This Newark group is not on a formal pedestal.

It stands upon a raised, grassy mound (again a note of naturalness) near the historic spot where Washington himself must have paused in his historic retreat before the British, in the early days of the War, to cheer and rally his discouraged men. There he stops with set, stern face—still the leader who only awaits the time to turn defeat into victory. The man and his horse make one of the most *human* pictures thus far achieved in our sculpture.

The occasion of the unveiling of this statue, in November, 1912, was a notable one. President Taft was present and made the speech of presentation. The poet of the day was Joseph F. Folsom. The opening and closing stanzas of his poem run:

> "To-day, Rhind's masterpiece unveiled, we feel
>   A sense of olden time. Light horsemen ride
>   On Jersey roads, and sleepless foemen hide
> In ambush. Everywhere the flash of steel.

> .   .   .   .

> Thus may he stand forever in our street,
>   Ready to mount and ride in our defense;
>   Or win us back with silent eloquence
> To nobler tasks, and daily lives more sweet."

In the same city of Newark stands another notable piece of sculpture, for which its citizens in future generations will have Mr. Rhind to thank. It is a replica, full size, of the famous "Colleoni" bronze equestrian statue in Venice, which dates back to the fifteenth century. "I regard the Colleoni as the finest statue of its type in the world," said he. "I shall never forget the impression it made upon me the first time I saw it. I could not leave the spot for hours."

So strong was the impression made upon him that when, some years later, an opportunity came to make a copy of it for Newark, he entered upon the work as eagerly as though the original had been his own. In fact, he suggested this statue to Mr. Christian Feigenspan, when that gentleman wished to bestow upon his city some great work of art, in honor of her 250th birthday. Naturally, Mr. Rhind encountered many difficulties in tackling this formidable commission. His first rebuff came when he applied to the Director of the Metropolitan Museum, for permission to make a plaster cast of their own copy, which stands in the main court of sculpture.

"To my astonishment," said Mr. Rhind, "this gentleman said coldly but politely that there would be no use in my applying to the Board of Directors for permission to take this mold, as he would certainly advise them to refuse it, on the grounds that the statue would have to be covered up for at least six weeks, and the court would necessarily be in disorder during that period. Disappointed at my first step, I made up my mind, as I walked away from the museum, to take the train that night for Chicago, and tell my story to the Director of the Art Institute there, where I had seen a very fine cast of the statue. In Chicago Mr. Newton Carpenter listened with great interest, saying that the Institute would do everything possible to assist me in my work. He accompanied me to the superintendent's office, where I made the necessary arrangements to begin the piece-mold the very next day."

The further details of this unique undertaking are most interesting, even to laymen, as showing how a fine work of art from the Old World was, to all intents, transported bodily to the New, to become an inspiration for all time. The copy is indeed so exact that photographs of the two reveal no difference. Even the railing around the pediment has been reproduced exactly. Such a replica is of more value to the public at large than the finest copied Velasquez or Rubens.

In discussing details, Mr. Rhind says: "As the pedestal is some twenty-seven feet high, with a statue of approximately fifteen feet rising above, it can readily be understood why it was decided to make a full-size plaster model of it. That was the only means of capably judging and studying the proportions of moldings, columns, capitals, frieze and bases. My friend, Albert R. Ross, architect of so many beautiful pedestals, criticized the full-size details for this model, and called at the studio many times to watch the progress of my work. When completed, this model was shown to several prominent architects, and many a time during these interesting consultations the remark was made: 'I wonder if the donor fully realizes how much he is doing for art in this country, by this generous gift.'

"Fortunately, on previous visits to Italy, I had procured squeezes or molds, taken from the original monument, of the most important decorations, including the bronze frieze, capitals, and two of the heraldic side panels, which proved invaluable when executing the large model. This model was the guide of the marble-carver. The commission was given to a marble company in Georgia, at whose quarry we found choice silver gray blocks of marble of just the right coloring to reproduce, as nearly as possible, the effect of the original."

The American replica was completed in 1916. A writer in the *Literary Digest* in summing up a consensus of critical thought on the subject says: "American artists are of the opinion that the $70,000 which the statue will cost could not have been devoted more wisely to the furthering of American art."

FAMOUS SCULPTORS OF AMERICA

Turning aside from this fine and successful effort to perpetuate the work of another hand and time, let us consider briefly some other examples of Rhind's original work. One of his earlier portrait statues was the colossal figure of John C. Calhoun, the South Carolina statesman of antebellum days. There are so many monuments to public servants in the large cities of the North that it is a distinct pleasure to find such examples as this in the South. The writer in *Munsey's* previously quoted says: "It was about 1860 that the people of South Carolina determined to erect a worthy monument of their great statesman, and gathered a fund of about $60,000. A romantic touch was given to the project by Calhoun's early sweetheart taking the matter in hand. Then the War came. The money was in charge of this lady, who regarded her task as a sacred one. When Sherman invaded the Palmetto State, she feared for her treasure. She finally sewed it into a part of her clothing, and wore it day and night until the danger was past. She is now ninety-six, is still president of the Ladies' Monument Fund, and expects to see her hero aloft within a few weeks."

This impressive statue is about seventy-five feet high, the pedestal alone being fifteen. Calhoun stands, a gaunt figure, alert, stern and vigorous. The pediment contains two bronze bas-reliefs, each ten by six feet, showing Calhoun in one of his great debates in the Senate, also in the War Department.

Some work along still different lines has been his public fountains, including the Rufus King Memorial in Albany, already mentioned. Another well-known example is the Corning Fountain in Bushnell Park at Hartford, Connecticut. This is a large circular basin surmounted by a bronze hart, suggested by the name of the city, while around the edges of the basin stand four separate Indian figures, in characteristic poses. One, dressed in a skin robe, is spearing fish. The second, shading his eyes with one hand, is on the lookout. The third, tomahawk in hand, is on the warpath. The fourth, asking for peace, is the finest, and remains to-day one of our best bits of Indian portraiture by any hand. It was thus described by Charles Dudley Warner: "With the fourth and last figure a great change comes. The Indian is making signs of amity and asking for peace. The war-hatchet is underneath the sitting figure. In his right hand he holds the pipe of peace, and the left is held up in a deprecatory attitude. The face is very noble, the finest type of the aboriginal character." There is a replica of this figure on the Wissahickon Drive, Philadelphia.

A fountain of totally different style was done a few years later for George Gould, to ornament the grounds

[267]

of his fine estate, Georgian Court, Lakewood, New Jersey. For this, Rhind chose a French motif, reminding one of Versailles. It was an ornate group with nymphs disporting around a boat, and done in an elaborate manner.

"I first made a full-size plaster model of the whole thing, and set it up in the exact spot," said the sculptor; "for that is the only way I could tell about the proper dimensions. The dwarf trees in the background did not admit of too large a fountain."

Mr. Rhind has a bubbling fund of anecdote, which might fittingly be called, "The Adventures of a Scotch Sculptor," and to hear him tell them is a treat indeed. He has a keen sense of humor and narrates a story with a dry chuckle that is infectious. Here is a fair sample:

"One of the first things I did after coming to this country, as well as one of the most interesting, was the statue of Stephen Girard, the Philadelphia philanthropist. It stands in the City Hall Plaza, and is the gift of Girard College, which he founded. It was done in bronze. Mr. Girard had long since passed away, but I had plenty of data to go on, for a likeness; my chief difficulty was as to costume. In middle life he dressed in a style which did not persist for very long. It was just after the knee breeches had gone out, and before our modern trousers had come in. The particular style was of long pattern but with two or three buttons at the bottom. And the waistcoat was of queer pattern, too. Well, I searched everywhere for a correct picture of that period, but couldn't find it. I was almost in despair. One day I was in the relic room of the college on another errand, when the caretaker pointed out some old articles of furniture which had originally belonged to Mr. Girard. One of these pieces was a large wardrobe with capacious drawers. We opened it to examine its workmanship, when I saw inside a good-sized bag like a pillow-case and tied at the top.

" 'What is in that bag?' I asked.

"The caretaker did not know; it had never been opened.

" 'Let's open it,' I suggested, and suiting the action to the word I speedily got inside of it. We brought to light a pair of trousers that Mr. Girard had actually worn; an embroidered waistcoat; and several other articles of apparel including a beaver hat, a pair of spectacles, and a pair of carpet-slippers. These gave me not only style but also the proportions of the man himself. They were one of the luckiest finds that I ever made. But you would be surprised at the amount of red-tape I had to unwind, to get that stuff out of the relic room. Nobody had known about it until I discovered it, but it required the united efforts of the Governing Board to get me the required permission. It would have been a lot easier to have watched my chance, grabbed the bag, and jumped out the window!"

And here is another.

"Up in Nova Scotia, where I have gone for several summers, there is a little town of Chester. It's pretty lively in the summer-time, but I imagine it's as dead as a mackerel in the winter. During the World War they did their bit, and some fifty soldiers from that section fell. They wanted to erect a memorial, and the usual fountains and flagpoles were discussed. They couldn't raise much money, and, of course, they couldn't consider anything very big.

"One night I attended a little public meeting, held in the schoolhouse, to consider ways and means—principally means. I hadn't given much attention to the project—I was up there to rest—but as I listened to them talking it over, I got hold of an idea. They gave me the floor, and I turned around to the blackboard and drew a rough sketch of what I had in mind.

" 'Why don't you do something like this?' I said, drawing a picture of a Canadian soldier in Highland garb, as I spoke. 'For the pedestal we can have two or three broad, simple steps, to begin with. Then the other day I saw a big granite bowlder standing near the road. One or two of you farmers with your teams can manage to haul that in, and we can set it up on the low platform, just as it is, without any shaping or carving at all. On top of that I would suggest that we place a square, chiseled block, which can have a bronze tablet for the inscription. Surmounting that will come our soldier boy done in bronze; and I will tackle that for you, if you cannot get anybody else to do it.'

"Well, they rose to that suggestion, like a fish to a worm, and the whole community put their shoulders to the wheel. The result is that they 'point with pride'—as the papers say —to this monument which now stands in their public square. Here is a postcard picture of it, such as they sell to every unwary summer visitor. That statue is eighteen feet high, and cost them about $3,000. If done in the ordinary way, it would have cost them about $25,000. But every other fishing community in Nova Scotia is camping on my trail, and wanting a monument of their own!"

[270]

JOHN MASSEY RHIND

On my last visit to his studio, Mr. Rhind was busily at work upon a heroic figure in clay of General Schuyler, for Albany. This is a standing figure, and the approach to the pedestal is treated in severely simple rectangular form. It is a design, by the way, which "won out" over many competitive designs submitted. The General is shown in a contemplative, rather than warlike mood, his graceful military cloak adding still further to his scholarly appearance.

"Schuyler was essentially a constructive soldier; he planned military works," explained the sculptor. "That is why I felt that he should be shown in an attitude of reflection."

Alongside of this study stood a large replica of his "Bobbie Burns"—a copy of the bronze statue which stands in Schenley Park, at Pittsburgh. A bonnie Scot he is, as he turns from the plow-handle to greet the spectator.

"I made him as handsome as I could," acknowledged this other Scot with a grin; "for he was essentially a ladies' man."

In this studio also is an interesting chair, if one knows its history; for in it have sat many famous men as they posed for their sculptured portrait. It is Mr. Rhind's intention to have a silver plate placed on the central standard of the back of it, which will be engraved with these sitters' names. Here are some of them: Andrew Carnegie, Theodore Roosevelt, William H. Taft, Elihu Root, Philander C. Knox, George F. Baker, Henry C. Frick, Elbert H. Gary, James A. Farrell, Speaker David B. Henderson, General Grenville M. Dodge, and Joseph G. Butler, a friend of President McKinley, and through whose efforts the McKinley Memorial at Niles, Ohio, took shape. Some of the above portraits, by the by, were done as bronze busts and placed in niches around this Memorial. It was not the sculptor's privilege to model the martyred President from life.

"How do you make a portrait study of a man who has passed away?" I asked. "The photograph is flat; while you have to show all sides."

"That is only one of the common problems of the sculptor," he replied. "It is true that we have to go back of the printed likeness and show the full contour of the head. Furthermore, we have to show the bust, the arms, the hands, and sometimes the entire figure. And the front face gives no conception of what the back of one's head looks like. If we can get good side views, that helps; but sometimes we don't get even that. I can't explain in a few words just how it is done. As the Scotch say, 'It's a gift.'"

That—it seems to the writer—explains many things in the career of such a man as Massey Rhind—not merely his high talent or his industry, but the rich stream of enthusiasm which bubbles as youthfully from his spirit and work, as it did when he first picked up mallet and chisel as a boy half a century ago: it's a gift!

IX

JAMES EARLE FRASER

THE SCULPTOR OF MEDALS

IX

JAMES EARLE FRASER

THE SCULPTOR OF MEDALS

"WELL, young man, so you have come to make my portrait."

The scene was in one of the rooms of the White House; the speaker, the President of the United States, Theodore Roosevelt. He had entered quietly and unattended, much to the surprise of the artist who awaited him, and who had always pictured the President as an eternally-guarded individual. But here they stood as man to man—the Chief Executive in the hey-day of his middle life—the artist a boyish appearing fellow even younger looking than his twenty-five years.

If the President was taken aback by the sight of so youthful a man awaiting him, he did not let that fact betray any lack of confidence. With characteristic brusqueness, but not unkindly, he opened the conversation.

"You are a much younger man than I expected, Mr. Fraser," he said. "It goes to show how merit must find its level, doesn't it? It can't be kept down.

I asked Saint Gaudens for the man who could do the job, with perfect confidence in his choice. The fact that he sent you proves that you are the man."

This, however, was not the first important commission the master had entrusted to his assistant. James Earle Fraser, like more than one other sculptor, owed his first start to the interest of Saint Gaudens, and has since justified his confidence. Fraser is a product of the Middle West. His early life was anything but conducive to an art career, except that he was given an unusual opportunity to travel and observe. He was born in Winona, Minnesota, November 4, 1876, the Centennial year. His father, Thomas Alexander Fraser, was a railroad builder then in charge of a section of the Chicago, Milwaukee and St. Paul Railway. Those were the days so graphically described in "The U. P. Trail," when the first uncertain lines of steel were pushing their way across the plains, displacing redman and buffalo alike. For months at a time the father lived in a construction car, and some of the boy's early memories were the sharing of this free and easy mode of life with him. He unconsciously imbibed much of the romance of the frontier. He saw the Indians at close range, and the tribes he met up with were evidently peaceful, as he has held a high regard for them ever since. He likewise followed the trail of the vanishing buffalo.

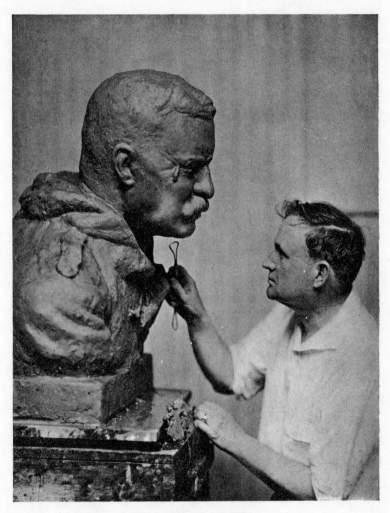

JAMES EARLE FRASER

At work upon his portrait bust of Roosevelt

Later on in life he perpetuated these two American types for all time. To-day every good American carries in his pocket the pictures made by Fraser of these boyhood associates—the Indian and the buffalo which adorn our five-cent piece.

Day by day as the rails were laid ahead of them the construction car pushed farther and farther into the wilderness. New scenes continually flashed before his interested eyes. Now it was a stampede of big, lumbering beasts across the prairie; now a file of prairie schooners wending their toilsome way along, their white tops bellying and flapping in the wind; now a bunch of cattle in charge of a half-dozen swarthy cowboys; now a string of ponies. As they neared the mountains there would be fleeting glimpses of wild game—the flaunting white banner of the antelope, the shaggy front of the goat, or the stately antlers of the elk. Each day was there something new, or the possibility of mystery lurking just around the corner. The old West of fifty years ago has vanished now; it is one of the penalties we pay for super-civilization. Fortunately, men like Fraser and Remington and the two Borglums grew up in it and have been able to transmit some of its vanishing charm to a later generation.

"We did not live in the construction car many months," said Mr. Fraser to the present writer, in talking over those early days. "My father had bought a ranch out near Mitchell, South Dakota, and about ten years of my boyhood were spent there. I cannot say that the romance of the West attracted me as strongly then as later. I was oppressed with the sadness, the tragedy of it all. The Sioux up around us had ceased to go upon the warpath, and were being pushed farther and farther back. They were not permitted to go off of their own reservations, even to hunt; and remember, their fathers and their fathers' fathers had hunted all over those broad plains, and considered them their own. Occasionally they would break loose and chase some small game across somebody's homestead, and then what a furore there was! The Indians were loose again! They would be herded back into their corrals like so much cattle, and really treated very little better. The Government meant well; but the men in charge were either indifferent to the needs of the Indians, or else grafters.

"And how proud those redmen were, despite the indignities they suffered! Not a whimper out of them. I have seen some idle white visitor go over to a brave and lift the blanket off his shoulders to inspect it, for all the world as if that Indian had been a horse. The Indian would stand there like a statue, never moving a muscle, and looking neither to the

[280]

right nor to the left. The moment the other man released his blanket, he would stalk sternly away.

"It was this idea of a weaker race being steadily pushed to the wall by a stronger, that I wished to convey in my equestrian statue, 'The End of the Trail.'" He indicated a small replica of this justly-famous work, which depicts a warrior bowed in deep dejection, seated on his pony which also crouches forward in dumb misery. They have come indeed to the end of all their hopes, and for them there is no turning back.

"This statue was shown at the San Francisco Exposition," continued Mr. Fraser, "and if I could only have copyrighted it I might have made a small fortune out of it; for it has seemed to strike a popular note of sympathy. I am told that the art concern which made prints of it have sold $150,000 worth—far more than it would have cost to erect the statue permanently."

"Where is the statue to-day?" I asked.

"It does not exist in life-size form. The one done for the Fair was only temporary, and there are one or two small replicas—at the Metropolitan Museum and elsewhere. But the work which is most generally associated with my name actually doesn't exist! It has been a dream of mine to erect this horse and rider in permanent form on some bold promontory just outside of San Francisco, and on the very edge of the Pacific. There they would stand forever looking out on the waste of waters—with nought save the precipice and the ocean before them—driven at last to the very edge of the continent. That would be, in very truth, 'The End of the Trail.'

"And the buffalo—that was my other tragedy of boyhood. If you could have seen those great, splendid beasts lumbering over the plains, a fitting complement to the great sweep of the landscape—then, only a few years later have seen nothing but their whitening bones! Those bones would run along in a zigzag line and in little heaps for miles. From that mute, whitening witness you could picture for yourself the details of that wholesale slaughter. The zigzag lines showed how the poor, frightened beasts sought to escape their butchers by running first in one direction and then in another, only to be headed off and slain. Were they killed by the Indians? No, by white men—organized bands of hunters who went out and killed them by the hundreds simply for their pelts. They would skin them and leave the carcasses to the wolves and coyotes.

"With two such impressions as these in my mind, you will perhaps understand why I chose the buffalo and the Indian as designs for the 'buffalo nickel.' A friend of mine remarked not long ago that of all the coins minted by the United States Government, this five-cent piece is the only one that is typically American—that would reveal to some later civilization its country of origin. I had not thought about it that way; all I tried to do was to express in these symbols —*America*, instead of merely copying some Greek temple or god."

"Perhaps"—I ventured—"numismatists of a thousand years hence will be eagerly searching for this little coin that we drop so thoughtlessly into the subway slot-machines."

"Who knows?" he mused smilingly. "But at any rate I feel that I have done my bit in helping to perpetuate these two so truly American symbols."

"Mr. Fraser, how did you come to take up art, out there in the Wild West?" I asked.

"It just came naturally, I suppose. I cannot remember when I didn't have the desire to draw or model something. My father was a bit of an artist. You see, he was a civil engineer and draughtsman, and used to make drawings along that line. He was an inventor, too. One of the things he invented was a contrivance for keeping the inside flanges of the railroad rails free from snow—a contrivance that is still in use. As I watched him draw things, the

[283]

natural impulse was to draw too. Then out near us was a queer deposit of stone, a beautiful creamy white, like chalk in substance except that after being quarried it remained soft for perhaps a month or two, then hardened. You could press or mold it into all sorts of shapes. The first settlers used to make blocks of it for the walls of their houses, and later it would become as hard as any other rock. I have often since wondered about that chalk, whether it could not be used in sculpture. I know that as a boy I had lots of fun making little figures out of it. And later, when I went to school in Minneapolis I still had the habit; I would take bits of blackboard crayon and make small objects."

The Fraser family removed to Minneapolis when James was about fourteen, and the boy attended school there for four years. His father would doubtless have been glad to have him follow his footsteps in railroad construction, but seeing that James was so much in earnest about wanting to study art, he consented for him to go to Chicago, to the Art Institute. He worked with Richard Bach, and kept hard at it, almost night and day, for six months, his first big individual study being a life-size "Head of an old Man" in marble, which, by the bye, he still treasures in his studio. This completed, he set forth for Paris, to "sink or swim." His objects were to get his work exhibited at the Salon and to study in the École des Beaux Arts, both of which were realized.

"When I was told that the 'Head' was accepted, I felt like I was walking on air. I went into that exhibition to look around—and there, right in the center of a semicircle of busts and portraits, stood my 'Old Man.' That was the thrill that comes once in a lifetime!"

The year of this Salon was 1898, and the sculptor was twenty-two. His "Head" won the prize offered by the American Art Association of Paris, for the best work exhibited by an American. Better still, it was the means of his making the acquaintance of Augustus Saint Gaudens. The latter was on the Jury of Award, and it chanced that just then he was in need of an assistant. He wrote to Fraser asking him to call, and Fraser lost no time in doing so. Saint Gaudens was at work on his Sherman statue for the entrance to Central Park, New York, and he could not get any French workmen to carry out his ideas to suit him. The work had been long under way, and meanwhile other commissions were pressing upon the master. He looked this quiet young Westerner over sharply, and asked him some pointed questions about himself and his aims.

"I hope you are not afraid of hard work," the older man said tersely, "for there's more hard work in art than anything I know of."

Fraser smiled. "That's what I have already found out, but I'm not afraid of it."

"Then come to my studio for awhile, and we'll see how we get along," invited Saint Gaudens. And Fraser nothing loath accepted.

For the remainder of his stay in Paris he assisted the master, working with him in the afternoons, and attending classes in the mornings and evenings. He came back to America with him, and for some months worked with him in his Cornish studio. It was a period of almost four years, of immense value to the younger man and not unprofitable to the older one; for together they worked on the Sherman statue, the Stevenson Memorial, "Amor Caritas," and other important subjects. While Fraser fell under the influence of his master, as has been later revealed in many a flowing line and graceful figure, his life out West and previous training have prevented him from being a mere imitator of the other's technique; his work has remained individual.

It was in 1902 that he came to New York and determined to start out for himself, and few could have been better equipped for the venture. His work at that time reveals all the maturity and skill of his later years. Among his first commissions was a bronze vase with delicate figures in bas-relief, ordered by the City of Buffalo in commemoration of the Pan-American Exposition. Then came the St. Louis Exposition, and for this he was given the opportunity to model a statue of Thomas Jefferson and also an equestrian Indian statue. The latter was the more congenial topic, for it carried him back to his boyhood on the plains. He depicted a stern and stately Sioux chieftain, his nude figure astride an active and wiry mustang, and the round war-shield at his side giving the balancing note to the composition. This warrior stood in the Court of Honor, as befitted an exposition held in the Middle West.

However, in these early days he did not win his reputation on Western subjects. It was in an entirely different *métier*—the depicting of child life. Mr. Fraser has always been fond of children, and he has been wonderfully successful in catching their characteristic moods and portraying them. In the Academy exhibition of 1902 he showed the first of what proved to be a long list of such subjects. It was the portrait bust of a child named Horatio Brewster, a commission obtained through Saint Gaudens, and so favorable was the comment it elicited that shortly the sculptor had more orders for children's portraits than he could execute. Among

[287]

others done about this period were studies of the children of Mr. and Mrs. Harry Payne Whitney, Mr. and Mrs. David Ericson, Mr. and Mrs. George D. Pratt, and others. One of the most charming of these is the head of little June Evans, the daughter of a fellow-sculptor. All are marked by a grace of line, set in low relief, which has all the freedom of a pencil sketch. That the children themselves "took to" the artist needs no argument, as one glances through a portfolio of their likenesses. They breathe the life and naïveté of artless childhood.

From children the artist turned to other portrait work. One of the best is a bronze bas-relief of Morris K. Jessup, which is now in the American Museum of Natural History, in memory of his services to that institution. Another is a bust of E. H. Harriman, sittings for which were given just before Mr. Harriman's last illness. And we have already spoken of his portrait of Theodore Roosevelt. The latter was undertaken primarily for an official bust of the President, to adorn the Hall of Statuary in the Capitol; but his first study was a much more faithful and unconventional likeness—so much so, that it now bids fair to be known as "the Roosevelt bust."

"I hated to conventionalize that likeness," says Fraser, "but the Senate Committee told me it had to be done to 'make it like the rest.' So I squared his shoulders back, put a frock coat on him, and let it go at that; but it isn't Roosevelt as I saw him. You may be interested to know that a replica of the one I like is to be placed on San Juan Hill, in Cuba."

A writer in *Scribner's* [1] has given an intimate picture of the sittings in the White House which resulted in "the Roosevelt bust." It is thus known to his friends because it is "the one that brings the great American back to them; and because artists approve it not only for its qualities as a likeness, but as a work of art."

"The President posed faithfully for me for two weeks, morning and afternoon, in the East Room," says Fraser. "And although he frequently had to receive cabinet officers and attend to business with other people, there were times when we had as much as two hours without interruption. I worked from eight o'clock until ten each morning, at which time the public was admitted; and in the afternoon, when business was over for the day and the President had had his ride, he would pose again."

The magazine writer continues: "For all his animation it seems that Roosevelt was far from being a 'difficult' sitter. Any artist who is accustomed to doing portraits will acknowledge that the mental attitude of the sitter is often the worst difficulty he

[1] October, 1920.

has to face. But Roosevelt neither expected a perfect likeness immediately, nor tried to help the artist by kind suggestions, nor did he have an idea that differed from all the world's regarding his own appearance. He candidly wanted the best that was due him, and was not a stickler for a too grim realism. One day he caught Mr. Fraser modeling two small moles—they may be seen on the left cheek of the bust—and exclaimed: 'Young man, I am not like Cromwell in being too particular about having such things as warts all represented. . . . '

"It was not long before Roosevelt found the specific point of contact between himself and the young artist—a mutual love of athletics. Boy fashion, the two stood up to measure themselves together. Now Mr. Fraser is a man whose breadth of shoulder apparently takes something from his height. Roosevelt was much shorter than he, yet to the artist's amazement the President's shoulders were two full inches broader than his. They compared notes on favorite sports. Roosevelt asked Fraser if he played baseball, and when the latter admitted it, the President looked positively wistful as he owned that he had never lived down his disappointment at not being able to play the game, because of his defective eyesight."

A day or two later, however, the President limped in from a game of tennis, and the artist fancied that he was genuinely proud of the fact that he had thus twisted an ankle; at any rate the President refused to sit down, and remained standing during this "sitting."

When the bust was finished, Roosevelt was frankly delighted with it, saying that it should be his official likeness. He was probably no better pleased than was the artist that a more conventional portrait had to be put in the Hall of the Capitol. He emphatically requested the sculptor to write the name "Theodore Roosevelt" under one ear of the bust. "For," said he, "in a hundred years the head will be broken off the base, and I don't want some one to pick it up and say, 'This is Charles W. Fairbanks, the great Idaho poet.'"

Some years later when Roosevelt passed away, Fraser was called in by the family to make the death-mask. Copies of this and the bust now stand side by side in his studio, in striking contrast—the one so virile, the other in the repose of eternal sleep. "I did not want to make the mask," says Fraser, "as I never want to make that of one of my friends. The man himself meant too much to me."

"Do you ever make life-masks?" I asked.

"Yes, occasionally. Do you recognize this one? Well, I'm sorry that you do not, for it is that of William G. McAdoo. Looks like Dante, doesn't it?"

The profile did indeed bear a striking resemblance to that of the Italian poet.

For a man of constantly varied activities such as Mr. Fraser, it is perhaps unfair to characterize him in a single phrase, as at the beginning of this chapter, "the sculptor of medals." Yet it is as good a single note as any, for he has probably modeled the designs for more medals than any other American artist. Such commissions seem to flow naturally to him. We have already mentioned the buffalo nickel as an outstanding instance. The first medal executed by him was one especially struck off by the Pan American Exposition at Buffalo, in honor of Saint Gaudens, who had made a memorable exhibit there. It came at the time when Fraser was closely associated with him, and thus could probably interpret him better than anyone else. The design was at once dignified and appropriate, and was the means of attracting other work of the same sort.

A partial list of such medals is: the Edison Medal, bearing a portrait of the inventor, and awarded for merit in electrical research; the Harriman Medal also with portrait, for those who promote safety in travel; the Medal of Award for the Academy of Arts and Letters; the Medal given by the American Institute of Graphic Arts; the Medal given by the Committee for Relief of Devastated France; the Williams

WILLIAMS COLLEGE MEDAL

MEDAL OF AMERICAN ACADEMY OF ARTS AND
LETTERS

By James E. Fraser

College Medal in honor of its students who served in the World War; the Distinguished Service Medal given by the Navy; and the well-known "Victory Medal" given to War veterans.

The artist shows regretfully another design for the Navy Medal which did not "get across." It is in the form of a steering-wheel of a vessel, with spokes in red, white and blue motif. "Secretary Daniels did not like it," he said; "he thought it too ornate, too much like the Belgian Service Medal; although I told him I had gotten the colors from the American flag."

Next to our five-cent piece, the Victory Medal designed by Fraser has had the most wholesale distribution of any coin of recent times. It was given to nearly five million veterans of the World War, not only soldiers, sailors and marines, but also nurses, doctors, and others who served the cause. A medal of somewhat similar design was given to the veterans of other Allied nations. Concerning this a writer in *Current Opinion* says: "Mr. Fraser has been repeatedly honored as a medalist, and his Victory Medal may be said to mark the culmination of his career. He was limited by a decision of the Interallied Military Commission that designers of victory medals in the Allied countries must follow the general specifications: 'On the obverse a Victory winged, standing full-length and full-face. On the reverse the inscription, "The Great War for Civilization" and a representation of the various allied and associated nations.' "

Despite these limitations, Mr. Fraser rose brilliantly to the occasion. Said Mr. F. P. Merritt, of the Numismatic Society: "Mr. Fraser in his execution of the design for the American Victory Medal has grasped completely the spirit of the decoration. . . . The Americanism of the figure is emphasized by the use of the spiked crown of the Statue of Liberty. The strength of the design and the character of the goddess are heightened by the use of an absolutely clear unornamental background." These medals were struck at the United States Mint in Philadelphia from a bronze of ninety per cent. copper and ten per cent. tin. Each section distributed bears its own serial number.

The artist was busily at work, on an afternoon recently when I called at his Macdougall Alley studio, on another medal. However, he was not concentrating on that. Several larger works were also in process. He likes to turn from one thing to another; he says it rests both brain and muscle. The three most important items just then were of widely differing character. There was a small sketch in clay of a statue of Thomas Jefferson, to go in front of the new

Missouri State Capitol, in Jefferson City. The subject is important locally both because of the name of the city itself, and also because it was through the efforts of Jefferson in consummating the Louisiana Purchase, that this great Western area became a part of the United States. For his studio model the artist has a painted panorama showing the front façade of the Capitol, with actual steps in miniature leading away from it. The statue will be placed in the center of this broad flight of steps, something like the position of the "Alma Mater" by French, up at Columbia University. The Missouri legislature is appropriating liberal sums of money to make this new Capitol beautiful without and within. At least half a dozen other well-known painters and sculptors are engaged upon details. The standing statue of Jefferson, which is Fraser's contribution, will be twelve feet high and done in bronze. The pedestal will be in a native red granite.

The second work is a statue and group commemorating John Ericsson, the inventor of the *Monitor*, that "cheese-box on a raft" that stopped the ironclad *Merrimac*, in the Civil War. This work is to cost about $70,000, half of which is appropriated by the Government, and the other half donated by Scandinavian citizens. It takes the form of a broad platform, about six feet high, in the center of which is a massed group of three figures, "Vision," "Adventure," and "Labor," rising some thirty feet above the pedestal. Down at the base of the pedestal rests a seated figure of the inventor. The whole composition is to be done in granite. It will be placed in the Mall, in Washington, near the Lincoln Memorial.

The third work of the series mentioned is a decoration for a pylon of a municipal bridge in Chicago, one of several such decorations by Mr. Fraser. It is a massed composition of figures in high relief, something like those done by MacMonnies for the Brooklyn Arch and elsewhere, except that here the outer contour is a flat spheroid. There are no sharply projecting lines. The subject is "The Pioneers," and depicts a party of early homesteaders going across the plains. Both face and figure express grim determination and a courage which argue no turning back. This is the white man's side of the Western epic, just as "The End of the Trail" is that of the Indian. The one is the complement of the other.

In the studio also were records of lately completed work, such as the "Alexander Hamilton," now in place in front of the Treasury Department, Washington. Hamilton is a young man of graceful carriage and well clad. At its unveiling President Harding spoke, paying a fine tribute to the sculptor as well as to his subject. It was one of the last public utterances of the President.

Then there was a plaster copy of the beautiful memorial erected in Rock Creek Cemetery, entitled "The Journey Through Life." Two life-size figures, a youthful man and woman, are walking forward in close communion. They are looking straight ahead, with clear-eyed calmness and confidence, facing the world together—and unafraid. While treated simply, there is a nobility of face and form which stamps this at once as one of Fraser's finest conceptions.

Mr. Fraser has had only three studios in New York. The present one in Macdougall Alley has been occupied by him now for twenty years. He might be called one of the "oldest inhabitants" of Greenwich Village, only his wife objects to his being called "old." Mrs. Fraser, by the bye,—known professionally as Laura Gardin—is herself a sculptor of distinction. Her work is widely known. She met Mr. Fraser while she was attending the Art Students' League and he was an instructor there. He held this position for some five years. They were married in 1913, and since then have been working happily side by side, as he has symbolized in the memorial to another couple, in his "Journey Through Life."

Laura Gardin Fraser has modeled some delightfully droll little "hound dogs," whose mournful expression would indicate that somebody had previously wanted to "kick 'em around." She has also done some exceedingly good medals—not to allow her husband to corner this market. One of her most widely advertised medals was that designed for the *Woman's Home Companion*, in 1914, and entitled "Better Babies." The design was particularly pleasing. She is said to have been the first woman employed by any government to design one of its coins; she was awarded the commission for the Alabama Centennial half-dollar, in 1921. She also made the War Medal for Army and Navy chaplains, awarded by the Federated Council of Churches.

Mrs. Fraser has done some clever little fountain figures, notably the "Grape Baby Fountain" in the rose garden, Delaware Park, Buffalo, and the "Goat Baby Fountain" for the interior of the Lockmoor Country Club building at Detroit. Her life-size group of a "Nymph and Satyr" in the Metropolitan Museum won the Barnett prize at the National Academy in 1916, and the Shaw prize was awarded to the "Baby Goat" in 1919. A greater honor still was her's in 1924, when the Saltus Medal was awarded to her. This is the highest award in the gift of the National Academy; it covers sculpture, painting, and all allied arts, and is open to both sexes. It was bestowed for her medals devoted to studies of

HEAD OF JOHN ERICSSON

By James E. Fraser; detail of the Washington group, taken in the sculptor's studio

horses and dogs.   Mrs. Fraser is an Associate Member of the National Academy.

On a recent visit to the Fraser studio, Mr. Fraser was apparently—though only apparently—taking it easy, while Mrs. Fraser was busily at work upon a life-size male figure, that of an athlete, splendid of torso and limb, suggestive of "The Discus Thrower," except that here the body was more erect. I am sorry to be unable to give the name of this creation, but the artist herself did not know. "I wish somebody would tell me the name!" she said.

Another critic who has seen this figure tells me that he considers it one of the finest nude studies by any artist of recent years.

Macdougall Alley, that haunt of many artists, is the Fraser domicile and workshop for the winter and spring months of the year. Then when the apple-blossoms become fragrant in New England they hie themselves to an old farm near Westport, Connecticut, a rambling place of some fifty-five acres of meadow, orchard, farm, and woodland, whereon is a house about a century old. Near-by Mr. Fraser has erected a big, roomy studio where he has lots of room to set up the larger pieces upon which he is at work.

Between-whiles up in the country he plays golf. "He plays *good* golf, too," supplements Mrs. Fraser loyally.

"Oh, come now," Mr. Fraser laughs embarrassedly. "I don't think it sounds right for an artist to be bragging about his golf game!"

"You don't have to brag about it," she reaffirms; "I'll do the bragging. Why he beats everybody he can get to play with him. He went up to Westport, the other day, for the first time this spring, and made two thirty-nines!"

Mr. Fraser is stockily built, and the set of his muscles would indicate that he could give a golf-ball a good long ride. In his boyhood he was good at baseball, as he admitted to Roosevelt. His broad shoulders give him the impression of being shorter than he really is, which I should say, at a guess, is five feet, ten. He is smooth-shaven, with a face inclined to the round; well-shaped nose, firm lips, square jaw, and hair beginning to show a trifle thin. But for all his indoor work, he looks qualified to take part at a moment's notice in a wrestling or boxing contest, or a swimming race.

He is a man without poses or prejudices, and waxes most enthusiastic when praising the work of somebody else. It was natural that he should speak in terms of reverence for his old mentor, Saint Gaudens, and he took up cudgels instantly at the suggestion that the latter was slow in finishing some of his work.

"Saint Gaudens did not work slowly," he said.

"The trouble was that he had too many big commissions to do at the same time; he was forced to turn from one thing to another, and for that matter he did not like to work at one thing continuously. But he worked very fast once he had settled down on a subject; and he was wonderfully stimulating in his suggestions to his assistants. You must remember, too, that he had to fight ill health. When you consider the output of his later years, you will realize how wonderful was its scope, as well as its quality. I can think of only one man, at present, whose work is commensurate with it, Daniel Chester French, and he has lived longer.

"When I consider the work that such men as French are doing, I feel it is a profound loss to the American people, that some adequate means of exhibiting it in mass is not provided. Mr. French is turning out, say, three big pieces each year; yet no one hears about them or sees them until they are set up in place, in widely scattered parts of the country. How fine it would be if, once a year, the big things of our big men could be grouped together in a place like Madison Square Garden. What a lesson it would be as to the progress of our American sculpture! Nowadays, the only shows we have are the ridiculously inadequate indoor exhibits at the Academy and elsewhere— mostly small figures badly assembled and still worse lighted. There is nothing inspiring about such a show, and I don't blame the public for not going. Now if we could only get these big things together, what an inspiring spectacle it would be!

"As a matter of fact, New York, like all our other cities, needs further awakening along art lines. Our æsthetic sense is still dull; it is swamped by commercialism. I mentioned Madison Square Garden, a moment ago. It looks now as though that fine building were doomed; and it is the only note of Old World beauty in our most prominent square. But out it must go, because they say it 'doesn't pay!' A big life insurance company is going to put up another office building 'in our midst.' What would you say if they tore down the Rheims Cathedral over in France, to make room for an office building? Of course, that is not quite commensurate, but it illustrates my point. We are too cocksure of ourselves over here. We are constantly changing. We build up only to tear down. We have no regard for things merely because they are beautiful; they must return us six per cent. on our investment—or, out they go!

"Against this spirit of commercialism our architects, our sculptors, and our painters are constantly striving. We are making some headway, as is evidenced by the fine single examples which continually arise. But we cannot go it alone. The public must keep step with us, and they can only do that when their sense of the æsthetic is prodded awake by such great public salons as mentioned awhile ago."

Such is the attitude of one of the foremost of our younger group of sculptors, and it is typical of the spirit of many studios. Our artists feel that they are giving expression to a definite phase of our national life, and they work not merely for individual glory but for that full-flowering of our art which can only come from united effort.

X

HERMON ATKINS MACNEIL

THE SCULPTOR OF INDIANS AND MONUMENTS

X

HERMON ATKINS MACNEIL

OUT on the Sound side of Long Island a little way from New York and about opposite One Hundred and Fiftieth Street, as the ferries cross, a rounded peninsula juts out. It is called College Point and is on somewhat higher ground than the country back of it. It is entirely built up with homes of workers in the metropolis, there being almost no stores or factories. If you go out by train to the rather dilapidated station, the only signs of life, other than arriving passengers, are the local taxicabs. If your final destination is the same as was that of the writer, not long ago, you need no street address. Merely go up to any of the drivers and say, "Drive me to Mr. MacNeil's studio," and he starts off without question.

Arriving at the very jumping-off place of the peninsula, the cab halts, and you perceive two buildings facing the water, with a bit of green intervening. They are connected only by an open passage-way. The one on the right is a sturdy frame structure, the home of the MacNeils; that on the left, of cobblestone, is taken up entirely by his workshop.

A kindly-faced man in middle life, of medium height, slender, alert, with brown hair and closely-cropped mustache greets you. (Not so many years ago his pictures showed him with a Vandyke beard, but that is not the MacNeil of to-day.)

"Shall we go into the studio first?" he inquires courteously, and leads the way into the sanctum sanctorum. A partition separates an office, its walls lined with photographs of completed work, from the big room in which the two or three young men assisting the sculptor are at work. This room is large enough and high enough to house models of quite heroic size. And, at that, it is likely to be "chock-a-block," for Mr. MacNeil is a man who seems unable to dodge work. If he has fewer than three large commissions going on at the same time, he begins to think he is loafing!

This is his home and workroom the year around, although he may be found in the city two or three times a week, at some one of the Clubs. He has lived in College Point for a score of years, and loves the rippling waters of the Sound, winter or summer. But he arrived at this little harbor by devious routes. His artistic path as well was not smooth and direct;

HERMON A. MACNEIL

From a photograph from life

his success has been achieved by no one *tour de force*, but by steady progress and unremitting toil.

Mr. MacNeil came of New England stock, having been born at Prattville near Chelsea, Massachusetts, in 1866. There was an artistic strain in his family. His uncle, Henry Mitchell, was a steel-engraver and gem-cutter, and was versed in heraldry.

"My mother painted," he says, "but it was the usual copy work of the good old days, when every girl was expected to have an accomplishment, and most of them did samplers. She evidently liked her painting, as I still have one of her pictures, a good-sized canvas which she had framed, and in the then-popular weeping-willow style.

"How did I come to take up art? I fell into it naturally. I·remember that as a boy in my teens, attending the public schools, I looked forward eagerly to Friday afternoon; for then it was that we had our one art class each week. It wasn't much to boast of —just some cubes and such like inanimate objects for pencil drawings on paper, but I thought it was great. I recall yet a trivial little incident of those days. Our teacher had been absent from the room, and boy-like some of the pupils took advantage of it. When he came back and found them skylarking he was displeased. Three or four of us had kept at work, and he remarked as he came up the aisle, 'Now if you would only turn out good work like this and this'—indicating some of the sketches he saw on the desk. As he came alongside my desk, I raised my head. 'Yes, and yours too,' he added. I had only been included in a general commendation, but that little remark has stuck with me to this day!"

From the public schools young MacNeil was sent to the State Normal Arts School, at his urgent request. "I told my parents it was what I wanted to do above everything else," he says. It was a stiff four-years' course, where everything was taught in the line of art—painting, draftsmanship, drawing for mathematical and engineering subjects, architecture, and sculpture,—and MacNeil took them all. It was not until the last year that he reached sculpture, and by that time he had determined this was what he wanted to make his life-work. "I went through the whole gamut, and the further I went the more it laid hold of me," he avers.

He was fortunate in his last year in winning the certificate of merit given by the School for the best work done by any pupil in the course; and this recommendation brought him to the attention of Cornell University, which just then needed an instructor in modeling. He went there and taught most acceptably for three years, as is shown by the fact that when he resigned in order to go abroad, they refused to accept his resignation as final, but told him they would hold the place open for him on his return.

In Paris, that focus of ambitious art students, he was a pupil of Chapu at the Julien Academy, and of Falguiere at the École des Beaux Arts. This was a two-year period full of inspiration and high hopes, and was only terminated by the depletion of the pennies saved up at Cornell. His return to this country was in the fortunate year of 1893, when the Columbian Exposition at Chicago had created a boom in the art world. MacNeil did not want to go back to teaching in Cornell, so went instead to the Western metropolis. He fell in with Martiny, and helped him with his decorations for various Exposition buildings.

"Before I got through," he says, "they gave me two figures of my own to do; they were for the Electrical Building, and I was mighty proud of them.

"After the close of the Exposition I stayed in Chicago for three years—and almost starved to death. I opened up a studio jointly with Charles F. Brown, but there wasn't much to do. The Fair resulted in a consequent slump. I was wondering how on earth I was going to manage it, when a restaurant keeper came along, who wanted some things done, and offered me my meal tickets for the job; and I was glad to take it."

"It was about that time that you became interested in Indian subjects, wasn't it?" I suggested.

"Yes, and you may find it an interesting yarn. Buffalo Bill's Wild West Show had been in Chicago during the Fair, and one of his braves was Black Pipe, a Sioux, a fine-looking fellow. He had stayed behind, and one day I met him on the streets, looking hungry and cold, and asked him if he wanted something to do. He did—there was no doubt about that. I took him into the studio, fed him up, and then set to work modeling his head. I finished it in four hours, for I was not sure that I would ever see my Indian again; but he stayed with me in all for a year and a half, helping me with odd jobs about the studio. That's his head there."

It was a life-size bronze, which he indicated, not done in full relief but resting on a plaque—a strong piece of portraiture.

"In this and your later work with Indians," I inquired, "did you have any trouble about making their likenesses? Some of them object to being photographed."

"Yes, many of the older Indians object; they think it takes the spirit out of them. But Black Pipe had been among white folks long enough to know better, and with others I managed to get around their superstitions. Black Pipe, by the way, posed for 'The

Primitive Chant' which is one of my best-known Indian subjects."

This is the spirited figure of a naked savage dancing to the music of his own flute. It has been widely copied in art prints.

"These first Indian subjects led to my first important commission," he continued reminiscently. "The Marquette Building was being completed in Chicago, and they wanted four decorative panels illustrating scenes in the missionary-explorer's life. As these would bring in Indians, they decided to try me. I don't mind admitting that it meant a lot to me, in those days. I felt that at last I was beginning to get my feet upon the bottom rung of the ladder."

The four Marquette panels, done in low relief, in bronze, show dramatic periods in the French priest's life. The last one, "The Burial of Pere Marquette," with its procession of figures is particularly impressive in its revealment of the peoples and customs in those formative days. It is a fine and permanent record of a man whose life-work was bound up intimately with the founding of Chicago, and whom in consequence they delight to honor.

"Curiously enough," said Mr. MacNeil, 'one of my latest pieces of work harks back to the same subject. You have doubtless heard of Mr. Ferguson who left a fund of a million dollars, the income of

[313]

which is to be devoted annually to the art embellishment of the streets, squares, or parks of Chicago. Knowing of this fund, the schoolchildren out there, to the number of fifty thousand, petitioned that a monument to Pere Marquette be set up in some public place. They acceded to the request, and the statue when finished is to be placed on the West Side, near two large public schools, where sixteen thousand pupils can see it daily. Not long ago I was out there doing some preliminary work on the site, when one of the school principals happened to notice me, introduced himself, and asked me to accompany him into his building. I did so, and was ushered into a large classroom seating perhaps several hundred pupils. He introduced me to them, told them what I was doing, and then asked if any student could tell about Marquette. Instantly not one but scores of hands went up, and faces looked eager. The principal picked at random a boy near-by, and that young fellow got up and made one of the best little speeches on Marquette you ever heard. I thought I was 'up' on Marquette, but I marveled at it. Later, I commented on the fact to the principal. 'Do you know,' he replied, 'that a large majority of these students are *foreigners*—yet they are keenly interested in Marquette as well as other figures in our history.' That incident heartened me and made me all the more de-

THE SUN VOW

By Hermon A. MacNeil; in the grounds of the Montclair (N. J.)
Art Museum

termined to give those children the best that was in me, for their chosen statue."

The statue will be a bronze group rising thirteen feet, from a five-foot pedestal, and will be so placed at the intersection of streets that it will be directly facing motorists and others, on the turn.

Born of his first work on Marquette and his Indian studies came a great desire to observe the redmen at close range. He went to the Southwest, among the Moquis and the Zunis. At times he was a hundred miles from the nearest railroad. He witnessed a Snake Dance and other tribal ceremonies, and lived their primitive life. For this reason he has interpreted them with a sympathy and insight peculiarly his own. As a writer in the *Craftsman* says:

"In 'The Moqui Runner,' 'The Primitive Chant,' 'The Sun Vow,' 'The Coming of the White Man,' and many others of his Indian statues, MacNeil always gives you the feeling of the Indian himself, of his attitude toward his own vanishing tribes, and his point of view toward the white race which has absorbed his country. It is never the Indian of Buffalo Bill's Wild West, trapped out for curiosity seekers, but the grave, sad, childlike man of the plains, faithful to his own tribe, once loyal to us, though now resentful; and always a thinker, a poet, and a philosopher."

And yet some of these portraits of our redmen were

completed thousands of miles away, amid the classic environs of Rome. But the classic atmosphere of that ages-old city could not stifle the Western inspiration which the sculptor had received on the Plains. He tells about the trip to Rome in these words:

"I had returned to Chicago and was teaching in the Art Institute, when I got an upsetting letter. It was from the National Academy offering me a year's scholarship, to study in Rome. I was perplexed; I didn't know whether I wanted to accept it or not. I realized that it was both a compliment and an opportunity, but I was chuckful of those Indian studies —and besides there were other reasons."

What those "other reasons" were, proved to be centered in the person of one of his most promising art students, Miss Carol Brooks. He had hoped that before long they could be married, and he wrote the Academy to this effect. They replied that while the scholarship was offered only to single men, they did not want to stand in the way of his marriage; however, if he took this step, the scholarship would be limited to one year instead of two. He took the step, and sailed with his bride for the Eternal City. Before the end of this year, however, the Academy wrote another perplexing letter.

"They said I might stay another year," he continued, "but that if I stayed that additional year, I

[316]

must stay three years. It was a curiously-worded
letter—I still have it—but after puzzling over it
some more, I decided to stay three, making four years
in all. It was a fine and profitable experience, but
I was glad to get back to America, and to make another start for myself."

The return was in the year 1900, and from this
time on, Mr. MacNeil has been identified with the art
life of New York. He had won a medal in the Paris
Exposition of 1900; and some of his first work done
after returning was for the Pan-American Exposition
at Buffalo, which gave him a gold medal. For the
latter exposition, also, he designed the official medal
of award, the first of several medallions later done by
him. Shortly afterward we find him busily engaged
at the Charleston and the St. Louis Expositions. At
St. Louis he executed the massive and elaborate cas-
cade fountain in the Court of Honor, one of the most
beautiful outside features of the Exposition. Still
later came decorations at San Francisco. There is a
photograph extant of a stately shaft which stood near
the sea-wall in the California city. It was fifteen feet
in diameter and over a hundred feet high—the
"Column of Progress," surmounted by an "Adventurous Bowman"—a landmark never to be forgotten by
any visitor to that Exposition. But alas! it was of
the flimsy stuff that exposition dreams are made of,

and passed with the demolition of the buildings. Now there is a movement on foot to rebuild it in the permanent stone which it deserves.

To this earlier period belongs the statue of President McKinley which stands in Columbus, Ohio. Those who knew the martyred president most intimately have been impressed by its naturalness. "Yes, that is the way he looked to his homefolks," they would remark. There is no pose about the portrait; McKinley stands there in a business-like manner as though delivering an address, one hand holding a state paper, the other resting by a thumb in a trousers pocket; the frock coat pushed carelessly back. The statue looks easy, and yet the sculptor confesses to having had more trouble with it than with any other work of the kind. In the first place, there is nothing essentially heroic in either the face or the figure. Then there was difficulty in procuring the death-mask for verifying measurements; and the work was nearly completed before this was secured. As for the figure, a neighbor in College Point, whose lower body was formed along McKinleyan lines, willingly posed.

"After the statue was completed," said Mr. Mac-Neil to the writer, "a curious thing happened. My doorbell rang one day, and I went to answer it— and there stood Mr. McKinley! At least it looked enough like him to have been him in the flesh. The visitor explained he had heard that I was having trouble in securing a model, and as he had often been called Mr. McKinley's double, he had come over to offer his services. I would have given anything to have met that man a little sooner."

The statue in Columbus stands upon an imposing pedestal, yet of classically simple lines, flanked by two groups in bronze: "Industry," a man of giant mold instructing a youthful student; and "Prosperity," a gracious woman who shields with one arm a little maid representing "Peace." Charming groups are these two, and the writer ventured the remark that he liked them better than the "McKinley" itself. "They *are* better," assented the sculptor at once. "I regard them as among my best things; but here I was not hampered by certain demands, as in the portrait; I could give free rein to my fancy.

"All portraits are not necessarily tedious, however," he continued. "There was my statue of Ezra Cornell, the founder of the University, which now stands on the campus. Apart from the fact that I had old associations with the college, the subject itself was much easier to do, than usual." He turned to a photograph of the monument, as he talked. "When I began to work on that, my heart fairly leaped within me. Mr. Cornell, I discovered, looked like my own father! It seemed to me that I was making

[319]

a portrait of my father. And so throughout it was a labor of love; it almost worked itself out."

In looking over a record of Mr. MacNeil's work for the past fifteen or twenty years, one is struck by the number of big commissions he has undertaken—"big" in point of physical dimensions. He says that he likes to work on large subjects; they appeal to him, and his work has gravitated that way unconsciously. He has done almost no busts or statuettes. His large outdoor work has created a demand for more and still more of the same character. One of the first of these was the "Soldiers and Sailors" monument, unveiled some fifteen years ago in Albany. Here again the lines of the pediment are classic; perchance his training in Rome crops out here. Along the face is a frieze in low relief summarizing incidents of the Civil War; while standing boldly away from the mass of stone is a heroic female figure in bronze, bearing in her arms sprays of palm. It is Columbia rewarding her battle-scarred sons, and the bas-relief which frames, as it were, her splendid presence, tells the story of their deeds.

Then there is his figure of Washington done in stone and setting off a companion piece, by Calder, on the supporting walls of the Washington Arch, on Fifth Avenue, New York. One shows "The President," and the other "The Soldier." "We had to

EZRA CORNELL

By Hermon A. MacNeil.   In the grounds of Cornell University

work together on those statues, Calder and I," said Mr. MacNeil, "and we had some hot arguments over them, though we are good friends. Of course, each of us had his own statue to do, but we had to treat them in the same restrained manner, to fit each other and the Arch itself."

Another large commission as yet uncompleted is two "Civil War Pylons," for a new parkway in Philadelphia. They will guard an entrance to the beautiful new boulevard now in process of making. The pylons are each fifty feet high and are slightly-tapering shafts flanked at the bottom by massed figures. Their lines are severely simple, yet dignified.

However, in point of size and detail, these are outranked by a frieze which has been ordered for the Missouri State Capitol. In the chapter devoted to James Earle Fraser's work, I took occasion to mention the elaborate art treatment which this magnificent structure is receiving. No less than six or eight artists of the first rank are aiding with brush and chisel to make this a temple of art, which will be an inspiration to the Middle West for untold generations. Mr. MacNeil's assignment is two side-wall panels cut in stone and flanking an entrance, and a frieze, semicircular in shape and one hundred and thirty feet long, just within. As this frieze is seven and one half feet high, the figures are larger than life.

There are so many of these figures, that the artist himself acknowledges he has never counted them. The whole thing will be cut out of Missouri stone.

These figures represent, first, the settlers who came across the Mississippi, received supplies and renewed strength from Missouri, and then penetrated the West bringing the civilization and the industries of the white race. It is a far-reaching conception, and again illustrates the point frequently mentioned in these pages, that our artists are now drawing their inspiration, not from Greece, or Rome, or France, but from the wellsprings of our own rich history.

The actual physical labor involved in the present work also impressed me, as I looked at a working model which was about a foot in width, and yet ran across the whole side of the studio. The molding of all these separate figures in wet clay and in miniature seemed formidable enough; yet it was only the beginning.

"It *has* been some job," assented the sculptor smiling; "but, do you know, I have discovered a short cut which will save me days and weeks of time, in the enlargements. I am having a photographer take pictures of these figures, which he afterwards enlarges in the prints up to the size I want. I then cut out these enlargements and lay them directly upon the larger mass of clay, and cut out my bigger figures by that. Of course, I can make minor corrections later, but the blocking out and measuring are all done for me, and I know they are accurate.

"I have used this idea quite successfully in work upon public monuments. I have enlargements made of my small working models, which I take to the site of the future monument and set up on a temporary pedestal against my actual background. I can then tell in advance if I have the right proportions. This is the method I am using for the new Marquette statue, and I also tried it out only recently over here in Flushing, where they want me to do their World War monument." He showed me a photograph of the street in Flushing with the memorial actually in place, or apparently so. "Looks natural, doesn't it? Yet the monument pedestal is right here"—pointing to one of the unfinished works in his studio—"and the group is somewhere else."

"Have you done any other Indians lately?" I asked, and recalled to him the fact that I had seen a fine replica of "The Sun Vow" out in the grounds of the Montclair Art Museum.

"No, only incidentally," he said regretfully. "This frieze will have some Indian figures, but my larger work has crowded out my figure studies. It has not been my choice, but as the gods have decreed. Why, I have done practically no single figures at all.   Here is one—not an Indian—which has created some discussion.   It was used last winter by the Sculpture Society for the 'seal' of their show.   It is called, 'Into the Unknown.' "

The figure is that of a female seated with mallet in hand, as though trying to chisel her way through the wall which she faces.   Her body is in bold relief, but as she tries to force her way forward, her face disappears entirely into the rock!   In fact, there is no face or head there.   The effect is quite uncanny. And it is unique as being probably the only human figure that never originally had any head.

Any record of a visit to the MacNeil studio would be incomplete without mention of the work of Mrs. Carol Brooks MacNeil, who has her separate workshop and won a reputation almost as soon as did her husband, for her sculptured works.   She is especially happy with her studies in childlife, her own two boys while little fellows being charming models.   She is the daughter of an artist and grew up with brushes and palettes, and when she laid them aside for mallet and chisel it was a disappointment to her father. The later success of her work has justified her decision.   She has exhibited at several Paris Salons, at the Chicago Exposition, and at the Paris Exposition of 1900.   She won an honorable mention at the latter, and a medal at the St. Louis Exposition.   One of her best known works is a statue of a "Foolish Virgin" with the inscription, "Too Late, Ye Cannot Enter Now," which is the property of Mrs. Cyrus Mc-Cormick of Chicago. Recently she has been devoting two days a week to an art class of girls, at Mamaroneck, New York. Between-whiles, she finds time for music, her friends, and her family.

As soon as the shut-in months are past, the MacNeil home takes on still more varied activities; for then the waters of the Sound beckon them. They have their own pier and boat-landing, and their own bit of shelving beach. A dip into the salt waves can be had on short notice. Then there is a big, roomy motor-boat with a decked-over cabin and deep sea-going lines. "It sleeps five," said Mr. MacNeil, "and we have spent many a fine night aboard.

"And to think," he added regretfully, "I shall have to miss all this for three months this summer! I am going to Hawaii. I have a brother out there, and have long planned to go out. On my way, too, I can stop and do some preliminary work at the Missouri Capitol. Yes, I guess it will be a fine jaunt, and maybe I can loaf for awhile. I worked hard all last summer. But I shall miss all this!"

The sweep of his arm embraced not only the dancing waves of the Sound, but also the bit of royal domain which enclosed his studio, his boat, his home, his family. Winter and summer he has lived there and toiled there untiringly. But he has looked on life and found it good, and I knew that the regret over even a temporary leave-taking was genuine.

XI
WOMEN SCULPTORS OF NOTE

I. HARRIET HOSMER: PIONEER OF OUR WOMEN
SCULPTORS

XI

WOMEN SCULPTORS OF NOTE

I. HARRIET HOSMER: PIONEER OF OUR WOMEN SCULPTORS

WHEN the roll is called of noted women sculptors of America, one of the first names that rises to the lips is that of Harriet Hosmer—both in point of time and because of the individuality of her work. Miss Hosmer was perhaps fortunate in living and working at a time when our sculptors of both sexes were comparatively few, and naturally her work attracted more attention than at a later and more crowded period; yet for all that, when viewed in relation to her contemporaries, it was worthy of the attention it received.

Mrs. Sarah K. Bolton, a biographical writer of a former generation, gives a picturesque account of the impression the artist made upon a group of schoolgirls. Remember, please, that the period was that of the Civil War and long before the day of the "emancipated woman." Says Mrs. Bolton: [1]

[1] "Girls Who Became Famous."

FAMOUS SCULPTORS OF AMERICA

"Some years ago, in an art store in Boston, a crowd of persons stood gazing intently upon a famous piece of statuary. The red curtains were drawn aside, and the white marble seemed almost to speak. A group of girls stood together, and looked on in rapt admiration. One of them said, 'Just to think that a woman did it!'

" 'It makes me proud and glad,' said another.

" 'Who is Harriet Hosmer?' said a third. 'I wish I knew about her.'

"And then one of us, who had stolen all the hours she could get from school life to read art books from the Hartford Athenæum, and kept crude statues, made by herself from chalk and plaster, secreted in her room, told all she had read about the brilliant creator of 'Zenobia.'

"The statue was seven feet high, queenly in pose and face, yet delicate and beautiful, with the thoughts which genius had wrought in it. . . . Since that time, I have looked upon other masterpieces in all the great galleries of Europe, but perhaps none have ever made a stronger impression upon me than 'Zenobia,' in those early years."

Who, then, was this woman artist of whom those girls were so proud—and who has been held up as an example to countless other ambitious girls? The following account of her early life is practically an autobiography.

[330]

ZENOBIA

By Harriet Hosmer

WOMEN SCULPTORS OF NOTE

Harriet Hosmer's birthplace was Watertown, Massachusetts; the date was October 9, 1830. Her father was a leading physician of the town; her mother a gentle invalid who died of consumption. Dr. Hosmer had lost his only other child by the same disease, and he was determined that Harriet should be an outdoor girl. As he said: "There is a whole lifetime for the education of the mind, but the body develops in a few years; and during that time nothing should be allowed to interfere with its free and healthy growth." Consequently, "her father encouraged her to follow a course of physical exercise such as boys only, at that period, were accustomed to take. She became expert in rowing, riding, skating, and shooting; developed powers of great endurance; scandalized the neighbors by climbing trees whenever birds' nests tempted her; filled her room, boylike, with snakes, insects, and other specimens of natural history, which she dissected or preserved; and in a clay pit in her father's garden modeled figures of animals.

"Her first instructor was a Mr. Peabody, brother-in-law of Nathaniel Hawthorne, who found it impossible to teach by his conventional methods the undisciplined child, and in despair returned her to her father. Mrs. Sedgwick, who had a school for young ladies at Lenox, was noted for her success in difficult cases of this kind. Harriet was placed under her

[331]

care, which was exercised with such tact that the child's breezy, independent nature was disciplined almost unconsciously, and the teacher gained the love and confidence of the pupil. Three years were spent at Lenox, and then Miss Hosmer went to Boston to study drawing and modeling under an artist, Mr. Stephenson. Her sex debarred her from entering the Boston Medical School, whose course in anatomy she was anxious to take; and hearing that the Medical College in St. Louis would admit her, she removed to that city. She made her home in the family of Wayman Crow, father of one of her old school friends, and from that gentleman she received her first order of a statue from Rome. Professor McDowell, of the Medical School, under whom the sculptors Powers and Clevenger had studied anatomy, was particularly kind to Miss Hosmer; and, in return, she made a medallion portrait of him after a bust by Clevenger."

Her art work, however, had by no means destroyed her athletic proclivities. No sooner was she out of school, in St. Louis, than she took an adventurous trip by steamer down to New Orleans, and then north as far as the Falls of St. Anthony. She smoked the pipe of peace with the Chief of the Dakota Indians, explored the lead mines of Dubuque, and scaled a high mountain which was later named for her. **And** she went without an escort, and safely.

Her father, who was a man of means, was very proud of his artistic daughter, and on her return home fitted up a studio for her where she carved and modeled to her heart's content, doing among other things a "Napoleon" and a "Hesper." She did all the marble work herself, after the block had been shaped down for her to within an inch or two of the desired outlines. Slight in build as she was, she "wielded for eight or ten hours a day a leaden mallet weighing four pounds and a half. Had it not been for the strength and flexibility of muscle acquired by rowing and other athletic exercises, such arduous labor would have been impossible."

She was now twenty-two, and well realized her own limitations. She wanted to go to Rome to study, and her father consented and accompanied her. She applied for admission to the studio of John Gibson, a leading English sculptor, but the latter at first demurred saying that "women wouldn't apply themselves to study." When showed photographs of her first work he relented and admitted her. Here she remained for seven busy years, earning her master's profound respect both for her ability and her perseverance. Her first works done in Rome, other than

copies, were a "Medusa" with serpent locks and a
"Daphne." Both were sent back to Boston for exhibition and were much praised. Mr. Gibson said
that "the power of imitating roundness and softness
of flesh he had never seen surpassed."

Her next works were "Œnone," a wood nymph,
and a reclining figure in marble, "Beatrice Cenci"
which was purchased by the St. Louis Mercantile
Library. Then came a turn in Fortune's wheel.
Her indulgent father met with financial reverses, and
wrote her that he could no longer pay her tuition
abroad, and suggested that she return home. At first
she was in despair, and then her natural pluck came
to her aid. "I cannot give up my art, and I won't,"
she said. Her trunks were unpacked again, she sold
her handsome saddle-horse, and settled down to work
indeed "as if she earned her daily bread."

"By a strange freak of human nature, by which we
sometimes do our most humorous work when we are
saddest," says Mrs. Bolton, "Miss Hosmer produced
now in her sorrow her fun-loving 'Puck.' It represents a child about four years old seated on a toad-
stool which breaks beneath him. The left hand con-
fines a lizard, while the right holds a beetle. The
legs are crossed, and the great toe of the right foot
turns up. The whole is full of merriment. The
Crown Princess of Germany, on seeing it, exclaimed,

'Oh Miss Hosmer, you have such a talent for toes!' Very true, for this statue, with the several copies made from it, brought her thirty thousand dollars! The Prince of Wales has a copy, the Duke of Hamilton also, and it has gone even to Australia and the West Indies." A companion piece is her "Will-o'-the-Wisp" which was also popular.

Another timely commission received when the item of living expenses was pressing was a memorial figure for a sarcophagus. A Madam Falconet, who had come to know and admire her work, gave her this commission in memory of her sixteen-year-old daughter who had recently died. It is in a church in Rome, and is a lovely representation of girlhood.

Nathaniel Hawthorne had known of Harriet Hosmer in her girlhood—it will be remembered that his brother-in-law had undertaken to teach her—and on a visit to Rome in 1857 he called at her studio. He has left a vivid impression of her and her surroundings, in his "Italian Notes":

"To-day we went to see Miss Hosmer,[1] and as her studio seems to be mixed up with Gibson's, we had an opportunity of glancing at some of his beautiful works. . . . We found Miss Hosmer in a little upper room. She has a small, brisk, wide-awake figure, not ungraceful; frank, simple, straightforward, and downright. She had on a robe, I think, but I

[1] The name was left blank in the original MS.

[335]

did not look so low, my attention being chiefly drawn to a sort
of man's sack of purple or plum-colored broadcloth, into the
side pockets of which her hands were thrust as she came forward to greet us. She withdrew one hand, however, and
cordially presented it to my wife (whom she already knew)
and to myself, without waiting for an introduction. She had
on a shirt-front, collar, and cravat like a man's, with a brooch
of Etruscan gold, and on her curly head was a picturesque
little cap of black velvet, and her face was as bright and merry,
and as small of feature as a child's. It looked in one aspect
youthful, and yet there was something worn in it, too. There
never was anything so jaunty as her movement and action;
she was very peculiar but she seemed to be her actual self,
and nothing affected or made up; so that, for my part, I gave
her full leave to wear what may suit her best, and to behave
as her inner woman prompts. I don't quite see, however,
what she will do when she grows older, for the decorum of age
will not be consistent with a costume that looks pretty and
excusable enough in a young woman."

Hawthorne was evidently more impressed with the
artist herself, and her mannish costume which was
strange then but common enough now, than with her
artistic ability; for he goes on to say:

"Miss Hosmer led us into a part of the extensive studio,
or collection of studios, where some of her own works were to
be seen: 'Beatrice Cenci' which did not very greatly impress
me; and a monumental design, a female figure—wholly
draped, even to stockings and shoes,—in a quiet sleep. I

liked this last. There was also a 'Puck' doubtless full of fun; but I had hardly time to glance at it. Miss Hosmer evidently has good gifts in her profession, and doubtless she derives great advantage from her close association with a consummate artist like Gibson; nor yet does his influence seem to interfere with the originality of her own conceptions. In one way, at least, she can hardly fail to profit,—that is, by the opportunity of showing her works to the throngs of people who go to see Gibson's own; and these are just such people as an artist would most desire to meet, and might never see in a lifetime, if left to himself. I shook hands with this frank and pleasant little person, and took leave, not without purpose of seeing her again."

Hawthorne had his wish gratified, for a few months afterward Miss Hosmer returned to America, where she worked on her masterpiece, a figure of Zenobia, the captive queen of Palmyra, led in chains through the streets of Rome. The artist studied for months on her subject, and while at work upon it, the famous author called again, and this time was more awake to her talent. He writes:

"This morning I went with my wife and Miss Hoar to Miss Hosmer's studio, to see her statue of 'Zenobia.' . . . There were but very few things in the room: two or three plaster busts, a headless cast of a plaster statue . . . 'Zenobia' stood in the center of the room, as yet unfinished in the clay, but a very noble and remarkable statue indeed, full of dignity and beauty. It is wonderful that so brisk a woman could have achieved a work so quietly impressive; and there is something in 'Zenobia's' air that conveys the idea of music, uproar, and a great throng all about her; whilst she walks in the midst of it, self-sustained and kept in a sort of sanctity by her native pride. The idea of motion is attained with great success; you not only perceive that she is walking, but know at just what tranquil pace she steps amid the music of the triumph. The drapery is very fine and full; she is decked with ornaments; but the chains of her captivity hang from wrist to wrist; and her deportment—indicating a soul so much above her misfortune, yet not insensible to it—makes these chains a richer decoration than all her other jewels. I know not whether there be some magic in the present imperfect finish of the statue, or in the material of clay, as being a better medium of expression than even marble; but certainly I have seldom been more impressed by a piece of modern sculpture . . . 'Zenobia' is a high, heroic ode."

The completed statue in marble was exhibited in America in 1859, and is said to have aroused much enthusiasm. The artist received five thousand dollars from these exhibitions. So great a work was it considered in London, that the critics ascribed it to the chisel of Gibson. Miss Hosmer promptly showed her "spunk" by bringing suits for libel, and the statements were speedily withdrawn. It is said that the Prince of Wales (afterwards Edward VII) wished to buy it, but the artist refused saying, "it must go to America."

In 1860 she again visited America, to see her father, who was seriously ill. While here she received a commission from St. Louis, the scene of her early studies, to make a bronze portrait statue of Thomas Hart Benton. It was not until 1868 that the statue was unveiled in Lafayette Park. Mr. Lorado Taft views it with very mixed feelings and exclaims: "It must have been very easy to do statues in those days!" Her "Sleeping Faun," shown in the Dublin Exhibition of 1865, was sold for five thousand dollars. It is one of her finest nude statues. Among the more important of her later works were a "Siren Fountain" for Lady Alford, and a "Queen Isabella of Spain" for the Columbian Exposition, at Chicago.

Miss Hosmer was always fond of Rome, and spent many of the closing years of her long life there. She knew a wide circle of famous people of both hemispheres, among them the Brownings, Tennyson, George Eliot, Thackeray, Carlyle, Ruskin, Whittier, the Hawthornes, and others. She was a great favorite with Pope Pius IX, who liked her independence and wit. Like Rosa Bonheur she affected a mannish attire, and used to ride around Rome unattended and astride, to the horror of the strict Italian matrons. She and Charlotte Cushman, the actress, frequently followed the hounds with the men, and leaped fences and ditches with the best of the riders. She turned at times from modeling to writing, both prose and poetry.

In her old age, she returned to the home of her childhood, Watertown, and here she breathed her last, February 21, 1908, in her seventy-eighth year.

2. ANNA VAUGHN HYATT: SCULPTOR OF ANIMALS

"On the northerly shore of Cape Ann, on the coast of Massachusetts, lies the sleepy little seaside village of Annisquam, long the refuge and delight of a handful of artists and discriminating summer visitors. [1] And the loveliest corner in this peaceful spot is a point of land comprising seven none-too-fertile acres, jutting out between two salt-water coves where the picturesque 'Squam River glides in and out to the sea. On a gentle rise of green lawn, shaded by noble trees, stands an old Colonial gray-shingled house, built in 1663, while-paneled, with big brick fireplaces, and a cool, white-wainscoted hall running breezily through it from door to door. This place was bought over forty years ago by Prof. Alpheus Hyatt, the well-known scientist and friend of Agassiz, then on the Harvard faculty. And it was there, in a room of that beautiful old house, that the first Marine Biological Laboratory of America was founded and in-

[1] *Touchstone*, July, 1919.

JOAN OF ARC
By Anna Vaughn Hyatt; on Riverside Drive, New York

stalled, the present important Laboratory at Woods Hole being the successor of this baby venture. But 'Seven Acres' has continued to be the Hyatt summer home, now sheltering the younger, as well as the older, generations."

This was the favorite haunt in childhood of Prof. Hyatt's daughter, Anna Vaughn, and it is still her chosen retreat in the summer months. In the winters she may be found among the busy artists of the metropolis. She is by birth and inheritance a New Englander. She was born, March 10, 1876, in the university town of Cambridge, Massachusetts, and came by her scholarly and artistic tendencies naturally. She was educated at a private school in Cambridge, conducted by the Misses Smith, and at first took up the violin, devoting several hours a day to it. Then her health failed and for a considerable time she was an invalid. While convalescing and to pass away the time, she took up clay modeling. Her first subject was a house pet, a Great Dane dog, and she amused herself for hours modeling him, entirely without instruction. The result was a very creditable first work, which was placed on view and later sold. In after years she perpetuated this study in marble.

Upon recovering her health she resolved to make sculpture, instead of music, her life-work, and studied

[341]

first under Henry H. Kitson, of Boston; then for some months at the Art Students' League, New York, where she came under the influence of MacNeil and others. But her earnest, searching disposition would not let her remain content with any one master; she wished to compare methods, to get as many viewpoints as possible, and then work out her own artistic salvation. Especially did she want to "do" her beloved animals. She was equally interested in doing domestic or wild animals. Now it was a horse pulling a heavy load uphill, or a frolicsome goat; again it might be a tiger or elephant. Bostock's Animal Circus came to Boston about that time, and it was a godsend to her. She obtained permission to study and model animals at close range, and sometimes in her eagerness she got too close for safety. Once a man-killing elephant got as close to her as his chain would allow and, filling his trunk with dirty water, squirted it all over her. At another time while absorbed in her work inside the tiger cage, one of the beasts crept around back of her and with one powerful sweep of his paw sent the clay model flying. If she had not instantly ducked, the second she sensed his presence, she would have been badly clawed.

On account of her interest in wild life, and consequent aptitude, she was employed by the Brooklyn Museum to work on the plaster restorations of prehistoric animals. She labored at this for several months.

An artistic partnership which she effected about the year 1904 with another ambitious young woman sculptor, Miss A. St. Leger Eberle, was of value to them both. They shared the same studio and for a time worked jointly on the same pieces—all animal groups—which met with favor in the exhibitions. One such work was a nude boy wrestling with a goat, a spirited interplay of muscles and hilarity. Soon, however, we find the partnership dissolved and the two artists working independently.

It was not long after the turn of the century that Miss Hyatt's work became nationally known, and eventually she attained the front rank of our sculptors of either sex in her especial forte. A writer in *Mentor* says: "Whether she presents the horse singly or in shivering groups, or depicts a significant attitude of jaguar, lion, elephant, bull, or dog, or represents the young of animals—colts, cubs, fawns—her work bears the mark of genius and understanding." And Lorado Taft confirms this opinion, saying: "Very exceptional it is to find a woman so completely master of her art as is Miss Anna Vaughn Hyatt, one of our foremost sculptors of animals. . . . There is not a sculptor in the land who does not pay homage to the able craftsmanship of Miss Hyatt's studies of wild

[343]

life. You can invest in these little bronzes of hers as confidently as you buy those of Barye, the French sculptor. Her "Great Danes" in blue Italian marble are a noble pair; her "Colts in a Snowstorm" are almost tragic in their new-found woe; but the things that one remembers best are those "Reaching Jaguars" which their author has planned for two gate-posts. Verily they are among the most original things in American art."

Among her larger pieces are a splendid "Lion," on the lawn of a public school, in Dayton, Ohio, and her "Fighting Elephants" in the Carnegie Institute, Pittsburgh. As one studies the smooth, graceful play of muscles of these wild beasts, one realizes the profound knowledge of animals that Miss Hyatt has acquired. She must have spent hours, days, and weeks before the cages of our great zoölogical parks. If she had done nothing in this line other than her pair of "Jaguars" her reputation would have been assured.

However, her larger fame rests not upon these but upon a nobler piece of work which, while introducing a spirited animal study, also introduces the human element. I refer to her equestrian statue of "Joan of Arc," overlooking the Hudson on Riverside Drive, New York. This is one of the most thoroughly satisfying pieces of sculpture to be found anywhere and one of the most beautiful in detail and surroundings. Even the careless passer-by involuntarily pauses to look a second time at it; and the reason is not merely its spirited pose but that it is so convincingly human. Here is no lay figure symbolizing a church saint, or mediæval soldier, but a vibrant, eager young girl, exultingly seizing and waving her consecrated sword, and confidently leading her troops forward to victory.

This monument was unveiled with impressive ceremonies, in the presence of the French Ambassador and other dignitaries of the city, state and nation, in the fall of 1915; but back of that unveiling is an interesting story.

For half a dozen years or more prior to that time, a "Joan of Arc Committee" had been quietly at work in New York planning for such a statue as a token of friendship to France. They had raised the requisite funds by private subscription, but their chief difficulty was in finding the right artist to do the work. They had not advertised for an artist officially, but through the underground channels of the art colony the tidings were no less thoroughly broadcasted, and many an ambitious sculptor, old and young, felt impelled to submit a sketch.

Before becoming aware of this search of the Committee, Miss Hyatt had already devoted some months to the study of the Maid of Orleans. It was a theme

[345]

which had long fascinated her. She had seen nearly every statue erected to the honor of the Maid, and had read every scrap of biography she could lay her hands on. And it was because none of the existing likenesses suited her, that she undertook to create her own "Joan."

Her first statue on the subject, a life-size model, was shown in the Paris Salon of 1910—and this was still antecedent to her trying for the New York commission. It was practically the same as the later work, except that the latter was larger than life and in many details is said to mark an advance. The Salon piece won an honorable mention, but the judges and others gave no credence to the statement that it was the product of only four months' actual work, and that the artist had done it unaided. "Impossible!" they averred; "on a group as large as that, even a man would require assistance. No woman would be physically equal to it—not even in a year!"

However, it was a cold fact. Miss Hyatt had gone out to her summer studio, filled to the brim with her subject, and had worked ten hours a day, seven days a week, for four months, until it was done. She herself had erected the sustaining iron framework, with its many radiating pieces of wood which sustained the clay, thrown that great mass of clay up into position, and then shaped it into its final form. None but a sculptor or his assistant can fully grasp what this means—the tremendously exacting physical labor it implies.

"It was a terribly brutal piece of work," admits Miss Hyatt. "Massing on three and a half tons of clay does entail great physical labor."

The artist likewise gives her conception of the militant Maid: "I thought of her there before her first battle, speaking to her soldiers, holding up the ancient sword. Her wrist is sharply back, to show them the hilt, which is in the form of a cross. Lamartine's life, more than others, shows her as a spiritual person, almost a fanatic. It was only her mental attitude, only her religious fervor, that could have enabled her to endure so much physically, to march three or four days with almost no sleep, to withstand cold and rain. That is how I have thought of her; that is how I have tried to model her."

From an excellent account of this statue, by Grace Humphries,[1] we quote other interesting details of the later work, which won favor over contestants representing six nationalities, and which now ornaments the Drive. So widespread was the competition that a Russian Jew is said to have been Miss Hyatt's nearest rival for the coveted honor. Says the writer in question:

[1] *International Studio*, December, 1915.

"Great attention has been paid in this statue to the cavalry mount, a splendid Norman horse, and to the armor. With the exception of a small headpiece, horse armor was not used in France until some hundred and twenty years later. Statues of Joan of Arc where the steed is encased in steel are anachronisms.

"As to the Maid herself, appeals to experts revealed the fact that there is not in existence a complete suit of Gothic armor of that period. All the details were supplied to Miss Hyatt from drawings only—rubbings of old tombs, old paintings, figures in stone and bronze were studied, and the data obtained by scholarly comparison on the part of Dr. Bashford Dean of the Metropolitan Museum and his assistants. For the first time in all her sculptured life, Joan of Arc is correctly dressed. And it is not stage armor, either; it fits the wearer, showing the play of muscles underneath. While it is a statue in armor, there is someone inside it. Indeed, Miss Hyatt began with careful studies from a nude model, and the armor was added later. . . .

"It is noteworthy that person after person who saw the statue in the studio used the same word in describing it, and that word was—convincing. The sculpture represents no extremes, no futile experimenting. Technically sound, the result of years of thorough training, plus hard and continuous labor, the workmanship of the statue gives the spectator the feeling that Miss Hyatt is certain of herself. The technique is there, but underneath or in the background."

Miss Hyatt has won many honors and medals. She has been elected to full membership in the National Academy, after having been an associate for several

years. She is a member of the National Sculpture
Society; and is Curator of Sculpture of the French
Museum of Art in this country. She was decorated
by the French Government with the Purple Rosette,
and in 1922 was made a Chevalier of the Legion of
Honor.

A replica of her "Joan of Arc," by the bye, was
presented to France, by Mr. J. Sanford Saltus, who
was active on the American Committee, and this statue
stands in Blois. It was unveiled in August, 1921.
The only other large replica extant is in Gloucester,
Massachusetts, in memory of men of that community
who served in the War, and also in compliment to the
artist who has made her summer home near by on Cape
Ann for so many years.

During the War, the artist turned war-gardener
and not only actively tilled the soil but also put up
large quantities of fruit and vegetables for winter use.
We are glad to give this picture of her, to show that
the woman has not been lost in the artist. After
listing her varied rural activities, a friend writing in
The Touchstone says:

"One might well think that the activities already described
would be more than enough to occupy a woman's full time,
but not at all; Miss Hyatt so masters her time that she is able
to spend several hours each morning in her studio on the place,
working on various commissions which she has in process of

[349]

completion, the most interesting being the two delightful boy-figure fountains which she has made for the beautiful gardens of Mr. Schwab's estate at Loretto, Pennsylvania.

"The genial amenities of human intercourse are not set aside, and on Sunday afternoons all roads over Cape Ann seem to lead to 'Seven Acres,' for on that day the family is known to be 'at home' and one is sure to find there representatives of almost every group of visitors to the North Shore of Massachusetts—artists, writers, musicians, officers, the purely ornamental, men and women engaged in every form of national and civic service.

"If guests linger beyond a certain hour a tall, slender figure clad in light buff breeches, leggings and tunic, carrying two shining milk-pails, will be seen gliding through the trees towards the cow barn, the dutiful cows accompanying her, all bent on the evening milking. No fuss of farewells, no excuses, just a simple turning to a duty waiting to be performed. This is the keynote of Miss Hyatt's character. Watch her as she swings slowly down the lane, every movement governed by instinctive grace and law of rhythm, an old buff-colored cloth hat crowning her shapely, exquisitely modeled head. And on either side of her a placid cow, both calmly content in her society."

Such a rural scene as this might well close our story, but this chronicle of a busy life has quite another ending. In the spring of 1924, the New York papers told of a "millionaire patron of arts and letters" and his "sculptor wife" who had set sail on a palatial yacht, on a voyage to the South Seas in quest of

[350]

treasure. Fired with the reporter's imagination it made a good story, especially the reference to pirates and their buried gold. Certainly there were both romance and treasure in this voyage.

After working out her own destiny quite capably, Miss Hyatt astonished her friends, one day in the spring of 1923, by marrying. Her choice was Mr. Archer M. Huntington, a son of the railroad king, Collis P. Huntington, and a litterateur and critic of ability. Their mutual interests had drawn them together, until a quiet wedding took place, in Miss Hyatt's studio on West Twelfth Street. The following March they embarked on the *Rocinante*, a seagoing yacht of luxurious design and fittings, with supplies enough on board for a two years' cruise.

Whither their final destination was to be, we do not know at this writing; but doubtless in years to come the artist will enrich her collection of animal studies with many a strange creature of both land and sea. To her the wild life which God made, wherever found, is always treasure trove.

3. JANET SCUDDER: SCULPTOR OF FOUNTAINS

The name of Janet Scudder is so closely linked with fountains, that the one naturally suggests the other. "That looks like one of Janet Scudder's fountains," is a common remark; and if the piece in question reveals a laughing, elfish child, it is more than an even chance that the speaker is right.

Miss Scudder comes from the Middle West. She was born in Terre Haute, Indiana, three years before the Centennial Exposition, the year when American art and especially sculpture was definitely waking up. And she came to maturity just at the time when the Columbian Exposition was calling upon our younger artists for the best that was in them. Consequently, she began her career under a favorable star.

After a common school education in her home town, Miss Scudder discovered a talent and an enthusiasm for wood-carving. She went to Cincinnati, where she studied this art for three years under Rebisso, at the Academy of Art; then returned home with the intention or supporting herself by teaching woodcarving, while she continued her own studies; but she herself declares it was a dismal failure. She next went to Chicago and took employment with a manufacturing concern, to do set pieces in carving. It was monotonous work, but the pay was fair, and she might have wasted some valuable time had not Fate stepped in in the guise of a walking delegate for a labor union, who declared that this young woman not being a member of his union must go. So she was "fired" and compelled to start on a wider career.

FOUNTAIN
By Janet Scudder

Miss Scudder was now twenty years of age. Her desultory schooling had given her a grasp of the technique of modeling, as well as of carving, and she attended special classes at the Art Institute, and was not long in deciding that clay and not wood was her forte. "That was about the time of the Columbian Exposition," says Leila Mechlin,[1] "when there was an uncommon abundance of work in Chicago for sculptors to do, and before very long Janet Scudder became a member of Lorado Taft's staff of energetic helpers. Those who have within themselves the germ of greatness need only opportunity to induce development, and in working for this great World's Fair under wise direction and the inspiration of goodly fellowship, not a few young sculptors discovered their own capability. None who belonged to that coterie but recalls those days with pleasure, when, in the midst of much con• fusion and some hardship, they endeavored to accomplish ideal results, and with a courage born of ignorance attained a standard which under less strenuous and congenial conditions would have been impossible. To Janet Scudder's share fell a statue for the Indiana Building, and a figure of 'Justice' for the Illinois Building, both of which she executed creditably, though, perhaps, without a great display of merit. Her work in Chicago, however, won her a medal and

[1] *Studio,* February, 1910.

[353]

brought her sufficient material reward to enable her to go to Paris and continue her studies there."

She is described by another at the time as a tall, slender girl with the light of eager enthusiasm shining in her eyes.

While in Chicago she had been attracted to the work of MacMonnies by his stately fountain in the Court of Honor, and it was not long before she had the opportunity of attending a class conducted by him, in the French capital. It was at Madame Vitti's on the Boulevard Montparnasse, where the inspiring young teacher was then surrounded by an adoring circle of women students of all ages. "None showed greater promise than Miss Scudder," says Mr. Taft, her earlier teacher, "and she was presently rewarded with an offer of employment in the studio of the brilliant American master. Now followed such a training as few women sculptors have ever had. Faithfully did the earnest pupil embroider Shakespeare's coat by the month, or stick *boulettes* (little pellets of clay or wax) on 'Bacchante'—it was all in the day's work. Meantime she was developing a new taste. Every now and then, MacMonnies in whimsical mood would dash a handful of clay into the form of an elfish little cupid as irresistible as any of Donatello's delightful wee figures. These babies seem to have made especial appeal to Miss Scudder. She tried one and

[354]

did it so well that she has been doing them ever since."

Those of us who remember the charming "Boy and Turtle" fountain by MacMonnies, as well as other child studies by him, can see the potent influence he has exerted upon his pupil's work. She remained with him for several years and attained proficiency in another field as well—that of modeling in low relief. It was an art which MacMonnies himself had derived from his master, Saint Gaudens, and now was passed on to the third generation.

Later still she went to Florence, where she opened up a little studio and made copies of interesting art works. It was here that she received her final inspiration for her fountains. There were many such examples in this Italian city both large and small; for in Florence the full flowering of the Renaissance had been attained, and both within-doors and without the art student could bask in its richness. Especially did she note the many small garden fountains, and she mentally resolved to transplant the idea to America.

When she returned home, she did indeed try to put her idea into practice; but orders, as is usual in such cases, came painfully slow. She tells an amusing story about the first fountain which she made in New York, where she had set up her modest shop, and how it came to be sold. She had in vain tried to induce Stanford White, the architect and patron of arts, to come to her studio, and had about given up in despair when suddenly one morning he hailed her on the street. It was the crowded intersection of Fifth Avenue and Thirty-fourth Street, and as the traffic one way was temporarily halted he caught sight of her.

"Good morning. This is Miss Scudder, isn't it?" he greeted.

"It is," she replied.

"Well I like that fountain of yours I saw exhibited the other day, and want to buy it. How much is it?"

Miss Scudder named the price.

"Well, send it around; I want it." Just then the whistle sounded, and Mr. White hurried across the street.

The fountain which he purchased in this summary style was not only her first, but still remains one of her best known—the "Frog Fountain," another copy of which was later purchased by the Metropolitan Museum of Art.

The joyous youngster who kicks at the frogs was the first of a goodly line of unclad babies, more sprite than human, that have braved both water and the small animals which usually accompany them. There is "Young Pan," who plays merrily on his pipes, seemingly not afraid of the crustacean so close to his toes. This was purchased by Robert Bacon when Ambassador to France, and found a place in the Embassy at Paris. There was the "Boy with the Crab," which adorns a grotto in the estate of John D. Rockefeller, in Pocantico Hills. There is the cupid who poises so airily upon the back of a tortoise, who snorts water angrily. This "Tortoise Fountain" was purchased by the artist's home town of Terre Haute, thus disproving the old adage about a prophet not being without honor, save in his own country. Then there was her "Fountain of the Fighting Boys," purchased by the Chicago Art Institute; her "Little Lady of the Sea," a small maiden decorated with dripping sea-weeds, which was exhibited at the Paris Salon of 1913; her "Young Diana," also shown at a Salon, and later bought by Harold McCormick for his summer retreat at Lake Forest, Illinois; and many another. The artist likewise found—or helped to create—a demand for very small fountains for table use, and some of her most exquisite things have been done in miniature.

But lest the reader consider her an artist of "only one bow," we must not forget her medallions in low relief—some of them being portrait studies. Five of these medallions were purchased by the French Government for its National Gallery. They may now be seen in the Luxembourg, not far away from the works of Saint Gaudens in the same vein—certainly a high compliment for this American woman's work. It was, in fact, the first work in sculpture by any American woman to be purchased for the Luxembourg.

The artist herself has alternated between New York and Paris. She has made many friends in the French capital and looks upon it as her second home. Certainly the Salons have been generous in their recognition of her ability. On one of her return visits to New York, in 1914, she made portrait busts of several of her friends, to take back with her abroad— "to keep me from getting lonely," as she declared. They were small in size and dainty in conception, like everything else that she models, and make one quite envious to be numbered upon her list of friends.

One of these friends thus describes Miss Scudder's home in France: "It is in Ville d'Arvray, near Paris, where she prefers to live and work. She says there is more space, more room to live and breathe there, than in the restricted spaces of New York. She is not particularly in sympathy with the rush and roar of life as it is lived in this great city, because we dash from one thing to another in a mad whirl and consequently do not give sufficient time to finish anything well. For this reason, the quiet, picturesque villa in the country of La Belle France, secluded by tall walls

[358]

over which the vines ramble at will, affords a shel-
tered spot most sympathetic to the mood of the artist.
A large garden surrounding the villa provides an admirable background for her sculptures, which are
wheeled out into the open while she is still at work
upon them, and can be seen to advantage under the
sunlight and shadows of their future surroundings."

That the artist loves her work is evidenced in
every line, which also reveals her painstaking artis-
try. Miss Mechlin says of it, in the *Studio* article
previously quoted: "Some spirit of mirthfulness, or
genuine delight in the work, finds its way into almost
all Janet Scudder's productions and lends them peculiar charm, for, after all, if the artist is not interested
in producing, why should others be expected to be
interested in the result? Not that Miss Scudder
produces thoughtlessly nor without effort, for she is
both a conscientious and a tireless worker. Like all
who really attain a measure of greatness, she destroys
her work again and again, until she is sure that it
represents her best effort—that at the time it is produced it measures up to the limit of her power. And
of this she insists upon being her own judge, yielding
neither to censure nor praise, reverencing her profession and respecting the opinions of her
fellow-workers, but first and always being true to
herself."

4. BESSIE POTTER VONNOH: SCULPTOR OF
STATUETTES

"Another eager spirit out of the West is Bessie Potter Vonnoh, whose little bronzes are welcomed the world over. Like Miss Scudder, she received her first impetus from the Columbian Exposition." Thus says her teacher, Lorado Taft, who first met this enthusiastic student when she came to Chicago as a young girl. She was born in St. Louis, in 1872, and received a common school education, without any special emphasis being laid upon art; yet she tells how as a child her hands instinctively sought the shaping of lovely things. In her early school days a happy opportunity presented itself to indulge in art studies as a side line. Here she was untrammeled by discipline, and allowed to work as her fancy dictated. For most students such a method would have been disastrous, but her teachers were wise in this instance, and beyond general suggestions gave her free rein.

Then came the announcements of the great exposition at Chicago, and the consequent pilgrimage of art workers thither. We have spoken of this as a great quickener of art life, in other chapters; but no reader who has not himself worked in stone or clay or color can appreciate the thrill which went abroad through the land, when the great buildings began to take

[360]

MOTHERHOOD

By Bessie Potter Vonnoh

shape, and the call came for workers. Bessie Potter was drawn thither also, but as an eager learner, an observer of the work of others. Already, however, her skill had begun to manifest itself. As Mr. Taft says: "When she came to us at the Art Institute her fingers were already skillful and her imagination had begun to recognize beauty in the casual incidents and groupings of daily life. The Columbian Exposition brought new revelations and new enthusiasms. From that time her pathway was clear."

When the archæologists of about a half-century ago first brought to light in Tanagra and other ancient towns of Greece those dainty little figurines—diminutive statues of persons and objects, sometimes faintly tinted—done by artists of bygone centuries—they almost caused the founding of a distinct modern school, so general was the interest. Every artist who worked in small was subject to the accusation of copying the Tanagra figurines. Miss Potter did not escape the same implication, as her work naturally fell into this channel. But as a matter of fact, she had modeled many statuettes before she ever saw these ancient art objects. She herself said that her first inspiration came from a group of charming small bronzes exhibited at the World's Fair by Prince Troubetzkoy, the eminent Russian sculptor. History does not say whether the Prince drew *his* inspiration from Greece, or not, but he did many clever bits of portraiture in this small form, one of the best being a study of his mother.

No sooner had the American girl seen these little bronzes than she fell in love with them. She studied them for hours, and later while working strenuously in her own studio she told her friends that she was busy "doing Troubetzkoys." But soon it was seen that here was no slavish imitation. She gave to her pieces a feminine grace and an innate sympathy peculiarly her own.

Then came an opportunity to go abroad, and she spent some months in Paris and Florence. In the former city she was fortunate in making the acquaintance of Rodin, and his influence was seen in some of her later work, in a species of haunting mysticism. But Rodin himself never attempted the minuteness of detail which is always evident in her work. While abroad she did not attend any one school but spent the months in travel and observation, comparing notes as to the respective merits of the French and Italian schools, and making valuable friends in the art world.

The years 1896 to 1900 were pivotal with her; she was finding herself. In the earlier year she made her first exhibition at the National Sculpture Society salon in New York. Her work, while still lacking in some respects, created a favorable impression, and she became known to the general public. Then came the two years or more spent abroad; followed by her marriage, in 1899, to Robert Vonnoh, the painter.

Mr. Vonnoh, then a man of forty, had already attained eminence as a painter and a teacher of art. He had been connected with the Boston Museum of Fine Arts and the Pennsylvania Academy of Fine Arts, in Philadelphia, among others; had traveled widely and exhibited his own canvases in many salons and expositions. He married Miss Potter at Rockland Lake, New York, in the early fall, and shortly afterward they went abroad again, where he served as a member of the Jury of Awards, in the Paris Exposition of 1900.

Their married life in the quarter of a century which has followed has been marked by that quiet happiness which comes from a congeniality of tastes. Each has continued busily at work on his or her own forte, but profiting no little from the viewpoint of the other. They have lived in New York, when not away on their travels, or indulging in the joys of their summer home at Pleasant Valley, Connecticut. However, while in the city they are not of it—at least to the extent of enjoying the roystering functions of Bohemia. As a writer in the *Studio* puts it: "There is one thing which cannot do otherwise than discourage the acute observer of the activities of Mr. and Mrs.

Vonnoh—the disquieting fact that they are people of refinement and intelligence. At a time when the idealisms of our artists and the appreciative capacities of our patrons of art are bounded on the one side by Castle House and on the other by the Persian Garden, we are forced, I think, to acknowledge the unhappy significance of so conspicuous a disqualification.

"I find, for example, in their home a Steinway parlor grand, in place of the inevitable Victrola, and it is from an atmosphere permeated with a gentleness of demeanor, a breadth of interest, an unobtrusive cultivation, that the work of Mrs. Vonnoh comes to us. It has been so extensively commented upon, that it would be superfluous of me to attempt an appraisal of its technical excellence. It is with its attitude of mind, of feeling, that I am concerned, maintaining, despite the hostility to this view of the literal-minded, that it is the duty of the writer to convey primarily the intentions, ambitions, idealisms of the artist, rather than to submit a mere cataloguing of certain mechanical proficiencies.

"When you meet Mrs. Vonnoh, you are impressed by a quiet absence of eccentricity, of over-emphasis, whether of dress, of manner, or of opinion. As you hear her talk, you realize that her work, because of the nature of the woman, cannot fail to oppose the thousand intricacies of that materialism and brutality

[364]

that has dominated so large a proportion of the art of
the times. Her point of view is a kind of diffident
defense, maternal rather than militant."

Indeed, the personality of the artist is as pleasing as
her art. Although intensely interested in her own
work, she is full of sympathy and interest for that of
others. In her first studio, in Chicago, might have
been found men and women representing varied lines
of industry, but all assured of a welcome. With later
success came no "pose" but always that ready friendli-
ness and understanding of others.

Perhaps if we were limited to one word to express
the art of Mrs. Vonnoh, it would be "maternal."
She is at her best when exhibiting phases of motherhood or childhood. We all remember her "Young
Mother," a tender, appealing bit of womanhood, as
she stands there with a babe in her arms and two
small children standing clinging to her skirts. She is
the universal mother, full of love, and ready to devote
the energies of her life to the rearing of these little
ones. This statuette is a permanent possession of the
Metropolitan Museum; and a replica was presented
to the Red Cross, during its War drives. The sculptor is fond also of depicting dancing children, "pre-
sentments of prettily costumed young girls taking their
dancing steps in easy grace." Her recent group of
young dancers in the more modern mode, called "Alle-

gresse," was awarded the sculpture prize in the
National Academy of Design, in 1920, and was purchased for the Detroit Museum. The Art Institute
of Chicago owns eleven of her statuettes, and the
Brooklyn Museum thirteen. She has won several
medals at expositions at home and abroad, and
her work has long been given recognition here through
full membership in the National Sculpture Society. A
"Dancing Girl" is in the possession of the Carnegie
Institute, Pittsburgh. In the Brooklyn Museum, the
Corcoran Art Gallery, at Washington, and elsewhere
in collections both public and private, her exquisite
little bronzes may be found. As one critic says:
"It would be useless and unprofitable to compare Mrs.
Vonnoh with any other American sculptor, because her
work occupies its own special and well-defined place.
In her own field—that of the statuette—she has no
superiors in this country."

Her work, however, is by no means confined to this.
Some of her busts of larger size are well known.
There is one of heroic size of General Crawford which
was done for the Soldiers and Sailors Monument of
Philadelphia. She has done some worth-while studies
of children, such as her "Mildred" and "Twin Sisters."
She made a half-length study of Julia Marlowe, and
a delightful statuette of Maude Adams, of the days of
Peter Pan. But whether working in small or in large,

[366]

her touch is ever feminine. Her specialty is, not
nudes, but figures adorned with finery or tricked out
in clinging drapery; yet still with the feeling of the
lithe body underneath. Most of her work is impres-
sionistic in character, perhaps a heritage from the influence of Rodin, but with that very definite suggestion
which "gets across" to the onlooker. Sometimes she
uses a dash of color—but only a dash—with much
success, just as the ancient artists of the Tanagra figurines. It is never blatant, but done with a prevailing
delicacy which heightens the charm. Working thus
in miniatures, she can go boldly out after certain effects which would be glaring in a life-size object.

Says still another writer: "Many of her best-liked
pieces have to do with motherhood. But whatever
the subject—'tall ladies in Greek draperies, young
mothers bending over their children, girls dancing and
fluttering their fans'—all her types are touched with
'the faint languor of a modern civilization.' A comparatively recent figurine of a little girl who is industriously engaged in eating a potato with a wooden
spoon suggests Boutet de Monvel, the French painter,
in its frank acceptance of the many varied little personal traits which are really the charm of childhood."

And the anonymous writer in the *Studio*, previously
quoted adds: "There has been no conscious imitative-
ness in her work; she has responded inevitably to

those things about her which have seemed beautiful to her, her fingers busying themselves in a glad and unpremeditated attempt to catch the lovely minuteness of life, rather than to labor at a conventional dignity of mere bulk. Her dominant note is her rendering of a sort of delicate domesticity. One feels that the touch which has evoked the nursery in the placid permanence of sculptures has been moved by that degree of tenderness with which it would caress a living thing."

BIBLIOGRAPHY

GENERAL

1834. HISTORY OF THE RISE AND PROGRESS OF THE ARTS OF DESIGN. W. Dunlap. New York.

1865. HISTORIC ANNALS OF THE NATIONAL ACADEMY OF DESIGN. T. A. Cummings. Philadelphia.

1867. BOOK OF THE ARTISTS. H. T. Tuckerman. New York.

1873. WONDERS OF SCULPTURE. L. Viardot. New York.

1877. GREAT AMERICAN SCULPTURES. W. J. Clark. Philadelphia.

1878. GREAT AMERICAN SCULPTURES. W. J. Clark. New York.

1880. ARTISTS OF THE NINETEENTH CENTURY. Clement and Hutton. Boston.

1880. ART IN AMERICA. S. G. W. Benjamin. New York.

1894. SCHOOLS AND MASTERS OF SCULPTURE. A. G. Radcliff. New York.

1899. TEXTBOOK OF THE HISTORY OF SCULPTURE. Marquand and Frothingham. New York.

1900. TWELVE GREAT ARTISTS. W. H. Downes. Boston.

1902. HISTORY OF AMERICAN ART. S. Hartman. Boston.

1903. HISTORY OF AMERICAN SCULPTURE. L. Taft. New York. (Supplemental chapter, 1924.)

1903. AMERICAN MASTERS OF SCULPTURE. C. H. Caffin. New York.

1905. OLD MASTERS AND NEW. K. Cox. New York.

1916. FAMOUS PAINTERS OF AMERICA. J. W. McSpadden. New York.

1921. SCULPTURE OF TO-DAY. K. Parker. New York.

1921. HISTORY OF EUROPEAN AND AMERICAN SCULPTURE. C. R. Post. New York.

1921. MODERN TENDENCIES IN SCULPTURE. L. Taft. Chicago.

1923. THE SPIRIT OF AMERICAN SCULPTURE. A. Adams. New York.

(See also general encyclopedias, "Who's Who in America," "American Art Annual," etc.)

SPECIAL BOOKS AND ARTICLES

(The references given below for individual artists are not complete. Only leading articles are cited. Saint Gaudens, for example, is particularly rich in references. For other articles dealing with his and others' work the reader is cited to the "Guides to Periodical Literature" to be found in every library.)

JOHN QUINCY ADAMS WARD

1873. "Ward's Statue in Central Park." Souvenir Volume. New York.

1878. "An American Sculptor." Anon. *Harper's.* June.

1902. "The Work of J. Q. A. Ward." R. Sturgis. *Scribner's.* October.

1909. "Work of a Veteran Sculptor." M. Schuyler. *Putnam's.* September.

1910. "Work of Ward." W. Walton. *Studio.* June.

BIBLIOGRAPHY

1910. "First of American Sculptors." E. Knaufft. *Current Literature*. June.

1912. "An Appreciation." A. Adams. National Sculpture Society.

AUGUSTUS SAINT GAUDENS

1897. "The Shaw Memorial and the Sculpture of Saint Gaudens." W. A. Coffin. *Century*. June.

1907. AUGUSTUS SAINT GAUDENS. R. Cortissoz. New York.

1907. "The Sculptor Who Typified American Character." *Craftsman*. October.

1908. A CHRONICLE OF FRIENDSHIPS. W. H. Low. New York.

1908. AUGUSTUS SAINT GAUDENS. C. L. Hind. New York.

1908. "Augustus Saint Gaudens." K. Cox. *Atlantic Monthly*. March.

1908. "Memorial Oration." G. B. McClellan. *Putnam's*. August.

1908. "Familiar Letters of Saint Gaudens." Ed. by R. S. Nichols. *McClure's*. October and November.

1908. "Reminiscences of Saint Gaudens." Ed. by H. Saint Gaudens. *Century*. (Serial)

1908. "Later Work of Saint Gaudens." H. Saint Gaudens. *Century*. March.

1911. "Letters of S. White and Saint Gaudens." Ed. by H. Saint Gaudens. *Architectural Record*. (Serial)

[371]

1917. "Recollections of His Friend, M. Armstrong." H. F. Armstrong. *Scribner's.* January.

FREDERICK MACMONNIES

1895. "Frederick MacMonnies." W. H. Low. *Scribner's.* November.
1904. "Frederick MacMonnies, Sculptor." H. H. Greer. *Brush and Pencil.* January.
1905. "Frederick MacMonnies, Sculptor." F. Strother. *World's Work.* December.
1906. "The Work of MacMonnies." C. Brinton. *Munsey's.*
1906. "Frederick MacMonnies, Portrait Painter." E. Pettit. *Studio.* October.
1912. "Frederick MacMonnies, Sculptor." C. H. Melzer. *Cosmopolitan.* July.
1922. "Early Days with MacMonnies in Saint Gaudens's Studio." R. de Quélin. *Arts and Decoration.* April.
1922. "Civic Virtue." *Architecture.* April.

DANIEL CHESTER FRENCH

1895. "New Figures in Literature and Art." R. Cortissoz. *Atlantic Monthly.* February.
1897. "Daniel Chester French." Mrs. H. B. Emerson. *New England Magazine.* May.
1900. "The Sculptor French." W. A. Coffin. *Century.* April.
1906. "Groups of the Continents." C. de Kay. *Century.* January.

BIBLIOGRAPHY

1906. "Groups for the New York Custom House."
Craftsman. April.

1912. "Later Work of French." W. Walton. *Scribner's.*
November.

1912. "An American Sculptor." S. Brinton. *Studio.*
May.

1916. "A Sculptor's Reminiscences of Emerson." *Art
World.* October.

1916. "Recent Sculpture of French." S. Brinton.
Studio. July.

1919. "Making a Great Statue." W. M. Berger.
Scribner's. October.

PAUL WAYLAND BARTLETT

1905. "Paul Bartlett, an American Sculptor." E. S.
Bartlett. *New England Magazine.* December.

1909. "A Sculptor who is also a Craftsman." K. E.
Chapman. *Craftsman.* July.

1910. "Bartlett's Pediment for the House of Representatives." W. Walton. *Scribner's.* July.

1913. "Recent Work." W. Walton. *Scribner's.* October.

1916. "Statues in Washington." *Art and Archæology.*
January.

1916. "The Power Plant and the Art Commission." P.
W. Bartlett. *Art and Archæology.* June.

1916. "Unveiling the Pediment Group, etc." *Art and
Archæology.* September.

1916. "Bartlett's Latest Sculpture." J. J. Klaber.
Architectural Record. March.

1916. "Sculpture for the New York Public Library." M.
Carroll. *Art and Archæology.* January.

[373]

1923. "Paul W. Bartlett." Pierre Darius. *La Peinture* (Paris). October.

GEORGE GREY BARNARD

1897. "A New American Sculptor." W. A. Coffin. *Century.* April.

1899. "A Great American Sculptor." L. C. Dennis. *Review of Reviews.* January.

1902. "George Grey Barnard, Sculptor." A. B. Thaw. *World's Work.* December.

1908. "The Spirit of the New World, etc." K. M. Roof. *Craftsman.* December.

1908. "A Virile American Sculptor." E. Knaufft. *Review of Reviews.* December.

1908. "George Grey Barnard." J. N. Lauvrik. *Studio.* December.

1916. "Cloister of George Grey Barnard." *Architecture.* March.

1920. "The George Grey Barnard Cloisters." I. F. Conant. *Studio.* October.

1920. "Barnard's Plan for an Art Acropolis in Memory of the War." *Current Opinion.* November.

GUTZON BORGLUM

1906. "Gutzon Borglum, Painter and Sculptor." Mechlin. *Studio.* April.

1906. "The Versatile Talent of Gutzon Borglum." *Current Literature.* May.

1908. "Individuality, Sincerity and Reverence in American Art." Gutzon Borglum. *Craftsman.* October.

BIBLIOGRAPHY

1908. "Esthetic Activities in America: An Answer to His Critics." Gutzon Borglum. *Craftsman*. December.

1910. "The Beauty of Lincoln." Gutzon Borglum. *Everybody's*. February.

1912. "The Betrayal of the People by a False Democracy." Gutzon Borglum. *Craftsman*. April.

1914. "Art That is Real and American." Gutzon Borglum. *World's Work*. June. Prefaced by short biography by George Marvin.

1923. "Moulding a Mountain." Gutzon Borglum. *Forum*. September.

JOHN MASSEY RHIND

1896. "A Genius of the Chisel." MacDonald. *Munsey's*. March.

1898. "Kindred Spirits After All." E. Newport. *Art Interchange*. September.

1902. "A Scotch-American Sculptor." J. A. Beckett. *Art Interchange*. April.

1902. "Scotch Notables in America." D. MacDougall. *Caledonian*. October.

1917. "The Newark Copy of the Colleoni." J. Massey Rhind. *Architectural Record*. May.

1917. "The American Indian in Sculpture." O. Payne. *Munsey's*. February.

JAMES EARLE FRASER

1905. "James Earle Fraser." Saint Gaudens. *Critic*. November.

FAMOUS SCULPTORS OF AMERICA

1910. "James Earle Fraser, Sculptor." A. Semple. *Century.* April.

1910. "James E. Fraser: American Sculptor." *Craftsman.* June.

1918. "James Earle Fraser." *Pan American Union Bulletin.* May.

1920. "The Fraser Bust of Roosevelt." Eberle. *Scribner's.* October.

1921. "The Sculptor of the Victory Medal." *Current Opinion.* April.

1924. "The Field of Art." Cortissoz. *Scribner's.* January.

HERMON ATKINS MACNEIL

1907. "The Sculptors MacNeil." J. S. Holden. *World's Work.* October.

1909. "The Art of MacNeil." *Craftsman.* September.

1916. "Two Bas-reliefs of Hermon A. MacNeil. *Studio.* September.

WOMEN SCULPTORS OF NOTE

GENERAL

1919. "Women Sculptors of America." Taft. *Mentor.* February.

1922. "America's Women Sculptors." T. Kohlman. *Studio.* December.

BIBLIOGRAPHY

HARRIET HOSMER

1911. "Life and Works of Harriet Hosmer." R. A. Bradford. *New England Magazine.* November.

1923. GIRLS WHO BECAME FAMOUS. S. K. Bolton. New York.

1924. HISTORY OF AMERICAN SCULPTURE. L. Taft. New York.

ANNA VAUGHN HYATT

1905. "Two Women Who Collaborate in Sculpture." B. H. Smith. *Craftsman.* August.

1915. "Anna Vaughn Hyatt's Statue." G. Humphrey. *Studio.* December.

1916. "Miss Hyatt's Statue of Joan of Arc." C. H. Caffin. *Century.* June.

1919. "An Artist Patriot." C. Morrow. *Touchstone.* July.

JANET SCUDDER

1910. "Janet Scudder, Sculptor." L. Mechlin. *Studio.* February.

1914. "Fountains Designed by Janet Scudder." A. Hall. *House Beautiful.* June.

BESSIE POTTER VONNOH

1903. "Sculptor of Statuettes." *Current Literature.* June.

1914. "The Vonnohs." *Studio.* December.

[377]